A TALE OF TWO CITIES

A TALE OF TWO CITIES

ADAPTED FROM THE ORIGINAL NOVEL BY
CHARLES DICKENS

ILLUSTRATED BY
RYUTA OSADA

COLORED BY
ROBERT DEAS

TEXT ADAPTED BY
DAVID ZANE MAIROWITZ

STERLING
New York

STERLING and the distinctive Sterling logo are registered trademarks of
Sterling Publishing Co., Inc.

10 9 8 7 6 5 4 3 2 1

Published by Sterling Publishing Co., Inc.
387 Park Avenue South, New York, NY 10016

First published 2010
by SelfMadeHero
A division of Metro Media Ltd
5 Upper Wimpole Street
London W1G 6BP
www.selfmadehero.com

Illustrator: Ryuta Osada
Adaptor: David Zane Mairowitz
Colorist: Robert Deas
Cover Designer: Jeff Willis
Designer: Andy Huckle
Publishing Director: Emma Hayley

With thanks to: Nick de Somogyi and Doug Wallace

Distributed in Canada by Sterling Publishing
c/o Canadian Manda Group, 165 Dufferin Street
Toronto, Ontario, Canada M6K 3H6

Sterling ISBN 978-1-4027-8045-5

For information about custom editions, special sales, premium and
corporate purchases, please contact Sterling Special Sales
Department at 800-805-5489 or specialsales@sterlingpublishing.com.

FOREWORD

Between one of literature's most well-known first lines ("It was the best of times, it was the worst of times...") and one of its most famous final sentences ("It is a far, far better thing that I do, than I have ever done...") sits an unequaled story.

Published in weekly installments in 1859, the French Revolution and the Great Terror are merely a few generations in the background. Dickens was strongly influenced by Thomas Carlyle's The French Revolution (1837), and clearly felt sympathetic to the initial grounds for the events of 1789. But, like many writers after him, he soon found himself driven by the historical cliché "the mob." "With a roar that sounded as if all the breath in France had been shaped into a detested word, the living sea rose, wave upon wave, depth upon depth, and overflowed the city..." Thus the Revolution loses its individual face and, on the Paris side of the "Tale," Dickens provides only one viable character with her own story, Madame Defarge. Nearly all the others are passing extras on a vague canvas, all speaking with one voice and often only one clichéd name: "Jacques."

It is also clear that Dickens bore a true horror for the guillotine, which prodded him to write, on the opening pages of his book, "...rooted in the woods of France and Norway, there were growing trees... to make a certain moveable framework with a sack and a knife in it, terrible in history." It will haunt him right up to the last paragraph of his book, when he sacrifices his central character to its caprices.

The usual rich tapestry of Dickens's supporting cast fills the book, but the restraints of our graphic novel form have obliged us to pare down the fingernails of some and decapitate others altogether. Instead we have chosen to concentrate on the central story and its small fate-knitted group of characters. But there is little doubt that A Tale of Two Cities is Sydney Carton's story. Fitting into a long line of dissolute heroes who would become pivotal in the twentieth century, it is difficult to fathom, from our contemporary standpoint, what Lucie Manette sees in the boringly "clean" Charles Darnay, the man she chooses as her life-partner over Carton. An incorrigible mix of alcohol and self-effacing cynicism, Carton finds a curious redemption only in the eyes of a doomed French seamstress, with whose skull his own is about to share a headsman's basket.

David Zane Mairowitz

BOOK THE FIRST: Recalled to Life

It was the best of times,
it was the worst of times,
it was the age of wisdom,
it was the age of foolishness,
it was the epoch of belief,
it was the epoch of incredulity,
it was the season of Light,
it was the season of Darkness,
it was the spring of hope,
it was the winter of despair,
we had everything before us,
we had nothing before us,
we were all going direct to Heaven,
we were all going direct the other way...

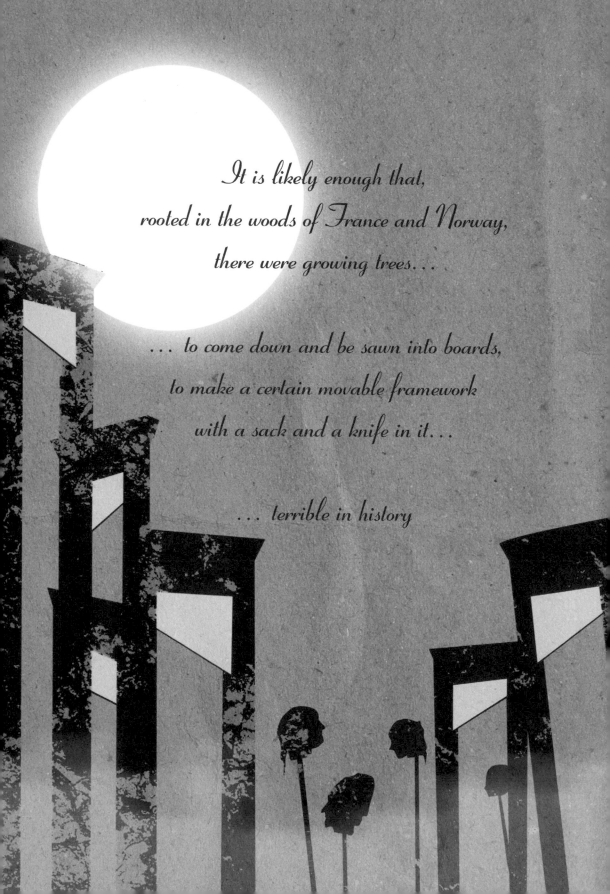

It is likely enough that,
rooted in the woods of France and Norway,
there were growing trees...

... to come down and be sawn into boards,
to make a certain movable framework
with a sack and a knife in it...

... terrible in history

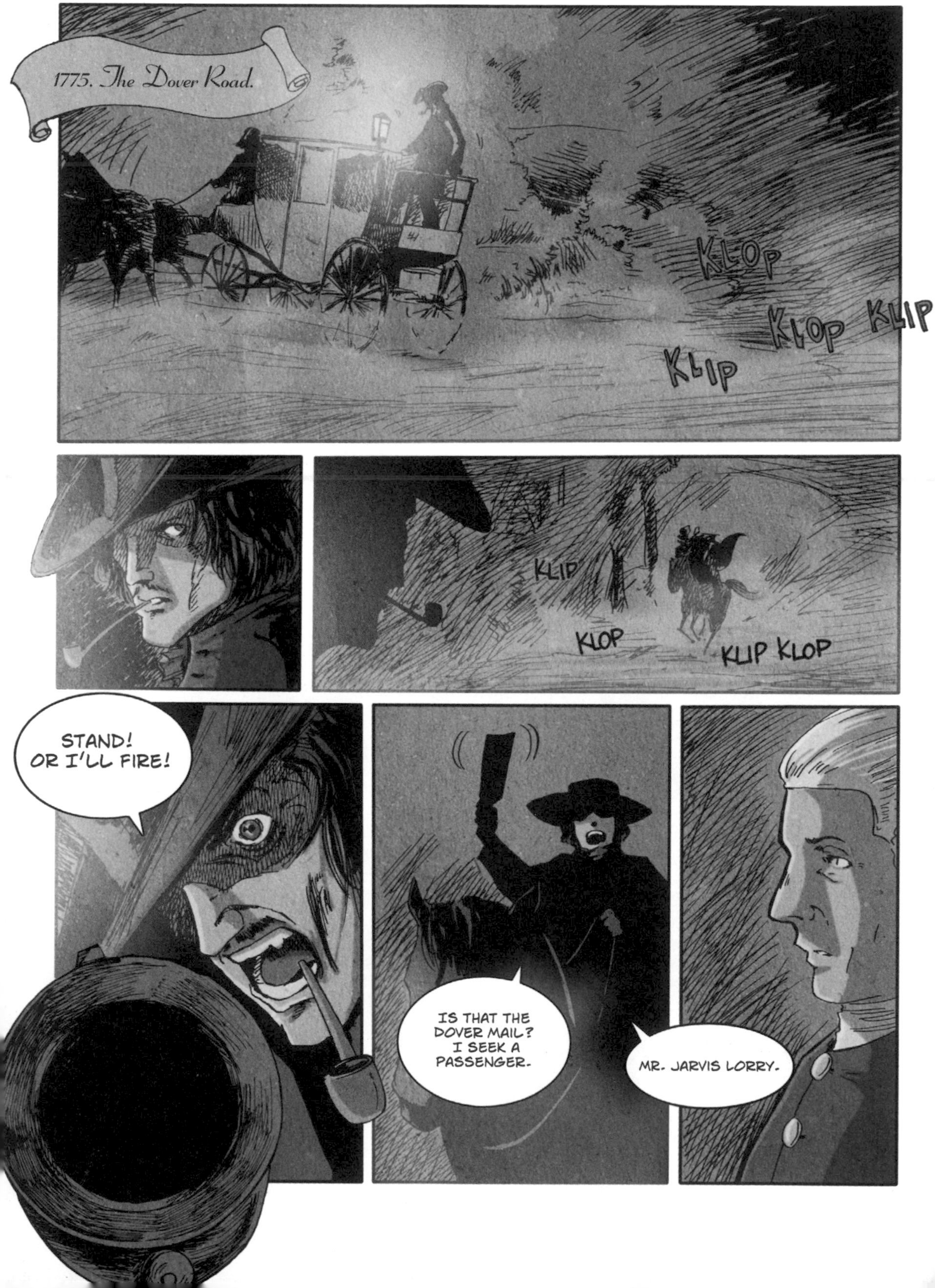
1775. The Dover Road.
KLOP
KLOP KLIP
KLIP
KLIP
KLOP
KLIP KLOP
STAND! OR I'LL FIRE!
IS THAT THE DOVER MAIL? I SEEK A PASSENGER.
MR. JARVIS LORRY.

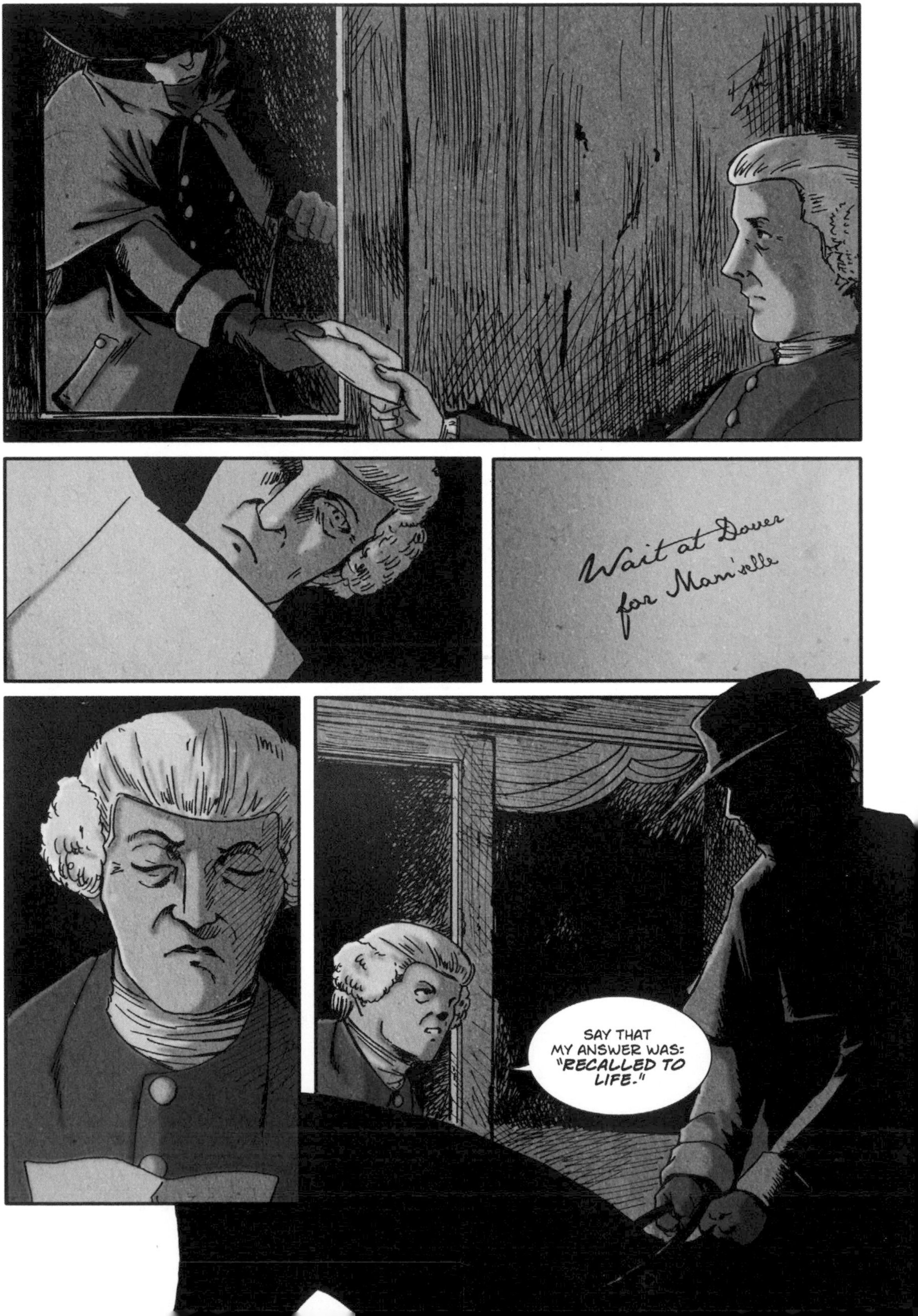
Wait at Dover
for Mam'selle
SAY THAT MY ANSWER WAS: "RECALLED TO LIFE."

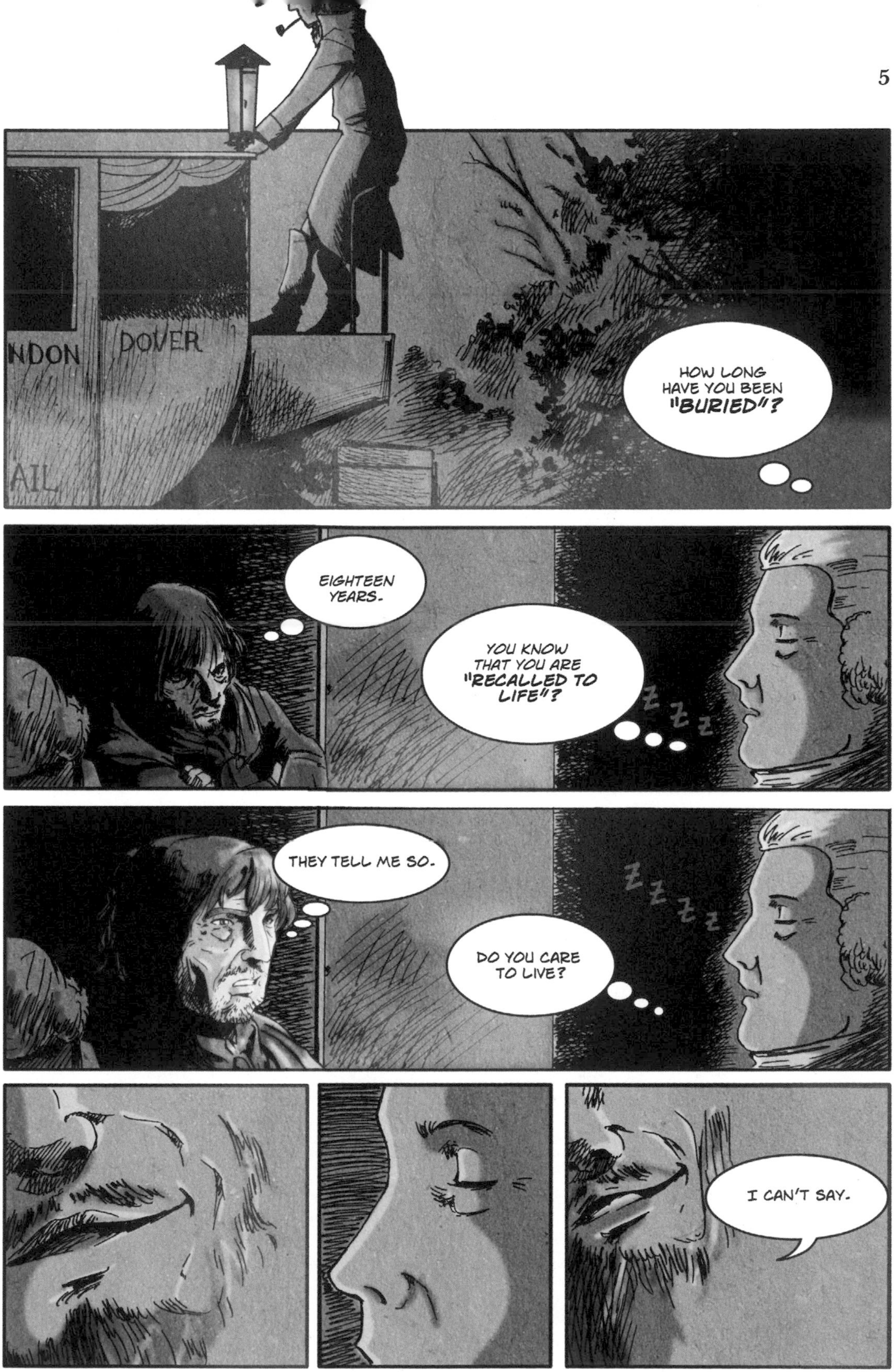
NDON
DOVER
AIL
HOW LONG HAVE YOU BEEN "BURIED"?
EIGHTEEN YEARS.
YOU KNOW THAT YOU ARE "RECALLED TO LIFE"?
ZZZ
THEY TELL ME SO.
ZZZZ
DO YOU CARE TO LIVE?
I CAN'T SAY.

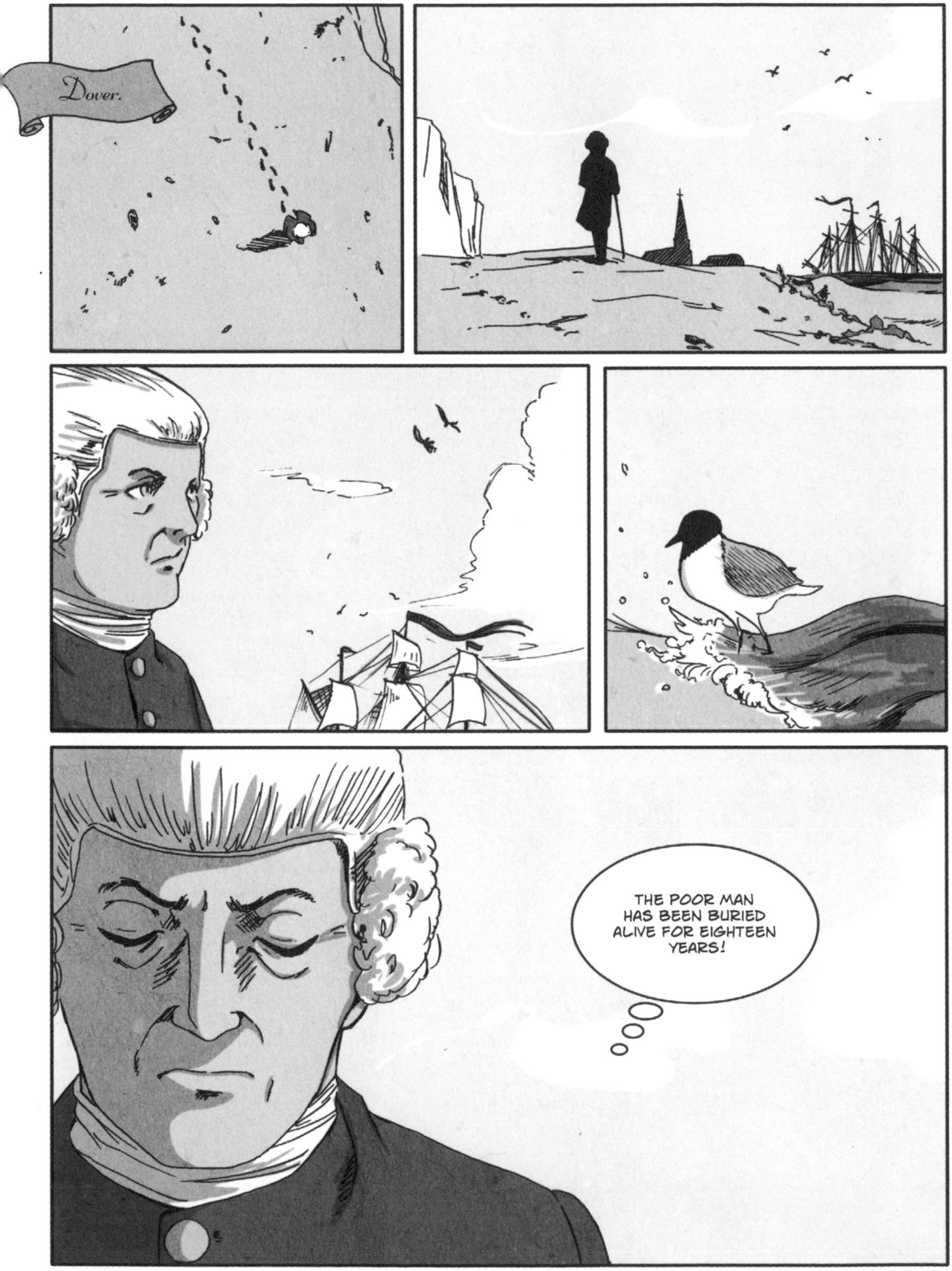
Dover.
THE POOR MAN HAS BEEN BURIED ALIVE FOR EIGHTEEN YEARS!

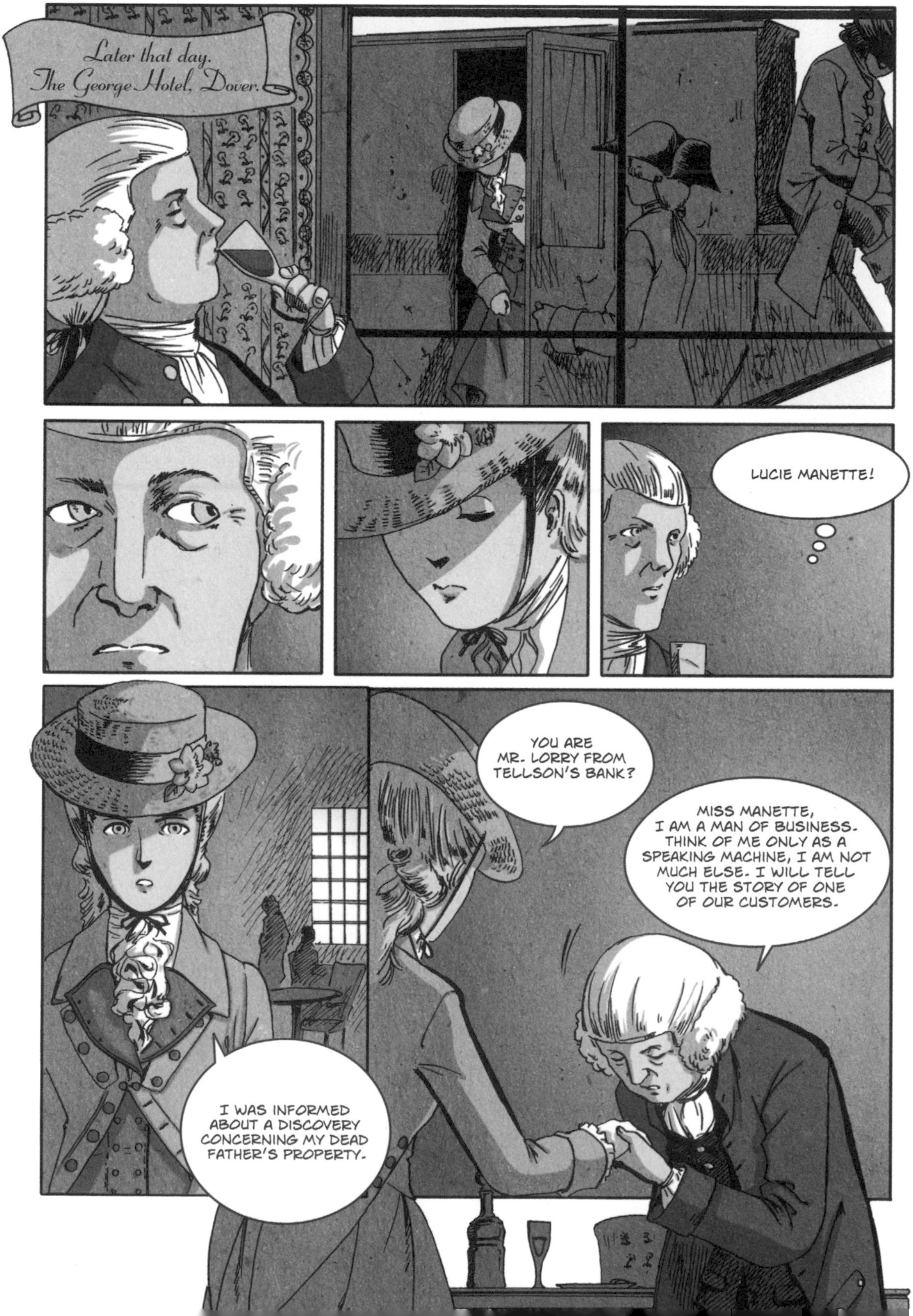
Later that day.
The George Hotel, Dover.
LUCIE MANETTE!
YOU ARE MR. LORRY FROM TELLSON'S BANK?
MISS MANETTE, I AM A MAN OF BUSINESS. THINK OF ME ONLY AS A SPEAKING MACHINE, I AM NOT MUCH ELSE. I WILL TELL YOU THE STORY OF ONE OF OUR CUSTOMERS.
I WAS INFORMED ABOUT A DISCOVERY CONCERNING MY DEAD FATHER'S PROPERTY.

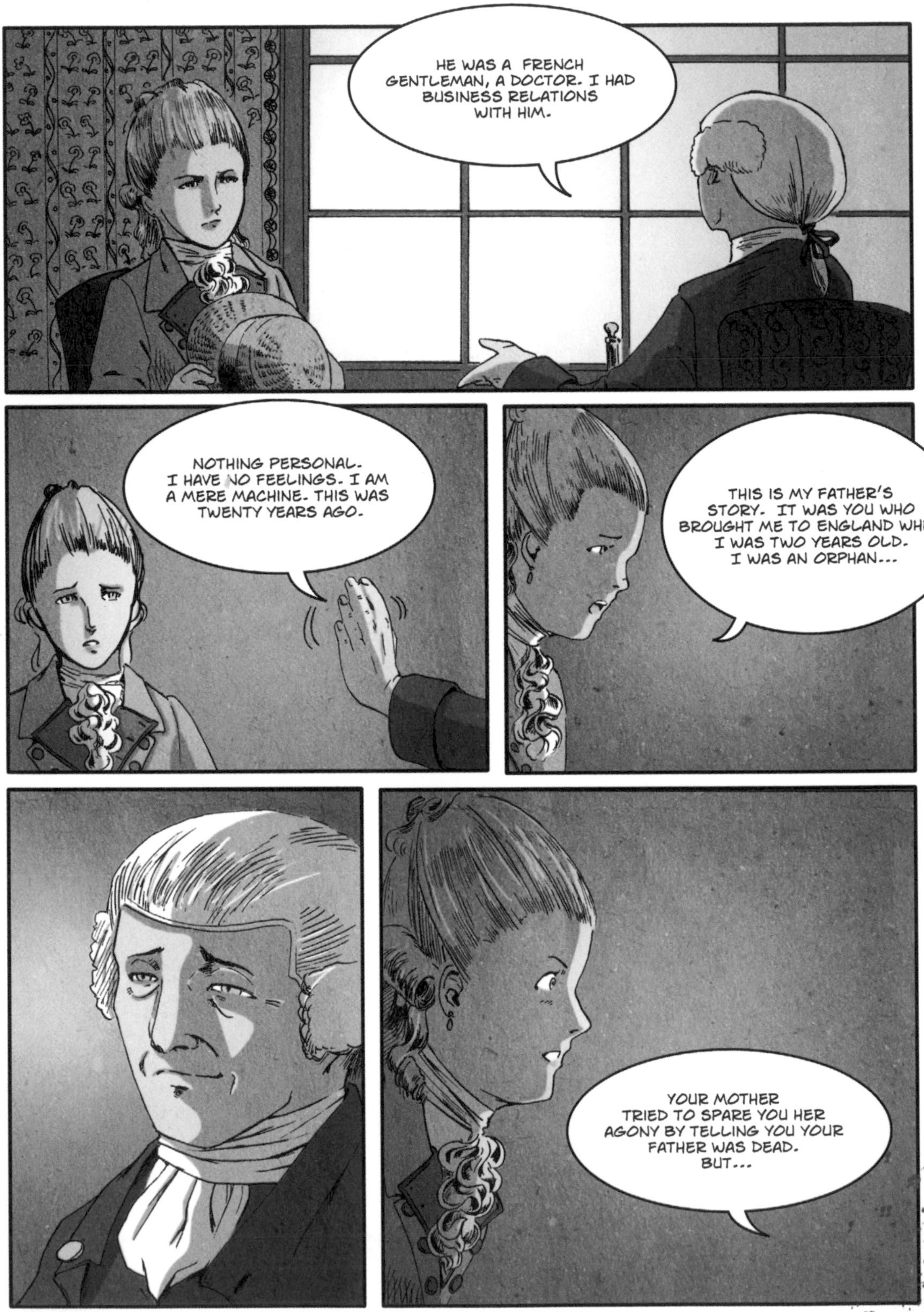
HE WAS A FRENCH GENTLEMAN, A DOCTOR. I HAD BUSINESS RELATIONS WITH HIM.
NOTHING PERSONAL. I HAVE NO FEELINGS. I AM A MERE MACHINE. THIS WAS TWENTY YEARS AGO.
THIS IS MY FATHER'S STORY. IT WAS YOU WHO BROUGHT ME TO ENGLAND WHEN I WAS TWO YEARS OLD. I WAS AN ORPHAN...
YOUR MOTHER TRIED TO SPARE YOU HER AGONY BY TELLING YOU YOUR FATHER WAS DEAD. BUT...

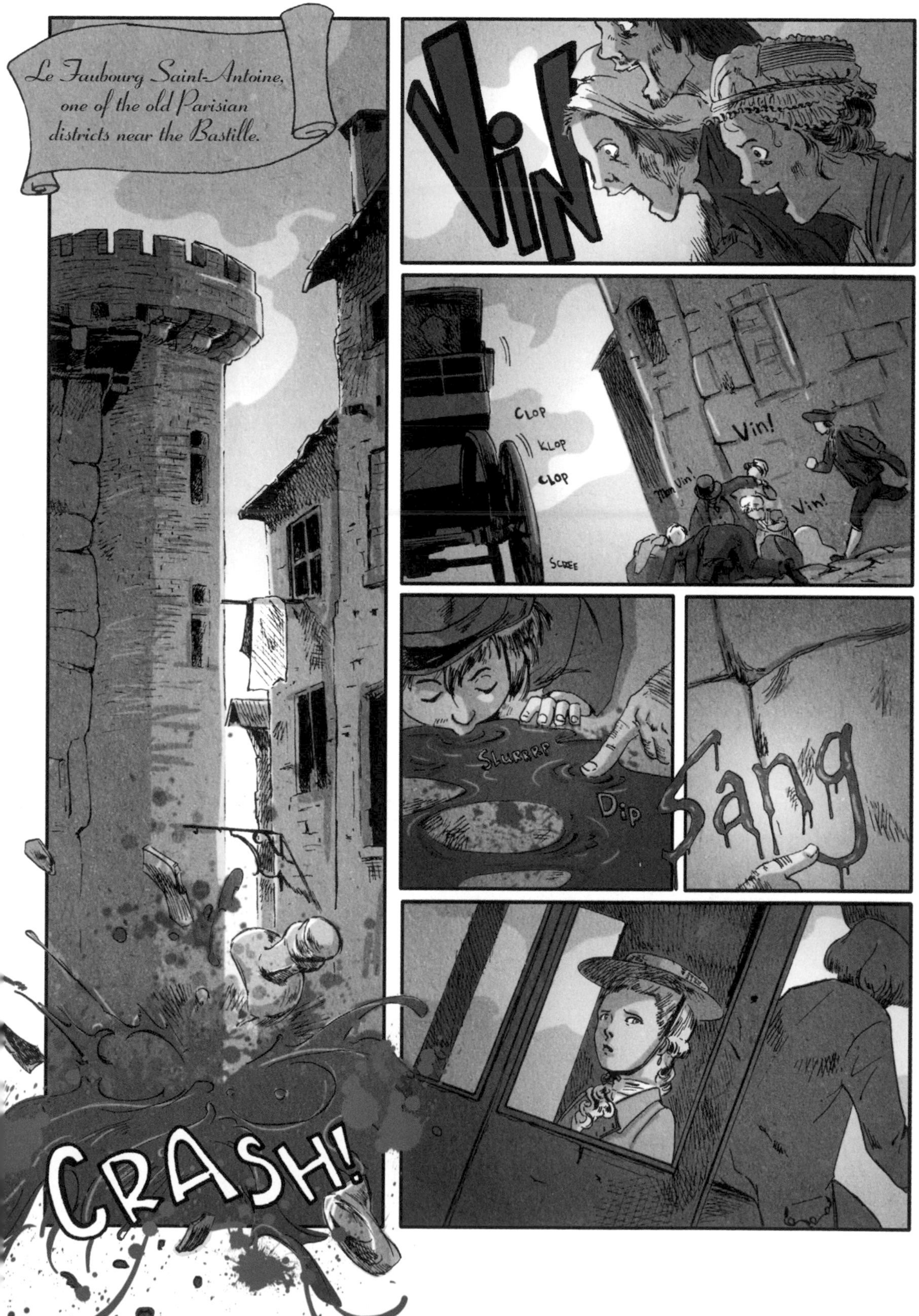
Le Faubourg Saint-Antoine,
one of the old Parisian
districts near the Bastille.
CRASH!
VIN
CLOP
KLOP
CLOP
SCREE
Vin!
Mon Vin!
Vin!
SLURRRP
Dip
Sang

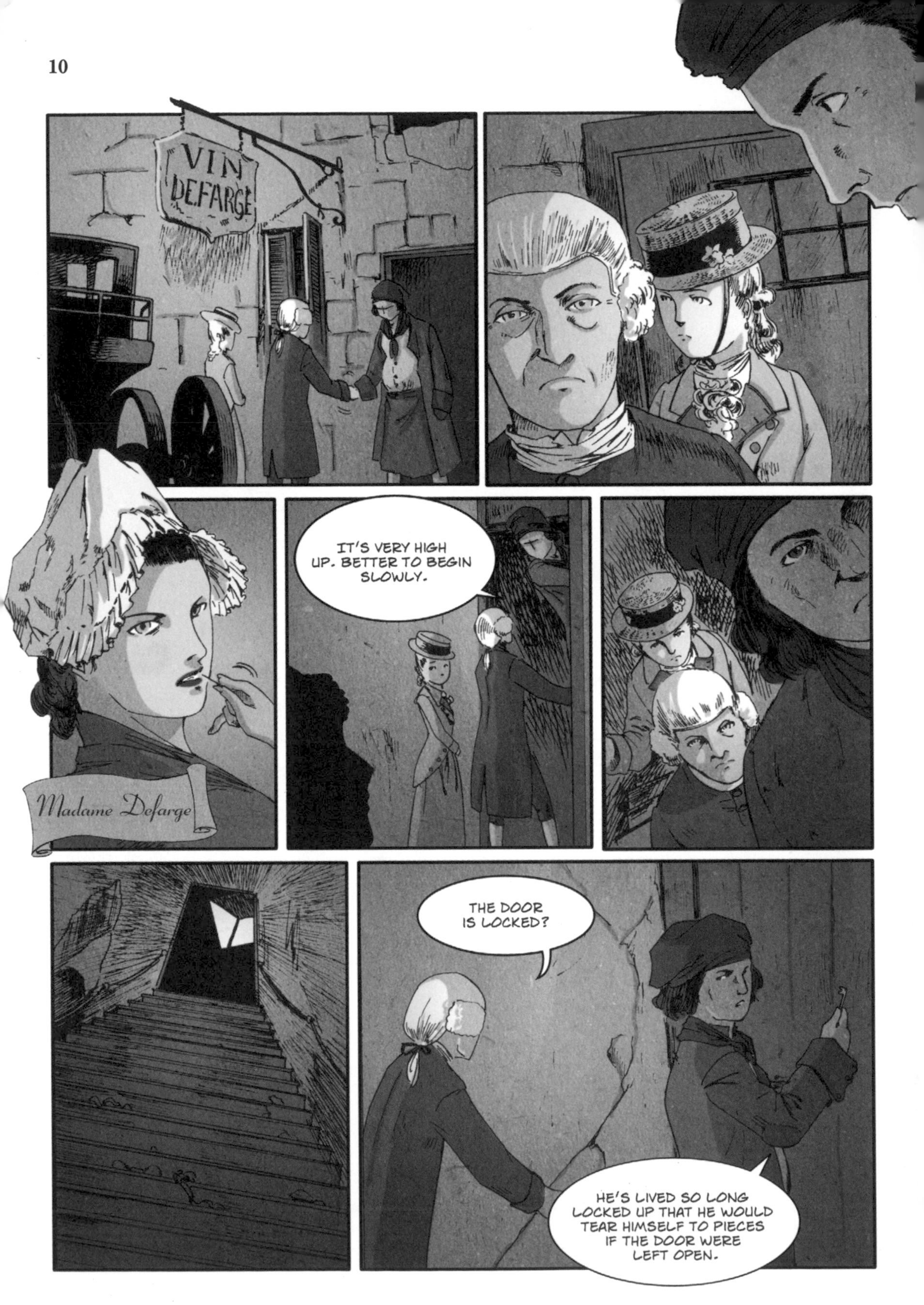
VIN DEFARGE
Madame Defarge
IT'S VERY HIGH UP. BETTER TO BEGIN SLOWLY.
THE DOOR IS LOCKED?
HE'S LIVED SO LONG LOCKED UP THAT HE WOULD TEAR HIMSELF TO PIECES IF THE DOOR WERE LEFT OPEN.

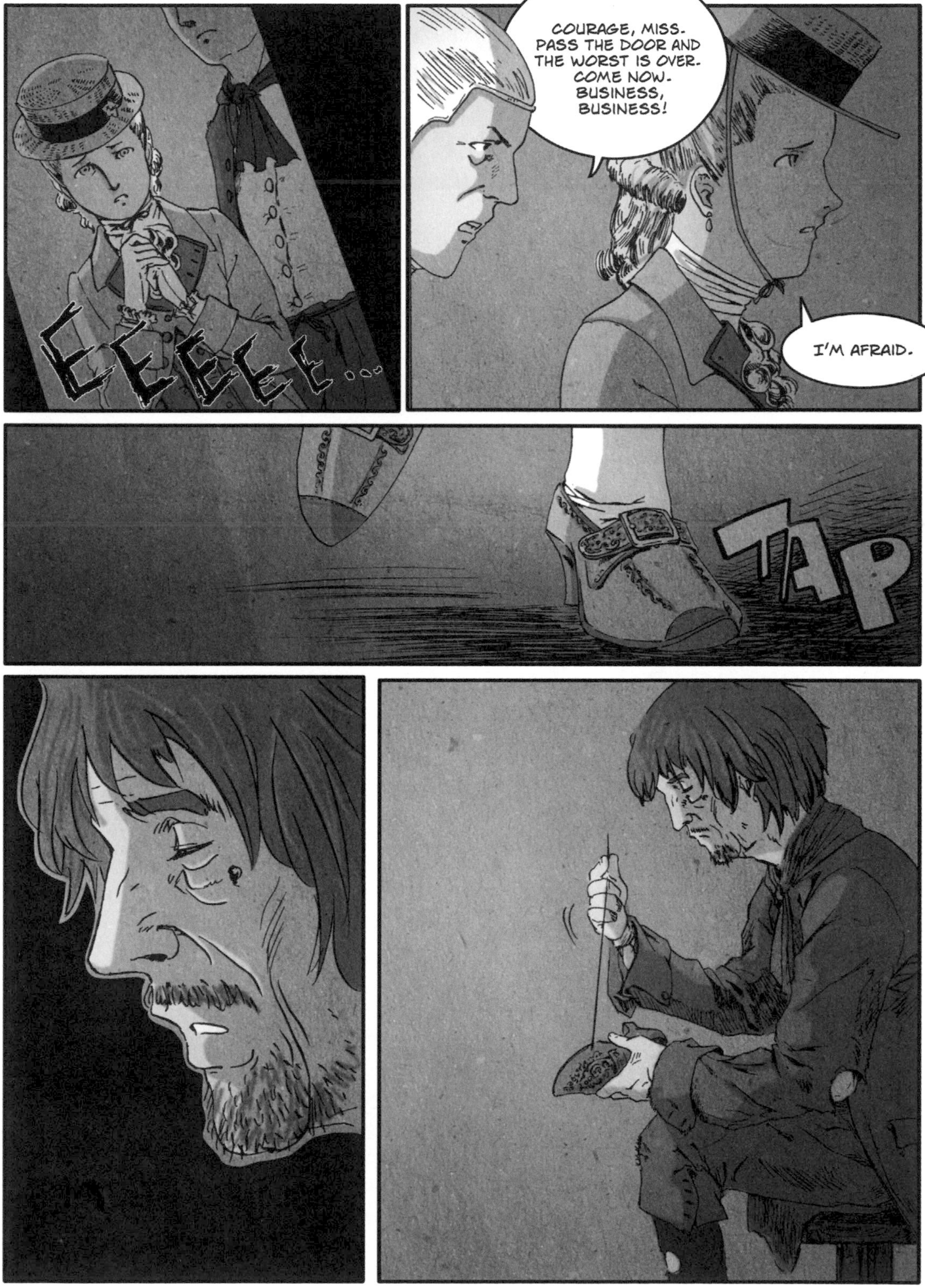
EEEEE...
COURAGE, MISS. PASS THE DOOR AND THE WORST IS OVER. COME NOW. BUSINESS, BUSINESS!
I'M AFRAID.
TAP

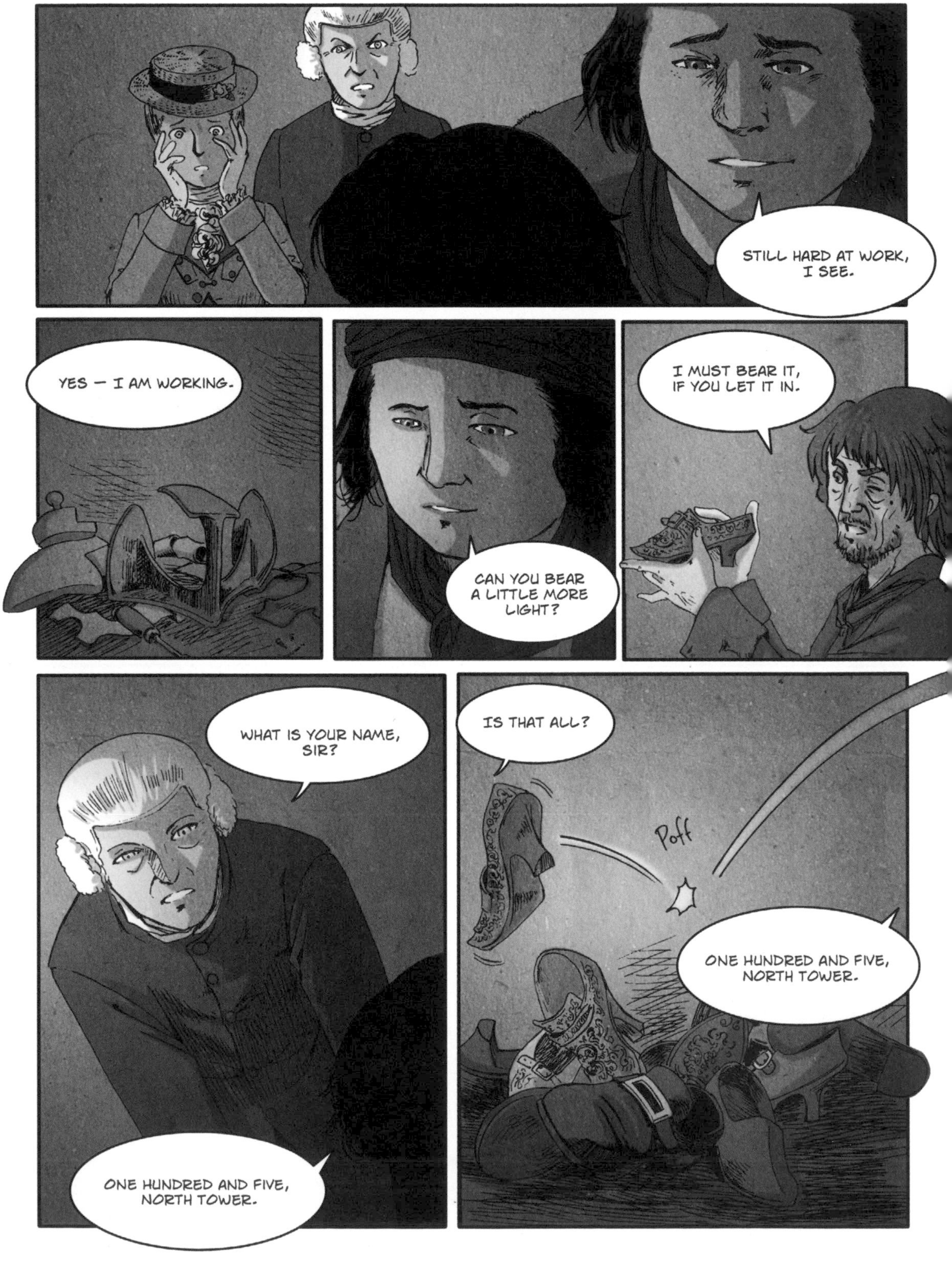
STILL HARD AT WORK, I SEE.
YES — I AM WORKING.
CAN YOU BEAR A LITTLE MORE LIGHT?
I MUST BEAR IT, IF YOU LET IT IN.
WHAT IS YOUR NAME, SIR?
ONE HUNDRED AND FIVE, NORTH TOWER.
IS THAT ALL?
Poff
ONE HUNDRED AND FIVE, NORTH TOWER.

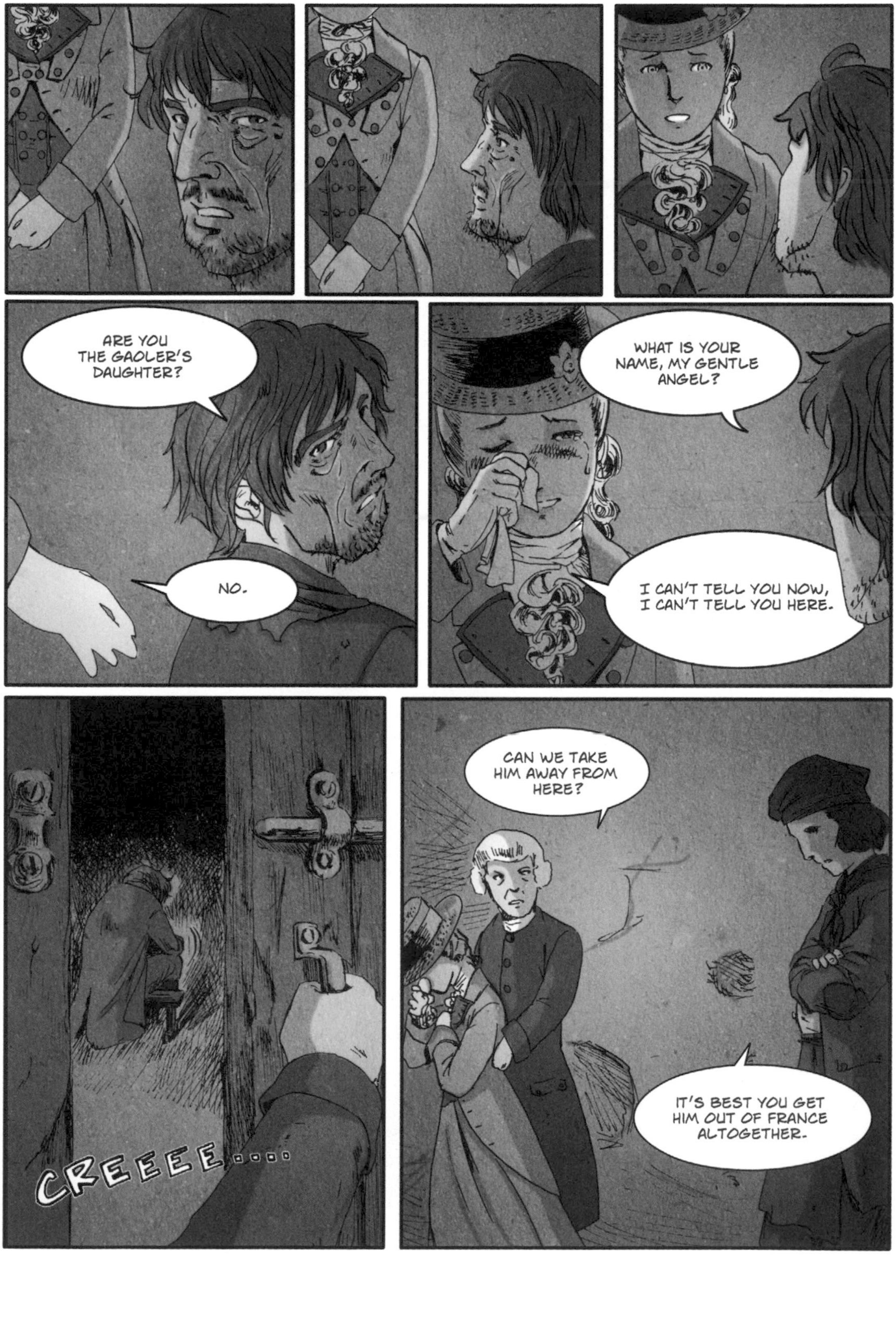
ARE YOU THE GAOLER'S DAUGHTER?
NO.
WHAT IS YOUR NAME, MY GENTLE ANGEL?
I CAN'T TELL YOU NOW, I CAN'T TELL YOU HERE.
CREEEEE....
CAN WE TAKE HIM AWAY FROM HERE?
IT'S BEST YOU GET HIM OUT OF FRANCE ALTOGETHER.

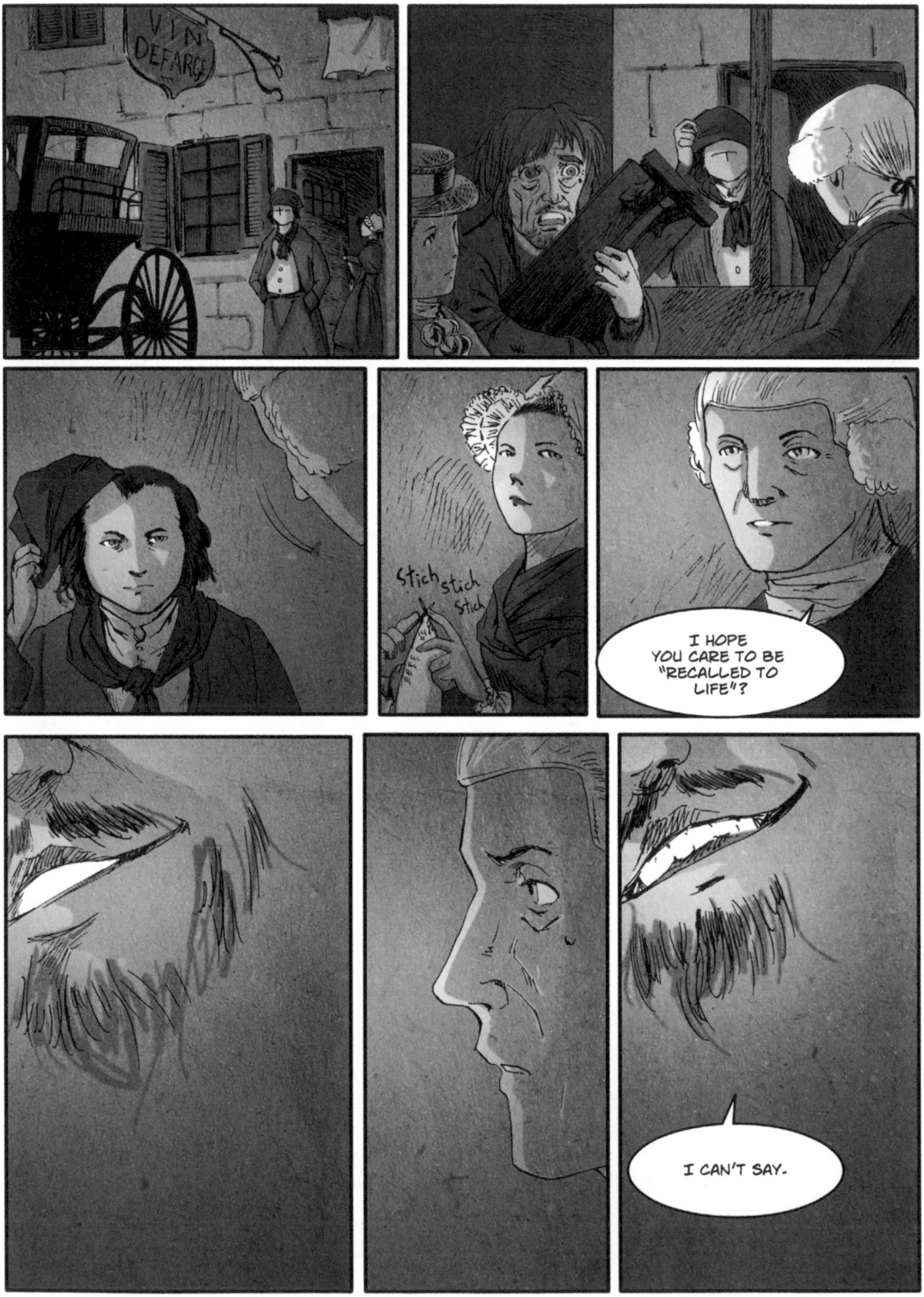
VIN
DEFARGE
Stich stich stich
I HOPE YOU CARE TO BE "RECALLED TO LIFE"?
I CAN'T SAY.

BOOK THE SECOND: The Golden Thread

*Putting to death was a recipe much in vogue
with all trades and professions.
The forger was put to Death;
the utterer of a bad note was put to Death;
the unlawful opener of a letter was put to Death;
the purloiner of forty shillings and
sixpence was put to Death;
the sounders of three-fourths of the notes
in the whole gamut of Crime, were put to Death...*

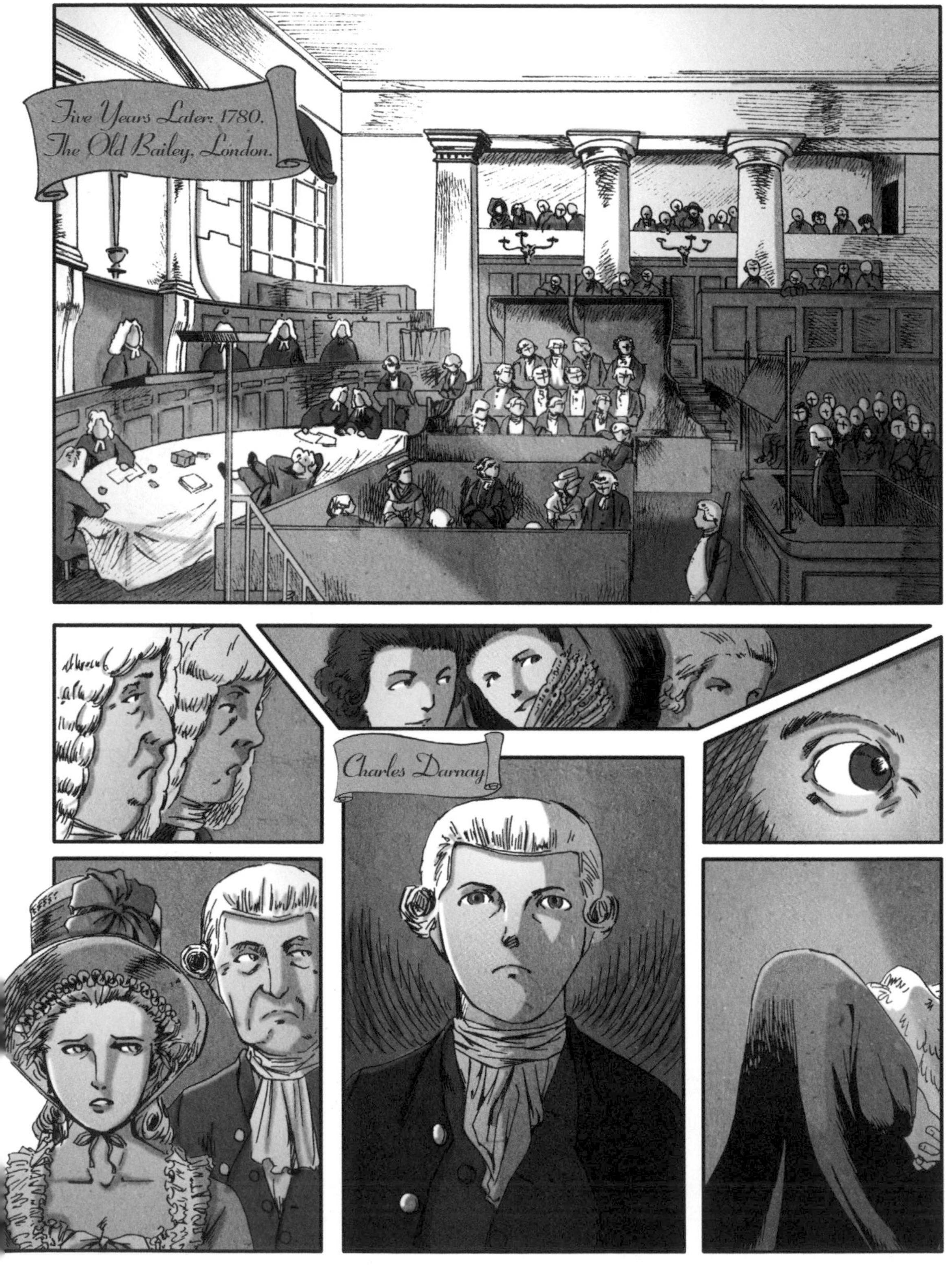
Five Years Later: 1780.
The Old Bailey, London.
Charles Darnay

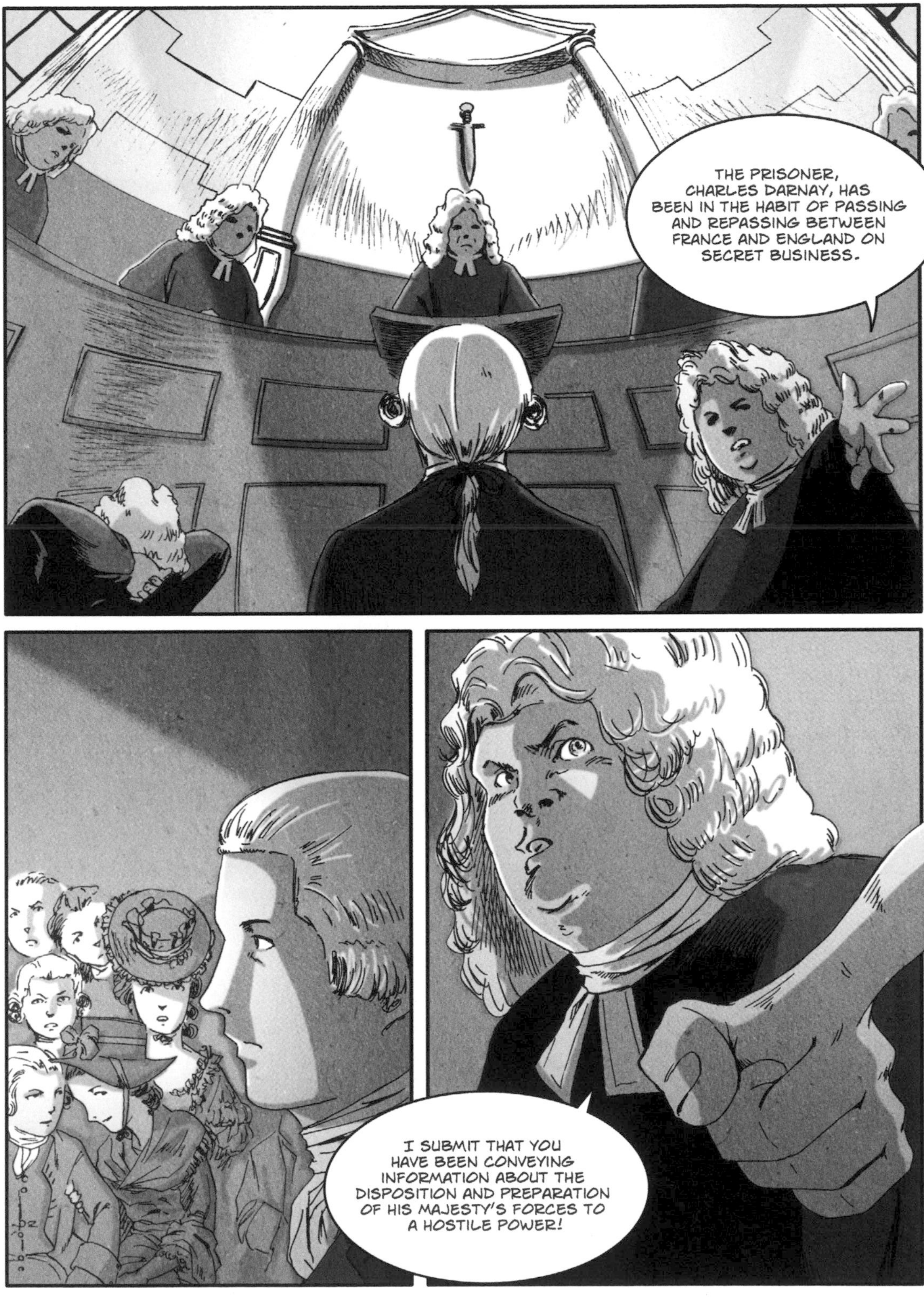
THE PRISONER, CHARLES DARNAY, HAS BEEN IN THE HABIT OF PASSING AND REPASSING BETWEEN FRANCE AND ENGLAND ON SECRET BUSINESS.
I SUBMIT THAT YOU HAVE BEEN CONVEYING INFORMATION ABOUT THE DISPOSITION AND PREPARATION OF HIS MAJESTY'S FORCES TO A HOSTILE POWER!

MISS MANETTE, HAVE YOU EVER SEEN THE PRISONER BEFORE?

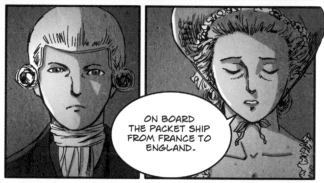

ON BOARD THE PACKET SHIP FROM FRANCE TO ENGLAND.

HE SAID HE WAS TRAVELING UNDER AN ASSUMED NAME, BETWEEN FRANCE AND ENGLAND, ON BUSINESS OF A DELICATE NATURE, WHICH MIGHT GET PEOPLE INTO TROUBLE.

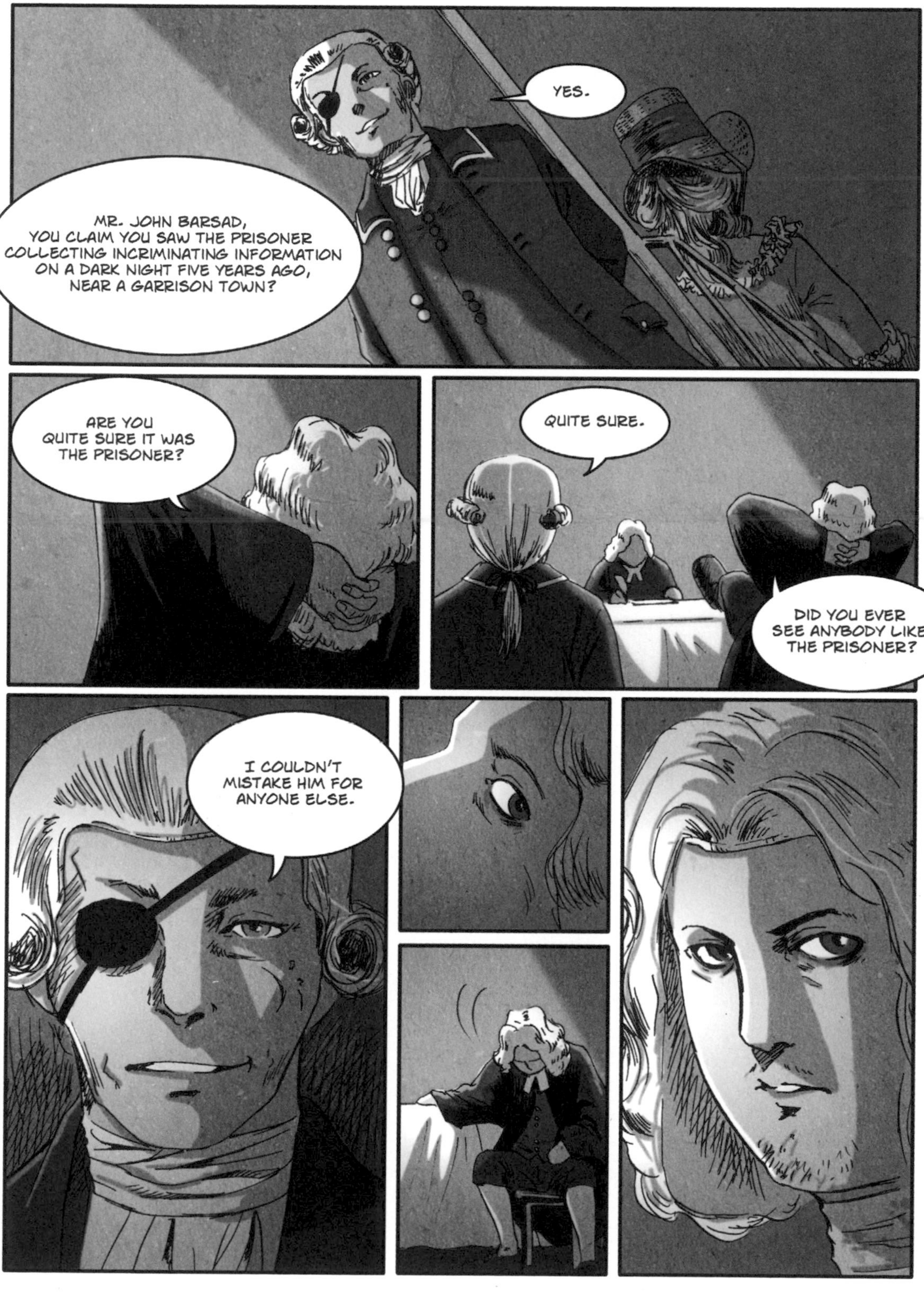
MR. JOHN BARSAD, YOU CLAIM YOU SAW THE PRISONER COLLECTING INCRIMINATING INFORMATION ON A DARK NIGHT FIVE YEARS AGO, NEAR A GARRISON TOWN?
YES.
ARE YOU QUITE SURE IT WAS THE PRISONER?
QUITE SURE.
DID YOU EVER SEE ANYBODY LIKE THE PRISONER?
I COULDN'T MISTAKE HIM FOR ANYONE ELSE.

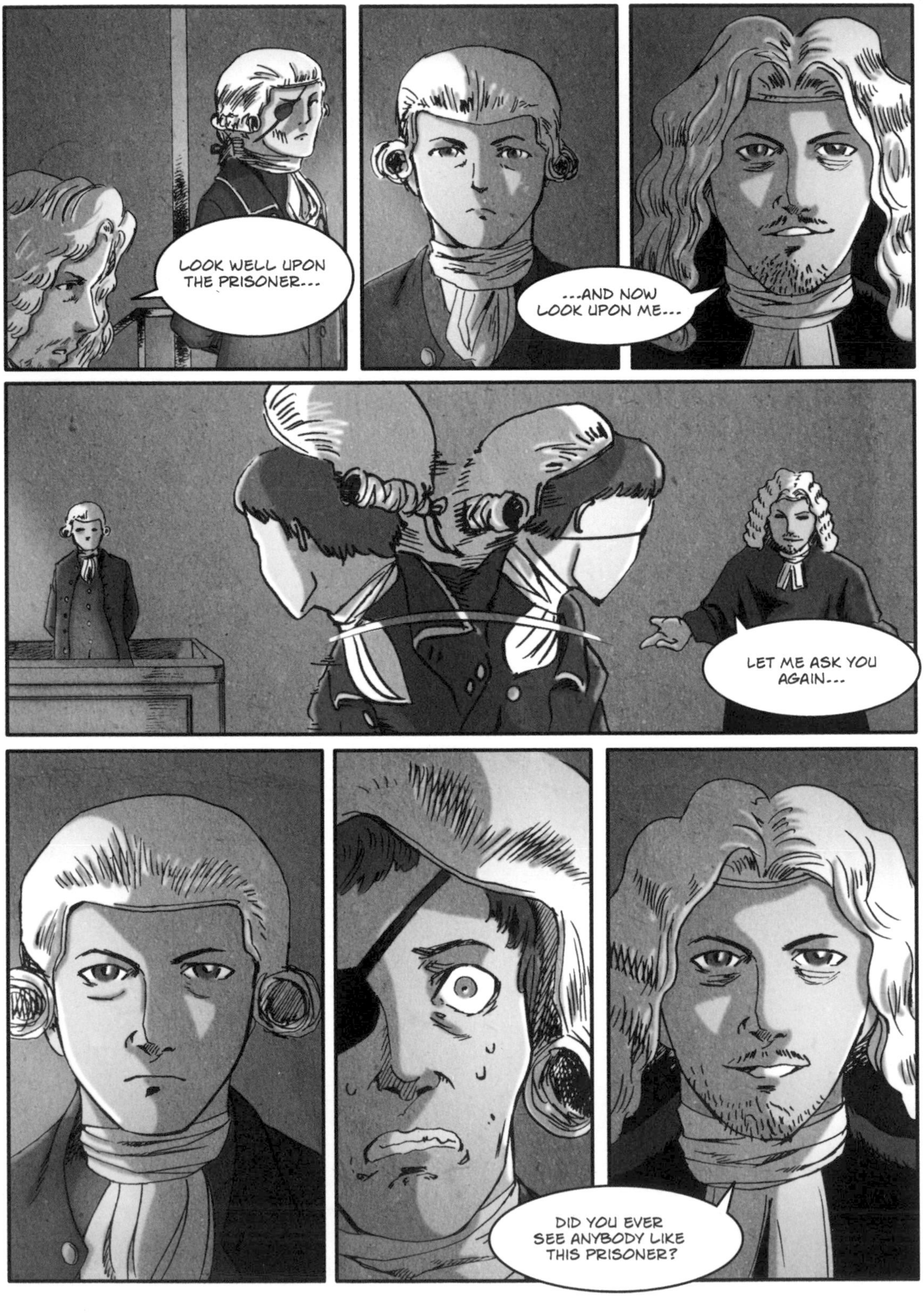
LOOK WELL UPON THE PRISONER...
...AND NOW LOOK UPON ME...
LET ME ASK YOU AGAIN...
DID YOU EVER SEE ANYBODY LIKE THIS PRISONER?

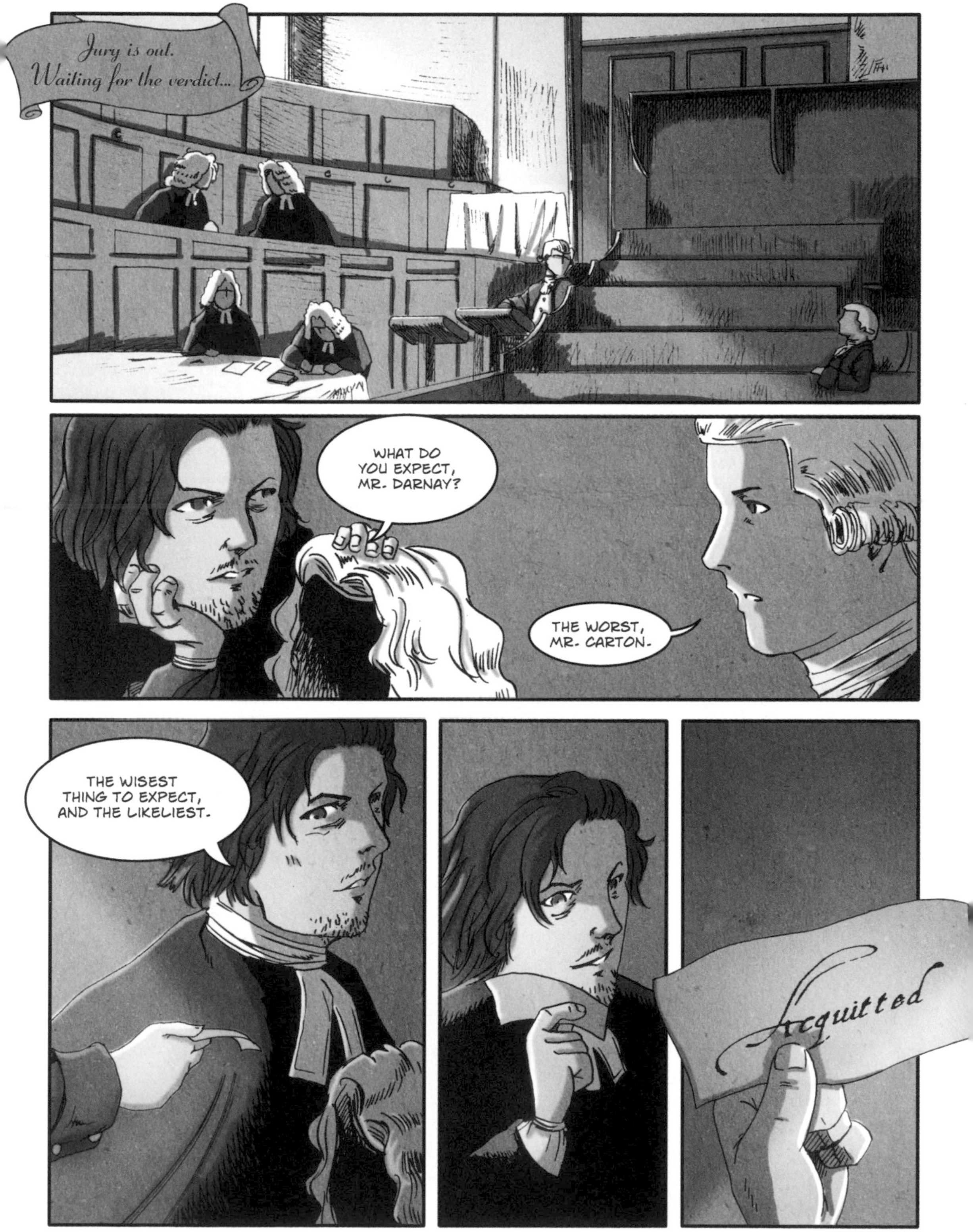
Jury is out.
Waiting for the verdict...
WHAT DO YOU EXPECT, MR. DARNAY?
THE WORST, MR. CARTON.
THE WISEST THING TO EXPECT, AND THE LIKELIEST.
Acquitted

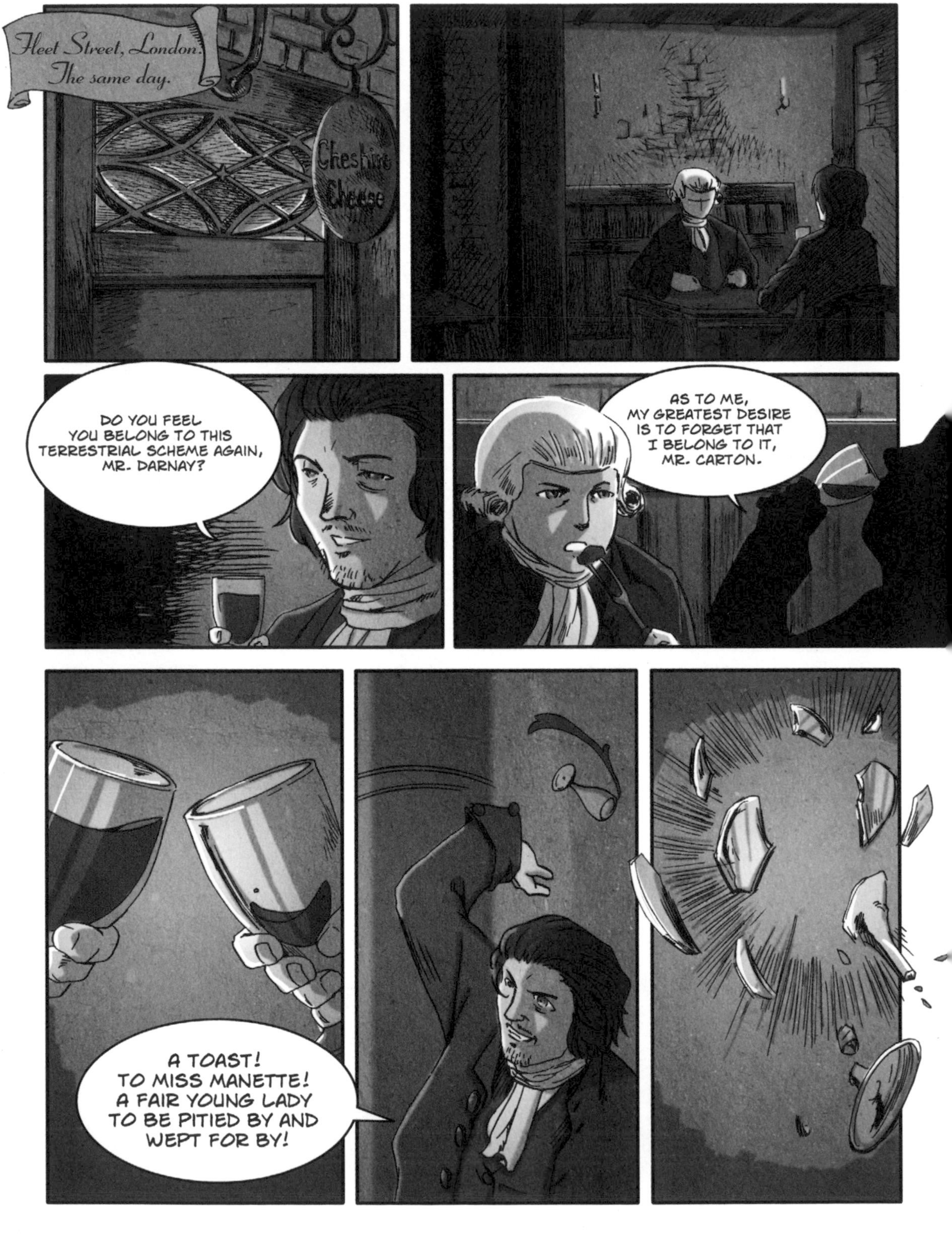
Fleet Street, London.
The same day.
Cheshire Cheese
DO YOU FEEL YOU BELONG TO THIS TERRESTRIAL SCHEME AGAIN, MR. DARNAY?
AS TO ME, MY GREATEST DESIRE IS TO FORGET THAT I BELONG TO IT, MR. CARTON.
A TOAST! TO MISS MANETTE! A FAIR YOUNG LADY TO BE PITIED BY AND WEPT FOR BY!

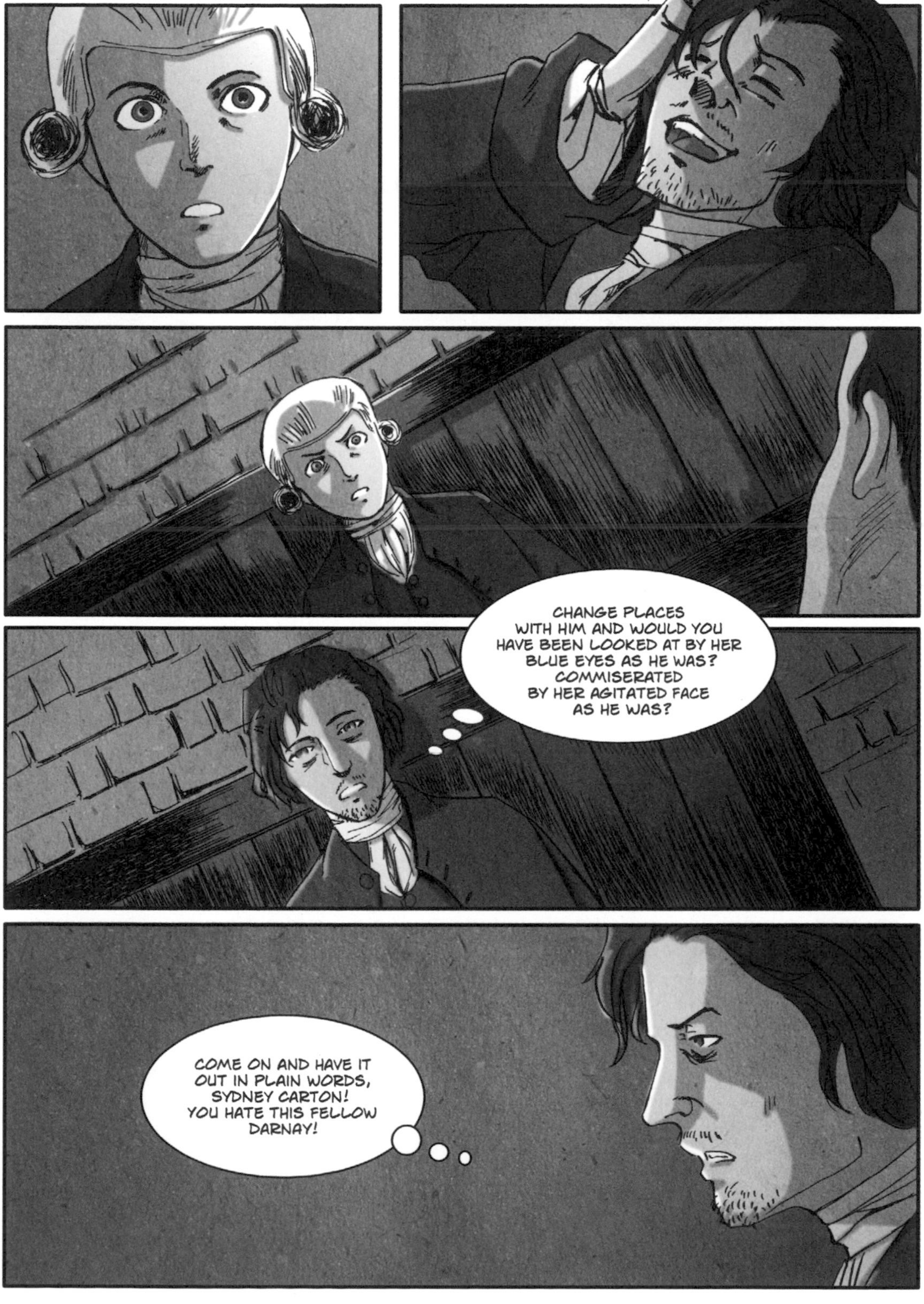
CHANGE PLACES WITH HIM AND WOULD YOU HAVE BEEN LOOKED AT BY HER BLUE EYES AS HE WAS? COMMISERATED BY HER AGITATED FACE AS HE WAS?
COME ON AND HAVE IT OUT IN PLAIN WORDS, SYDNEY CARTON! YOU HATE THIS FELLOW DARNAY!

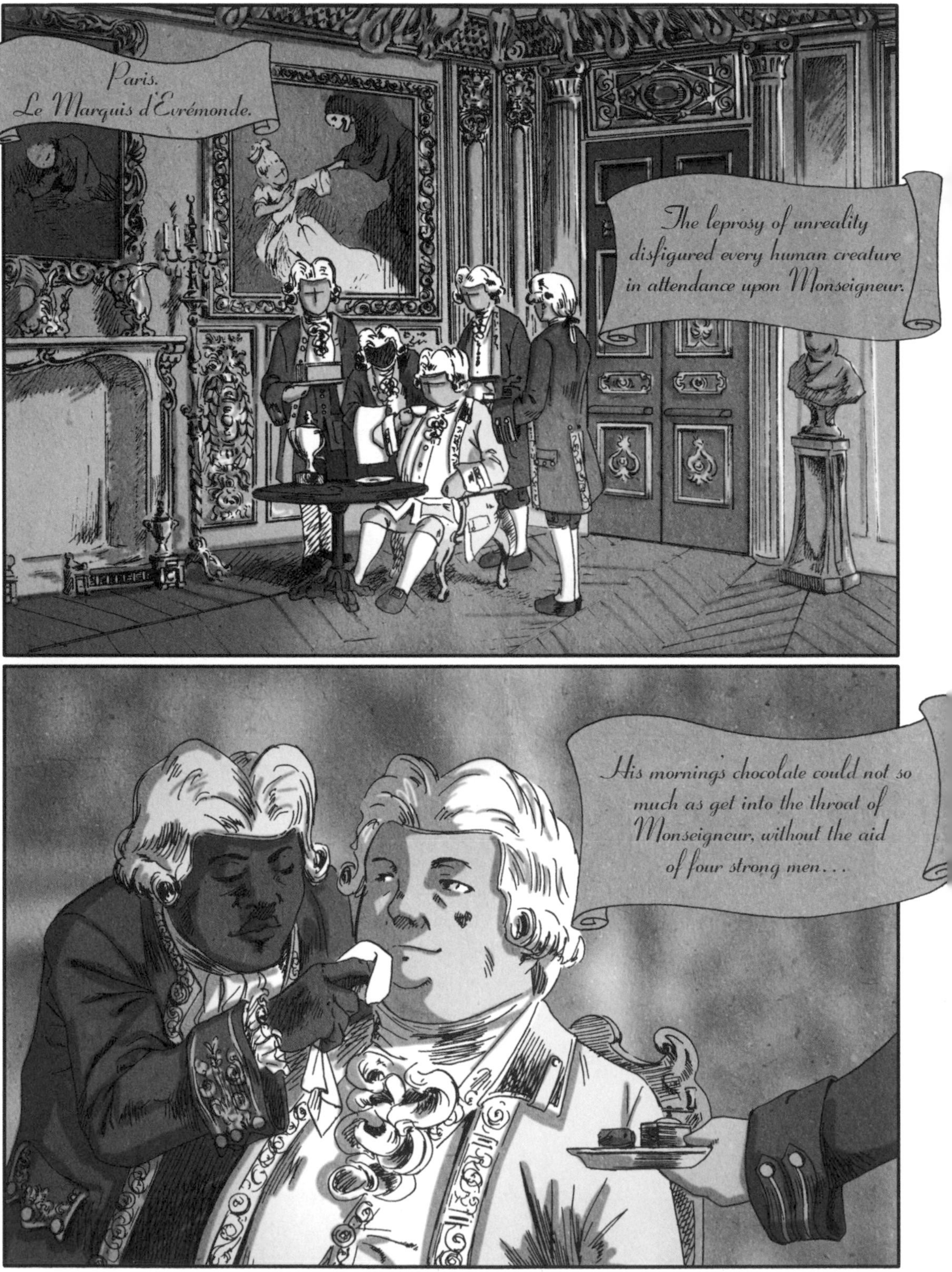
Paris.
Le Marquis d'Evrémonde.
The leprosy of unreality disfigured every human creature in attendance upon Monseigneur.
His mornings chocolate could not so much as get into the throat of Monseigneur, without the aid of four strong men...

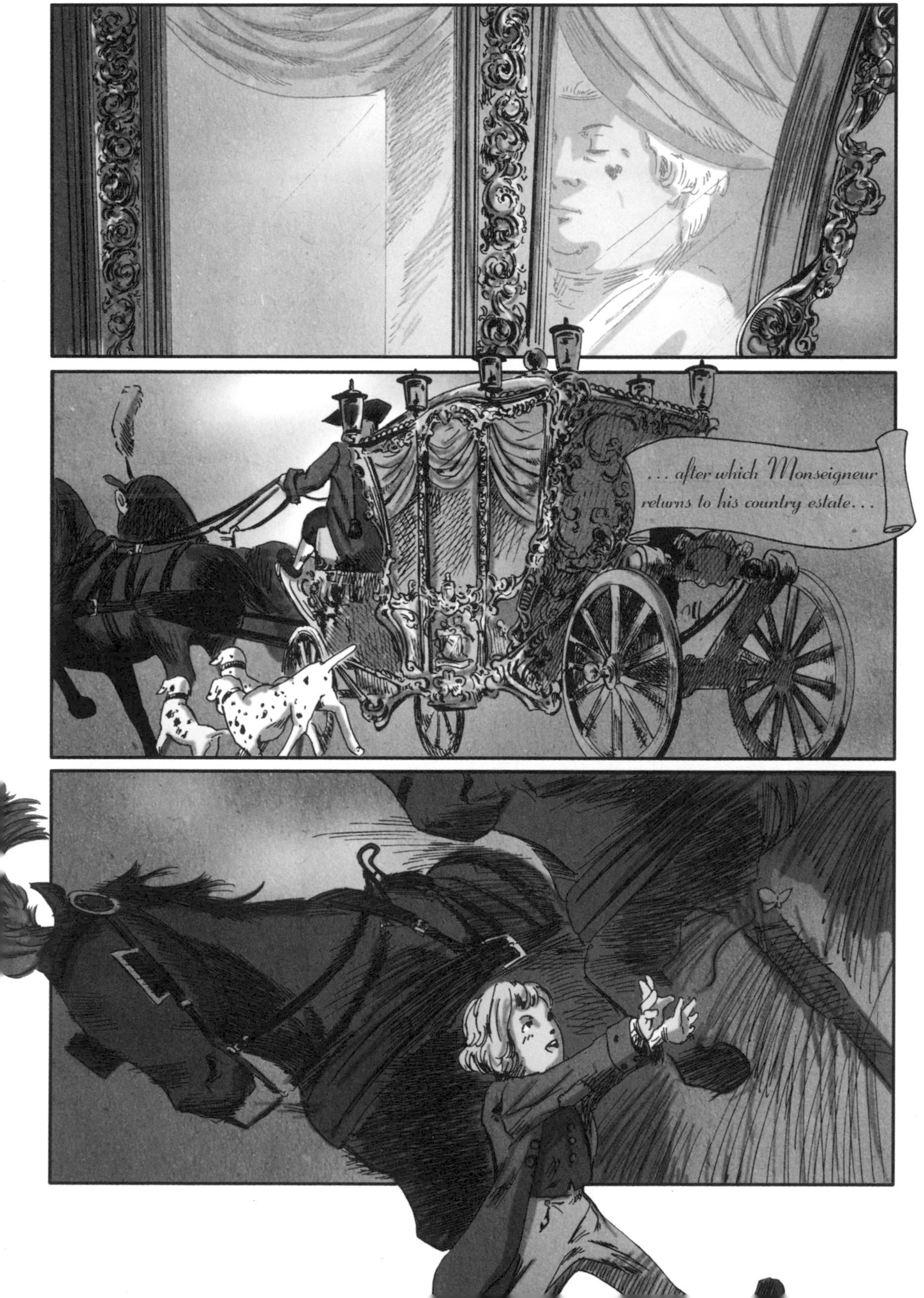
. . . after which Monseigneur returns to his country estate . . .

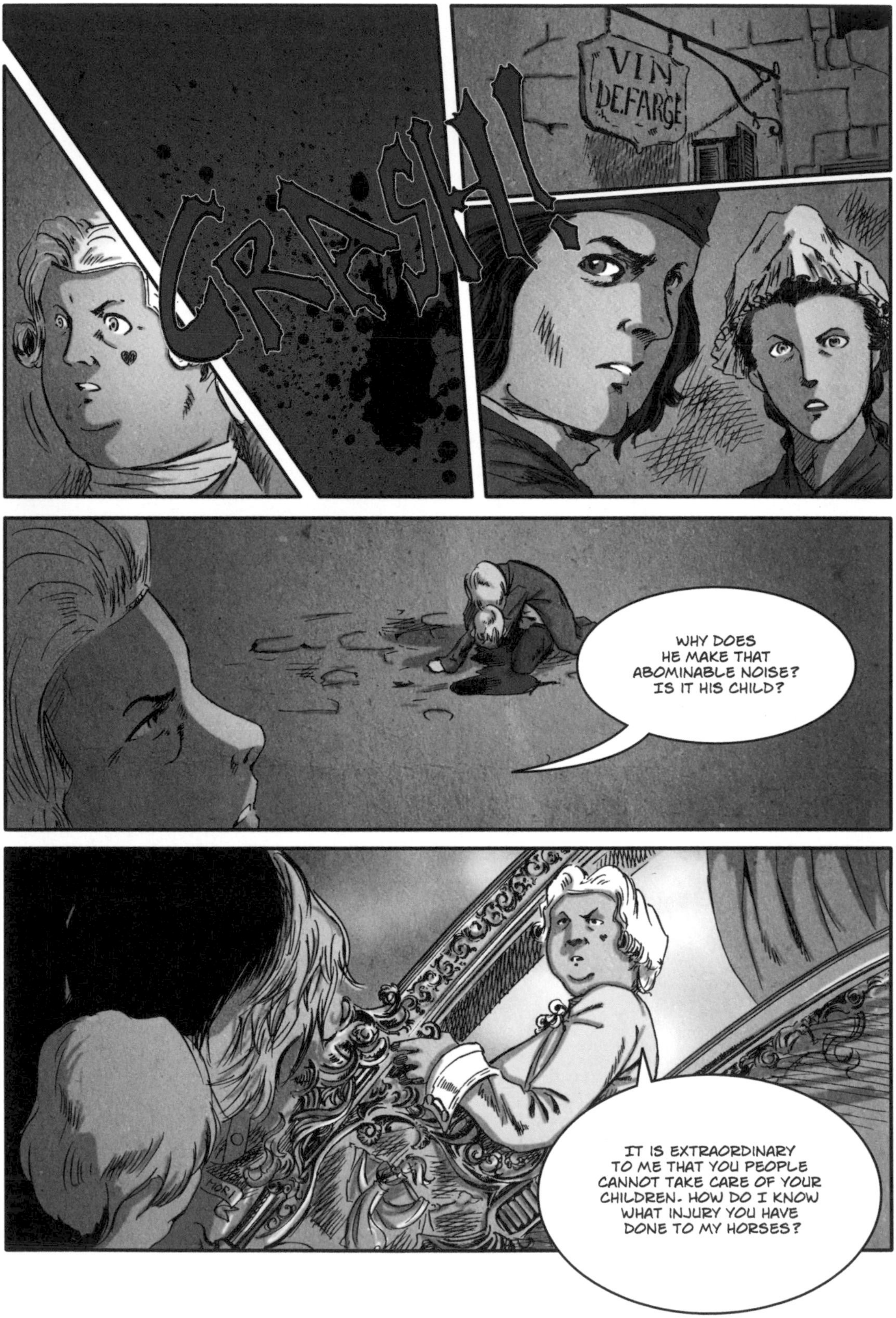
VIN DEFARGE
CRASH!
WHY DOES HE MAKE THAT ABOMINABLE NOISE? IS IT HIS CHILD?
IT IS EXTRAORDINARY TO ME THAT YOU PEOPLE CANNOT TAKE CARE OF YOUR CHILDREN. HOW DO I KNOW WHAT INJURY YOU HAVE DONE TO MY HORSES?

HE DIED IN A MOMENT WITHOUT PAIN. COULD HE HAVE LIVED AN HOUR AS HAPPILY?

YOU ARE A PHILOSOPHER. HOW DO THEY CALL YOU?

DEFARGE.

PING

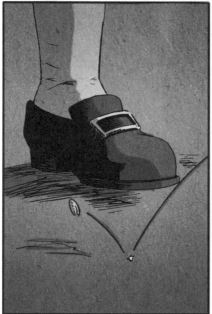

PICK THIS UP, DEFARGE. AND SPEND IT AS YOU WILL.

CLOP

CLOP

CLOP

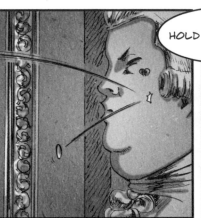

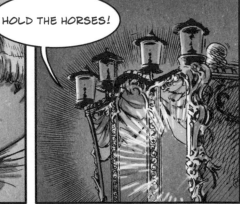

HOLD THE HORSES!

SCREEEEEEE

YOU DOGS! I WOULD RIDE OVER ANY OF YOU VERY WILLINGLY, AND EXTERMINATE YOU FROM THE EARTH.

IF I KNEW WHICH ONE OF YOU THREW THAT COIN, HE SHOULD BE CRUSHED UNDER THE WHEELS!

knit knit

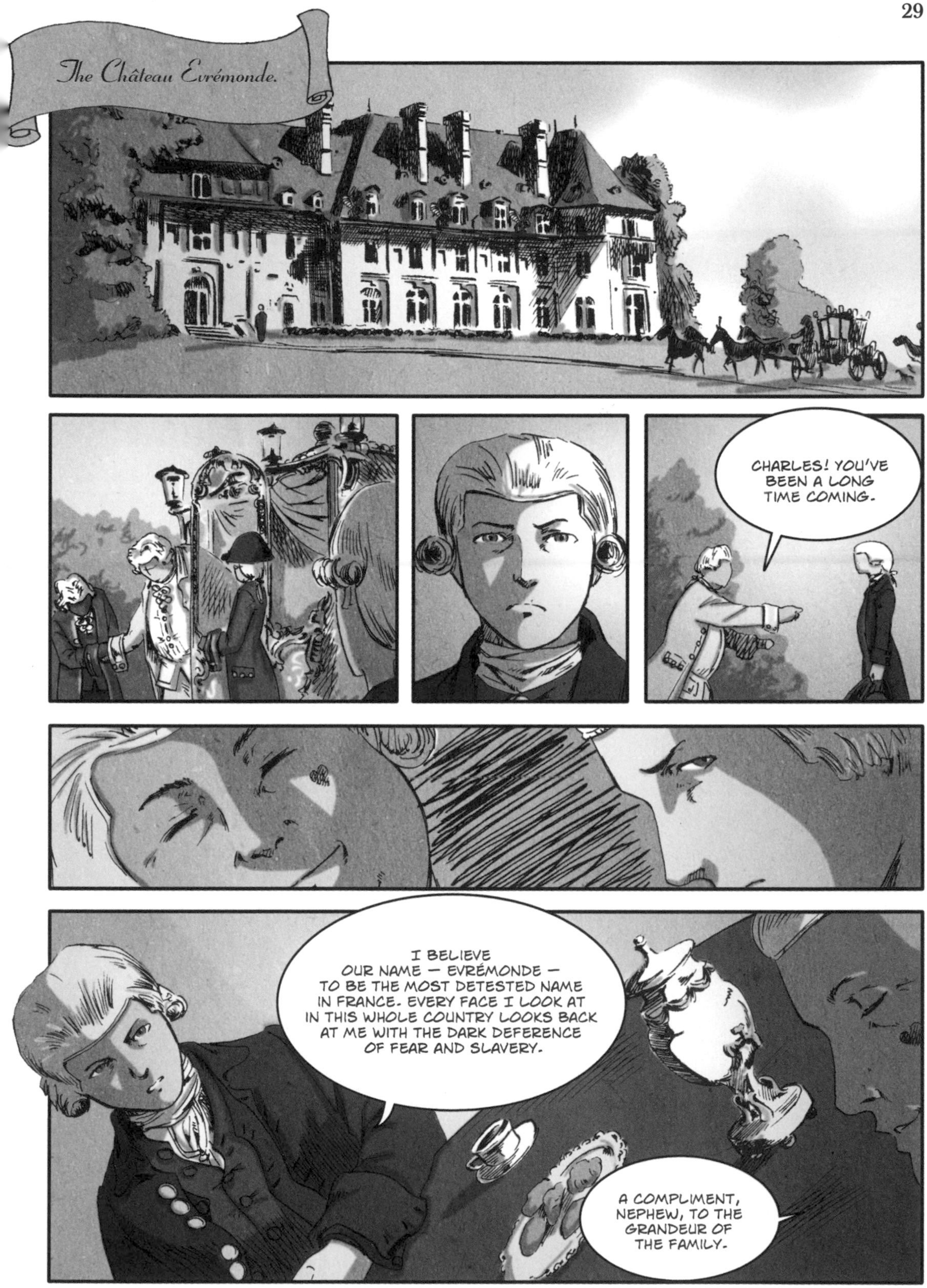
The Château Evrémonde.
CHARLES! YOU'VE BEEN A LONG TIME COMING.
I BELIEVE OUR NAME — EVRÉMONDE — TO BE THE MOST DETESTED NAME IN FRANCE. EVERY FACE I LOOK AT IN THIS WHOLE COUNTRY LOOKS BACK AT ME WITH THE DARK DEFERENCE OF FEAR AND SLAVERY.
A COMPLIMENT, NEPHEW, TO THE GRANDEUR OF THE FAMILY.

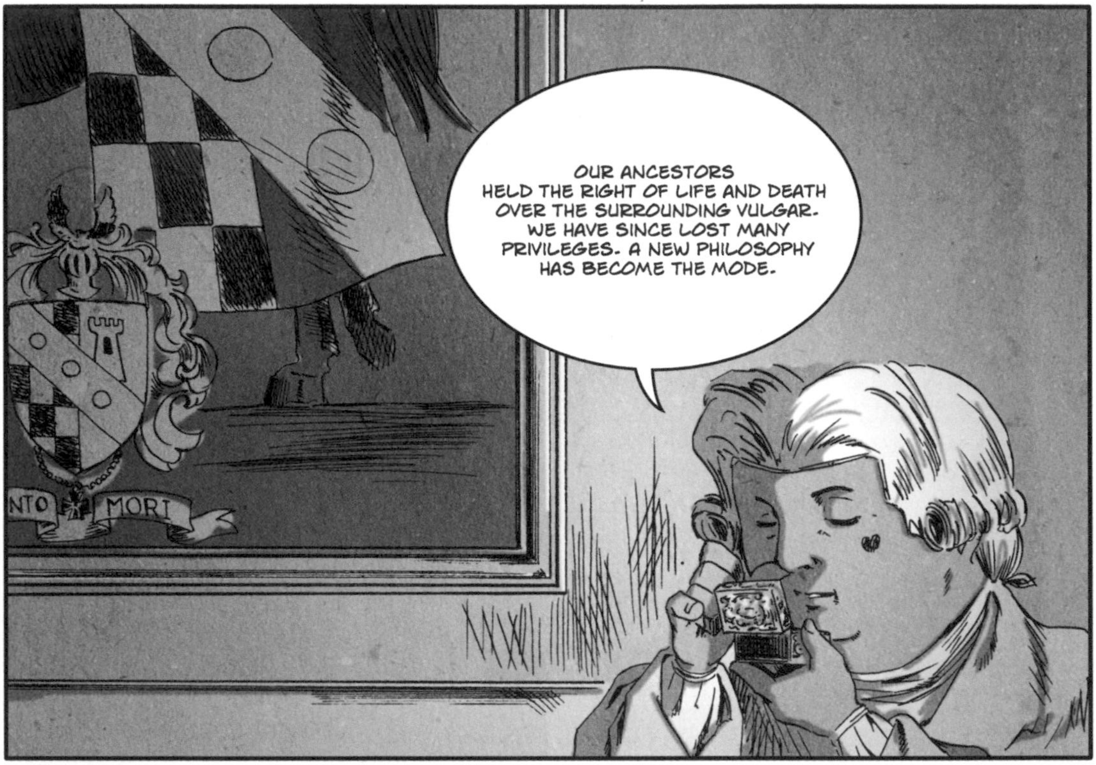
NTO MORI
OUR ANCESTORS HELD THE RIGHT OF LIFE AND DEATH OVER THE SURROUNDING VULGAR. WE HAVE SINCE LOST MANY PRIVILEGES. A NEW PHILOSOPHY HAS BECOME THE MODE.

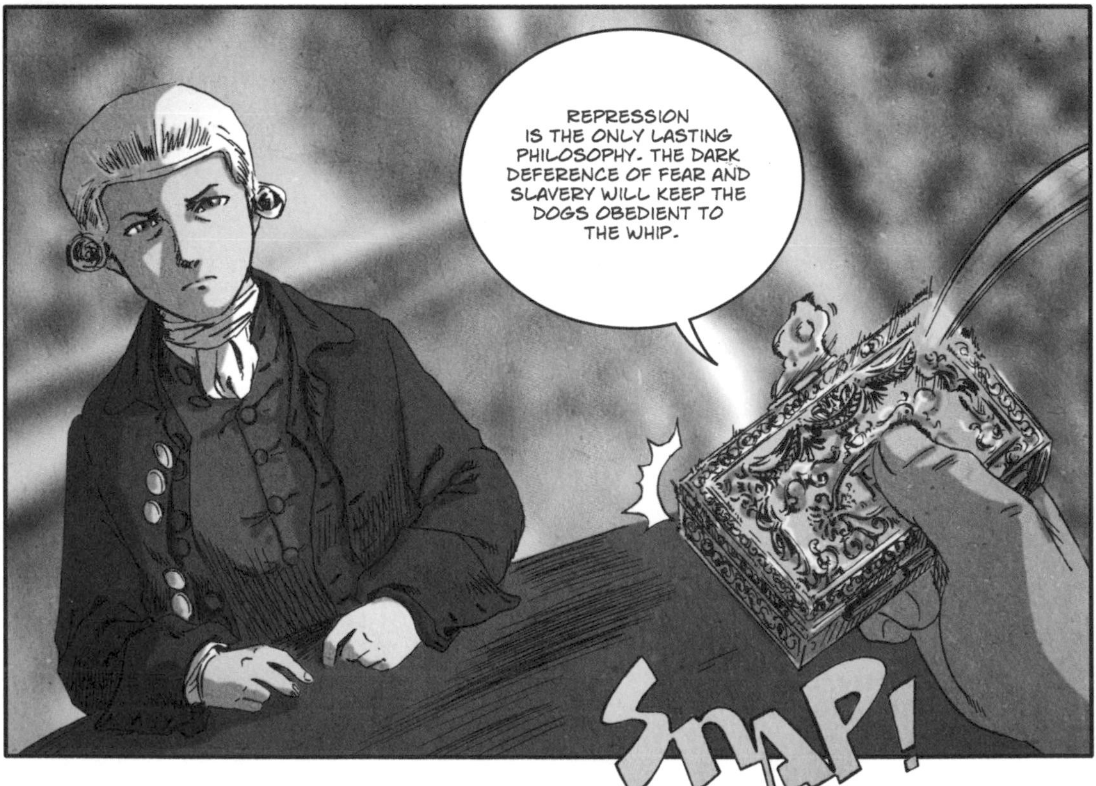
REPRESSION IS THE ONLY LASTING PHILOSOPHY. THE DARK DEFERENCE OF FEAR AND SLAVERY WILL KEEP THE DOGS OBEDIENT TO THE WHIP.
SNAP!

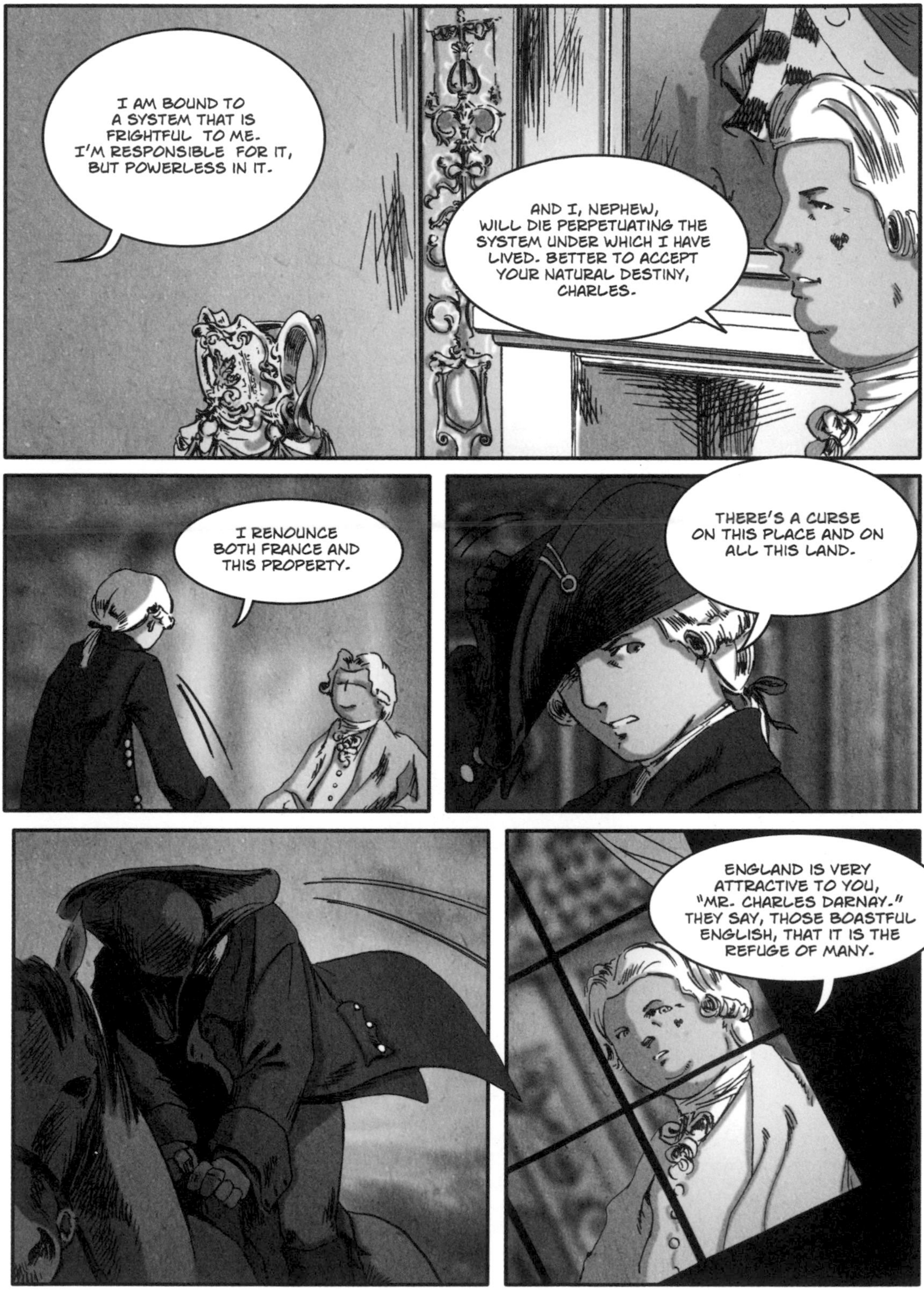
I AM BOUND TO A SYSTEM THAT IS FRIGHTFUL TO ME. I'M RESPONSIBLE FOR IT, BUT POWERLESS IN IT.
AND I, NEPHEW, WILL DIE PERPETUATING THE SYSTEM UNDER WHICH I HAVE LIVED. BETTER TO ACCEPT YOUR NATURAL DESTINY, CHARLES.
I RENOUNCE BOTH FRANCE AND THIS PROPERTY.
THERE'S A CURSE ON THIS PLACE AND ON ALL THIS LAND.
ENGLAND IS VERY ATTRACTIVE TO YOU, "MR. CHARLES DARNAY." THEY SAY, THOSE BOASTFUL ENGLISH, THAT IT IS THE REFUGE OF MANY.

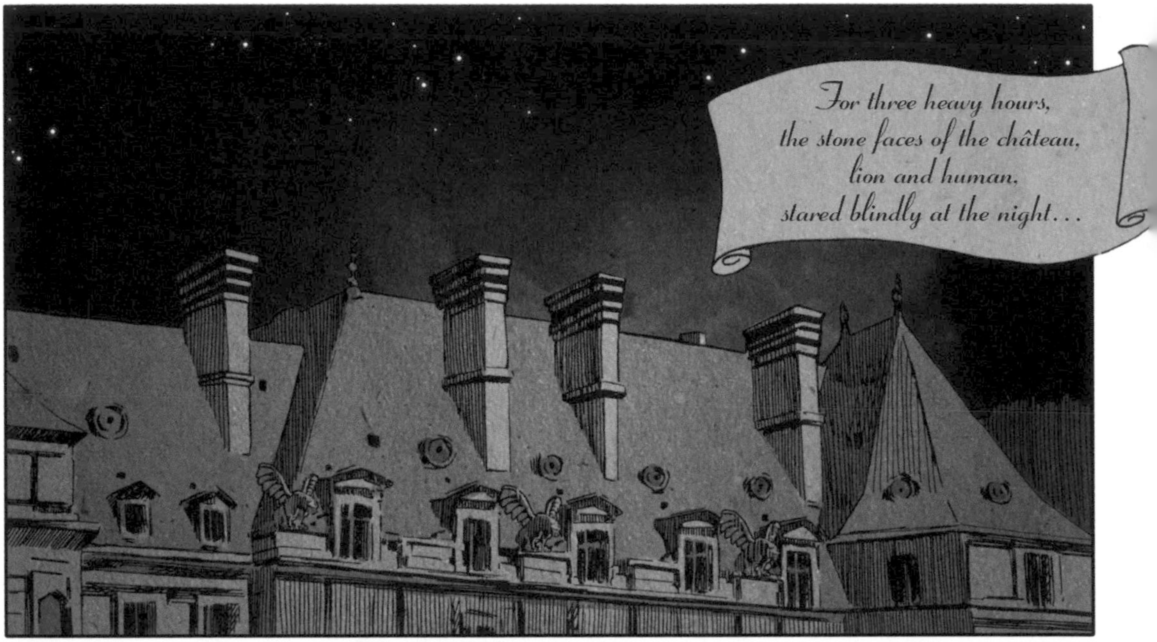
For three heavy hours,
the stone faces of the château,
lion and human,
stared blindly at the night...

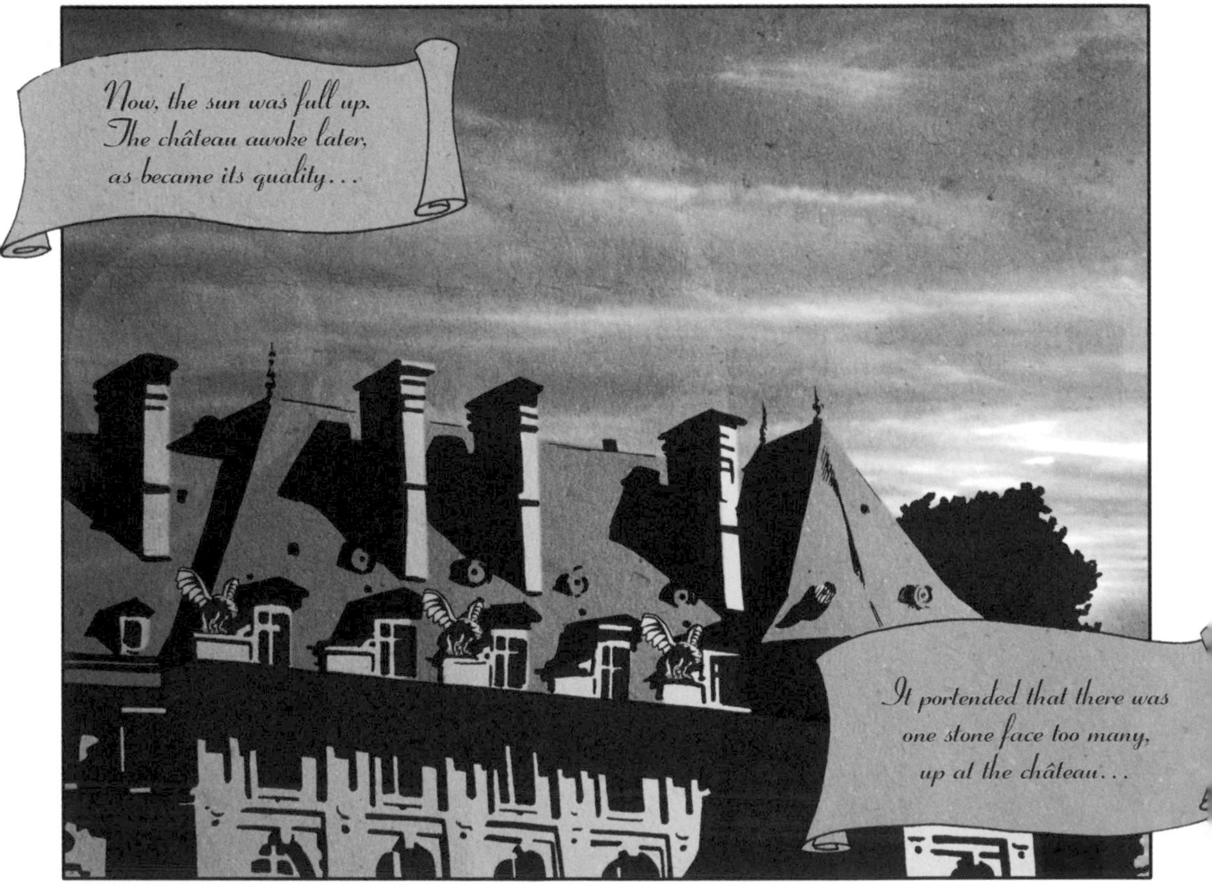
Now, the sun was full up.
The château awoke later,
as became its quality...
It portended that there was
one stone face too many,
up at the château...

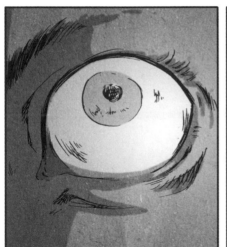

Drive him fast to his tomb.
This, from Jacques!

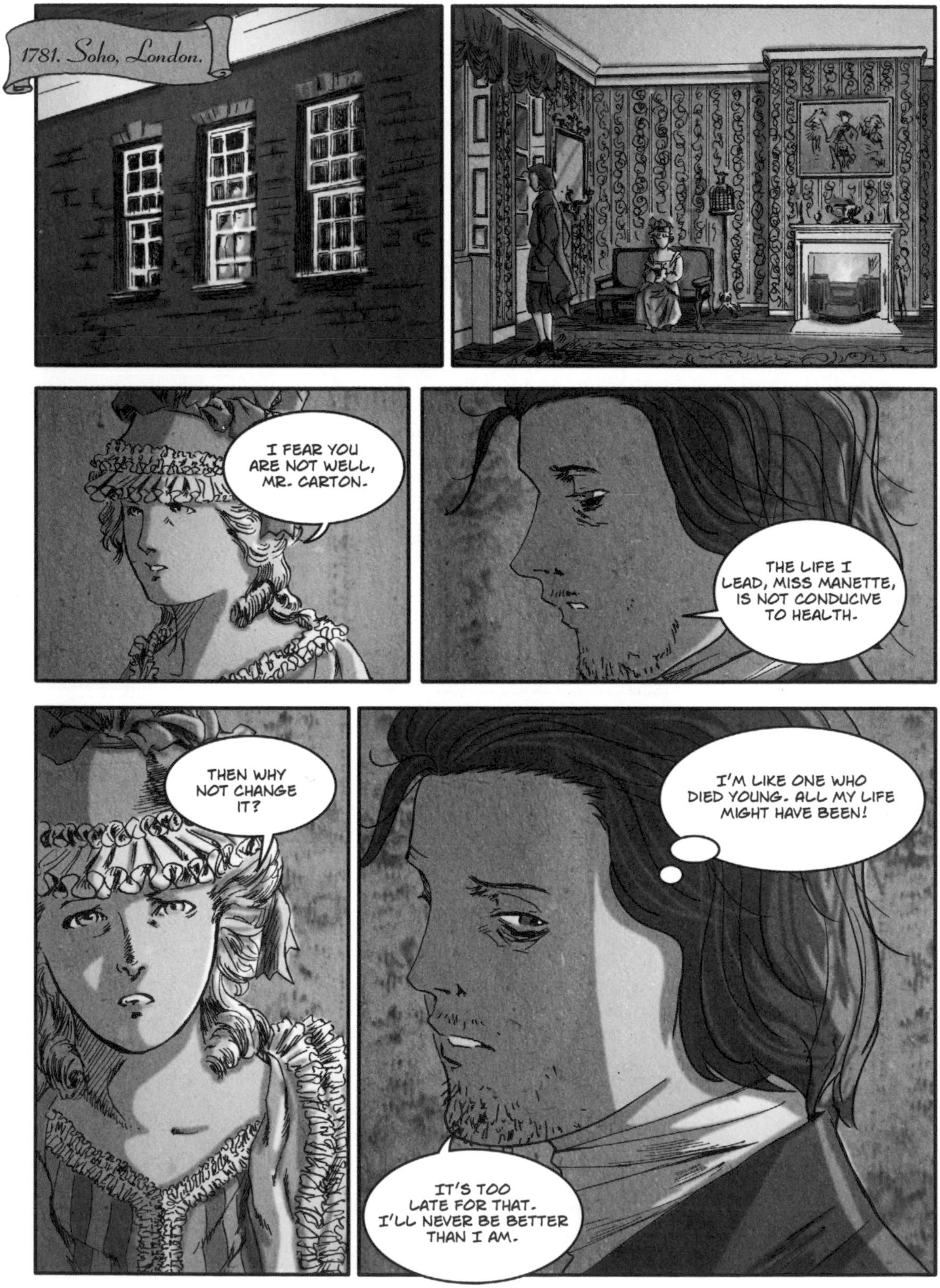
1781. Soho, London.
I FEAR YOU ARE NOT WELL, MR. CARTON.
THE LIFE I LEAD, MISS MANETTE, IS NOT CONDUCIVE TO HEALTH.
THEN WHY NOT CHANGE IT?
I'M LIKE ONE WHO DIED YOUNG. ALL MY LIFE MIGHT HAVE BEEN!
IT'S TOO LATE FOR THAT. I'LL NEVER BE BETTER THAN I AM.

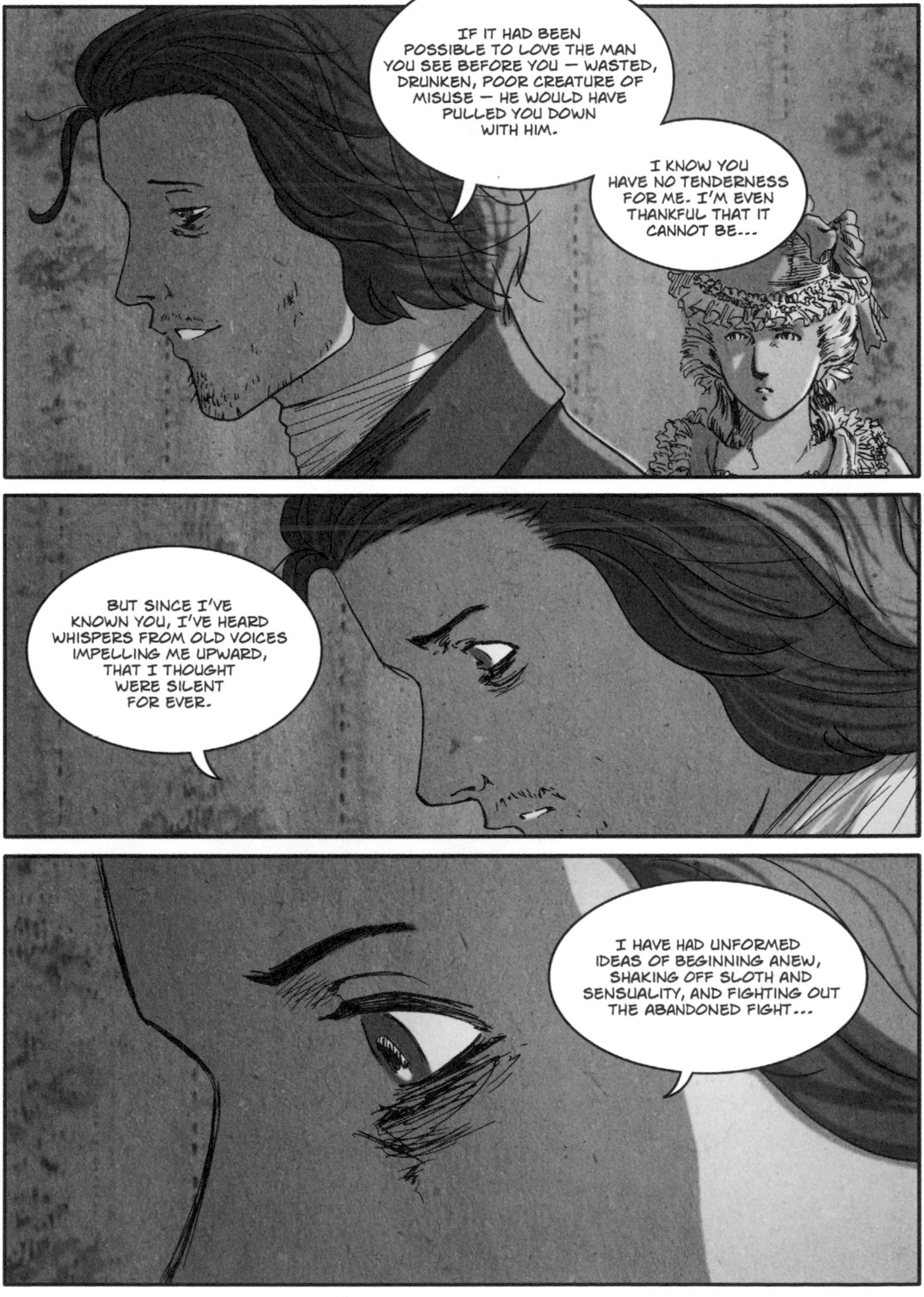
IF IT HAD BEEN POSSIBLE TO LOVE THE MAN YOU SEE BEFORE YOU — WASTED, DRUNKEN, POOR CREATURE OF MISUSE — HE WOULD HAVE PULLED YOU DOWN WITH HIM.
I KNOW YOU HAVE NO TENDERNESS FOR ME. I'M EVEN THANKFUL THAT IT CANNOT BE...
BUT SINCE I'VE KNOWN YOU, I'VE HEARD WHISPERS FROM OLD VOICES IMPELLING ME UPWARD, THAT I THOUGHT WERE SILENT FOR EVER.
I HAVE HAD UNFORMED IDEAS OF BEGINNING ANEW, SHAKING OFF SLOTH AND SENSUALITY, AND FIGHTING OUT THE ABANDONED FIGHT...

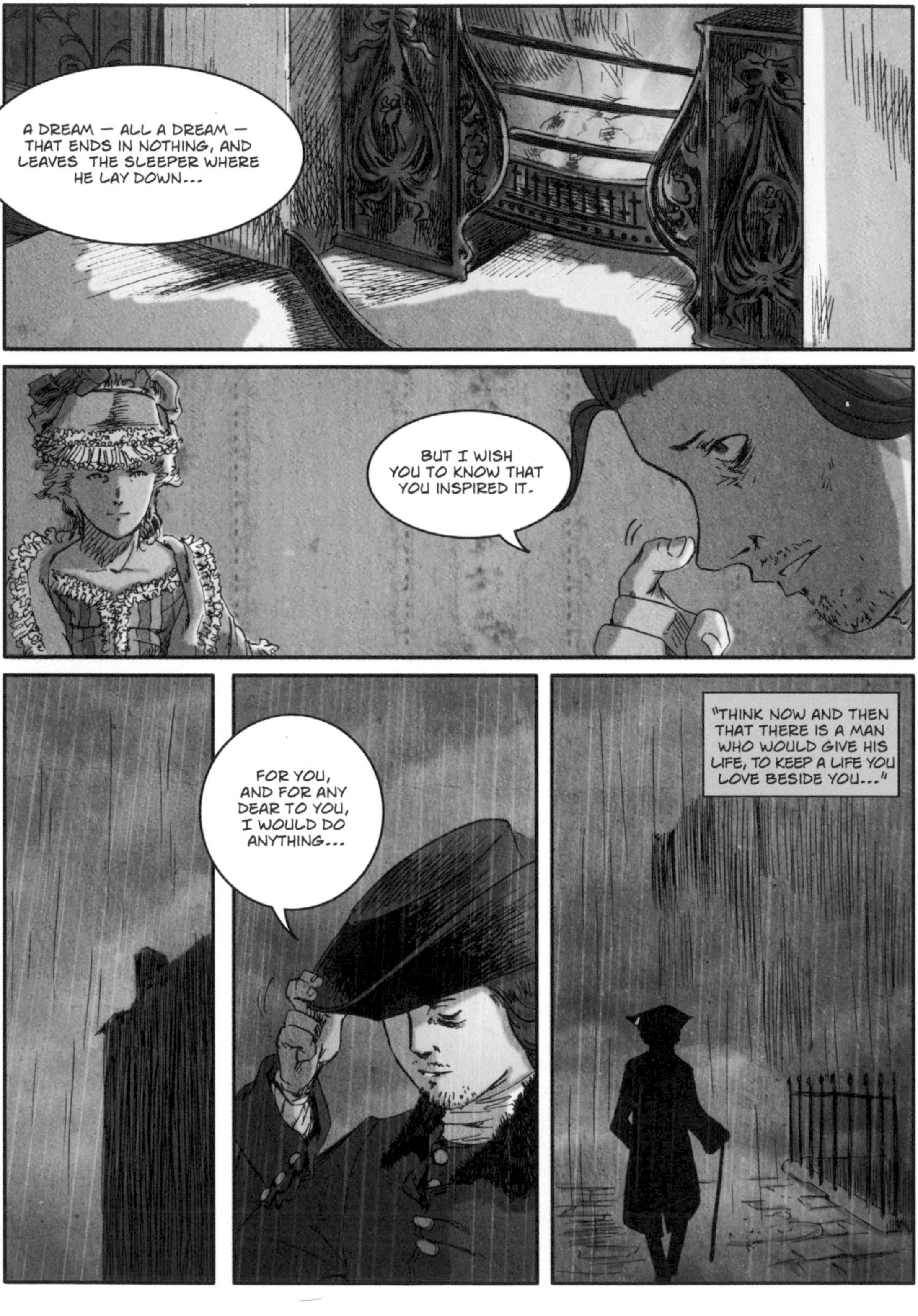
A DREAM — ALL A DREAM — THAT ENDS IN NOTHING, AND LEAVES THE SLEEPER WHERE HE LAY DOWN...
BUT I WISH YOU TO KNOW THAT YOU INSPIRED IT.
FOR YOU, AND FOR ANY DEAR TO YOU, I WOULD DO ANYTHING...
"THINK NOW AND THEN THAT THERE IS A MAN WHO WOULD GIVE HIS LIFE, TO KEEP A LIFE YOU LOVE BESIDE YOU..."

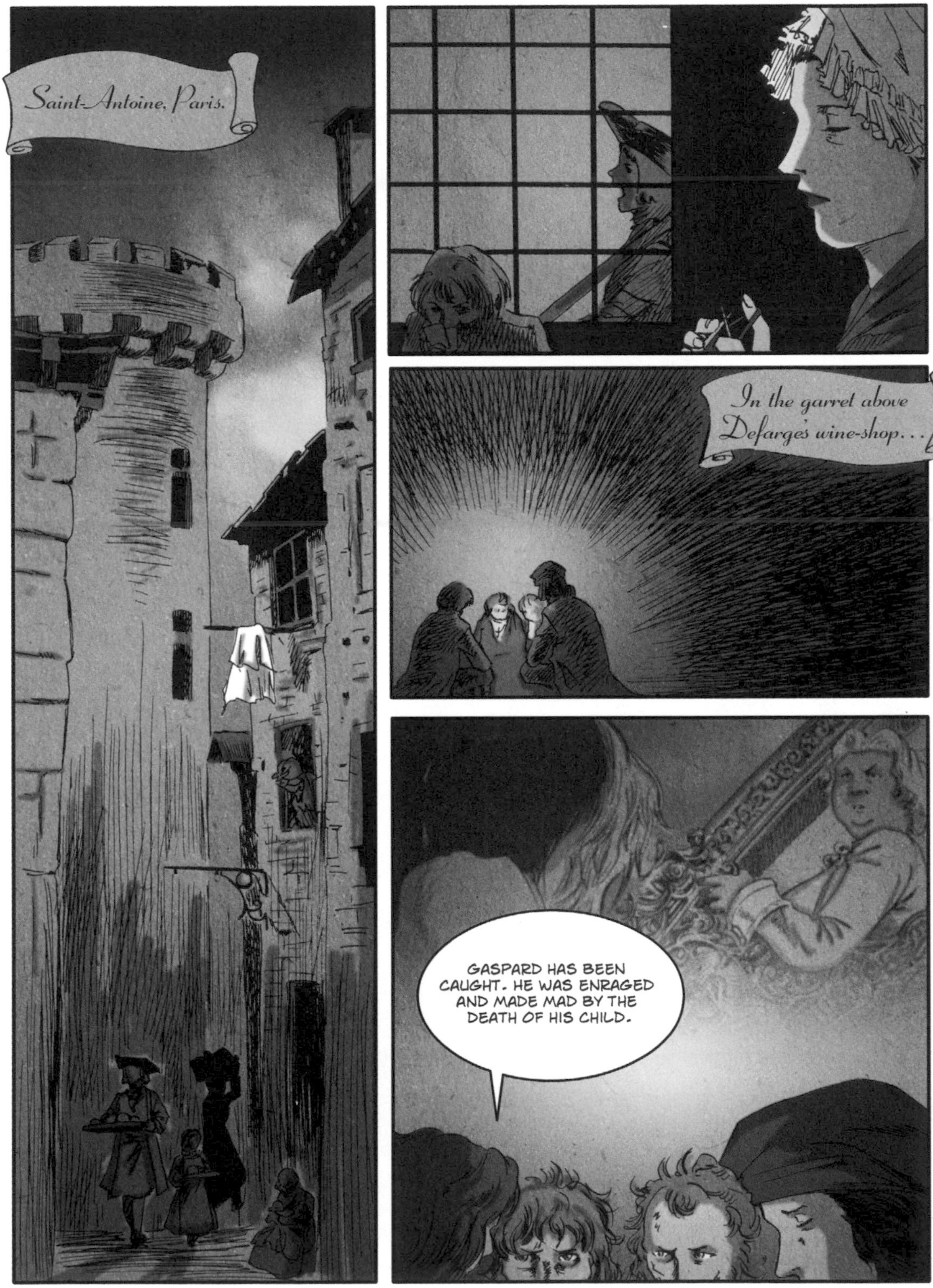
Saint-Antoine, Paris.
In the garret above Defarge's wine-shop...
GASPARD HAS BEEN CAUGHT. HE WAS ENRAGED AND MADE MAD BY THE DEATH OF HIS CHILD.

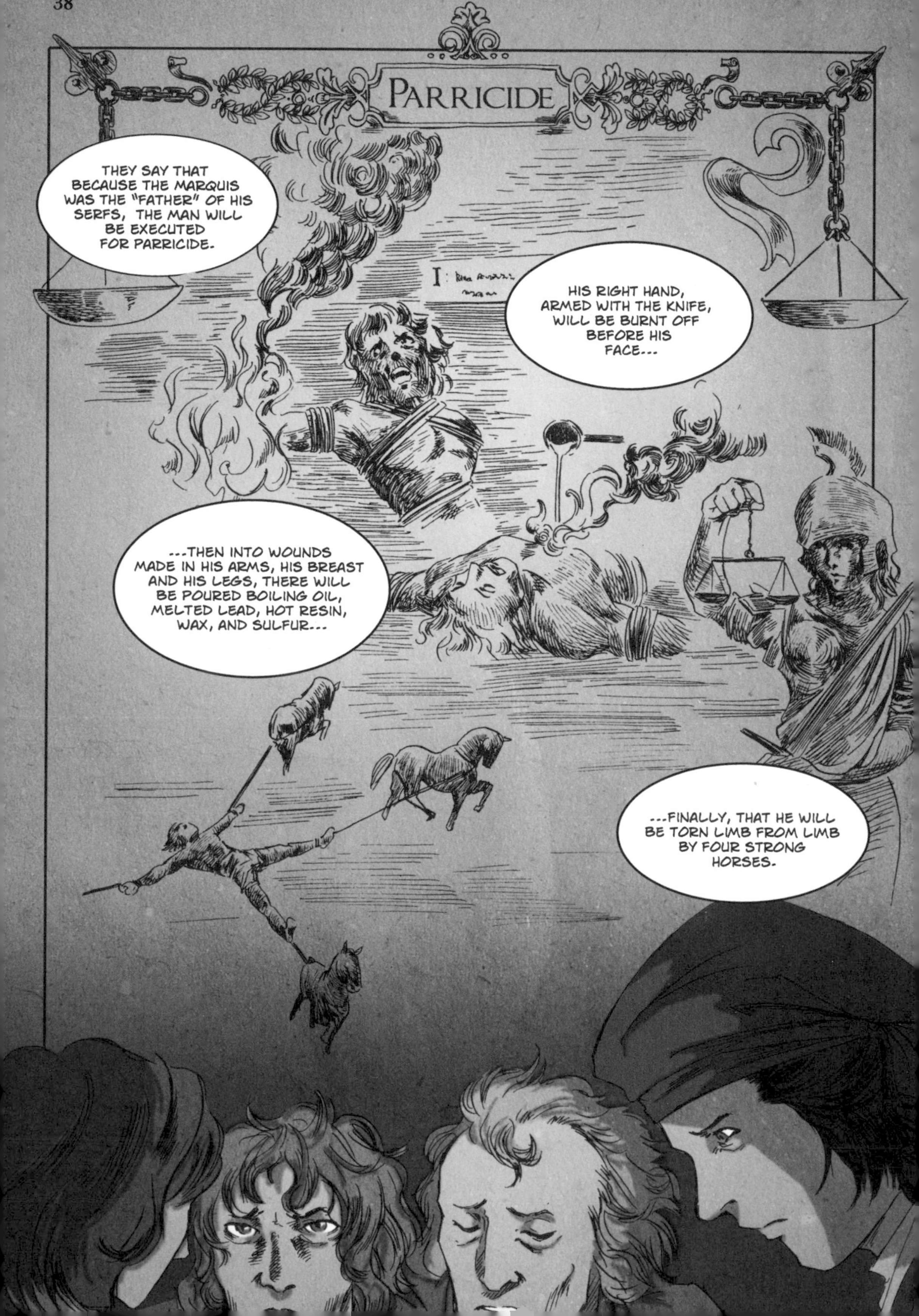
PARRICIDE
THEY SAY THAT BECAUSE THE MARQUIS WAS THE "FATHER" OF HIS SERFS, THE MAN WILL BE EXECUTED FOR PARRICIDE.
HIS RIGHT HAND, ARMED WITH THE KNIFE, WILL BE BURNT OFF BEFORE HIS FACE...
...THEN INTO WOUNDS MADE IN HIS ARMS, HIS BREAST AND HIS LEGS, THERE WILL BE POURED BOILING OIL, MELTED LEAD, HOT RESIN, WAX, AND SULFUR...
...FINALLY, THAT HE WILL BE TORN LIMB FROM LIMB BY FOUR STRONG HORSES.

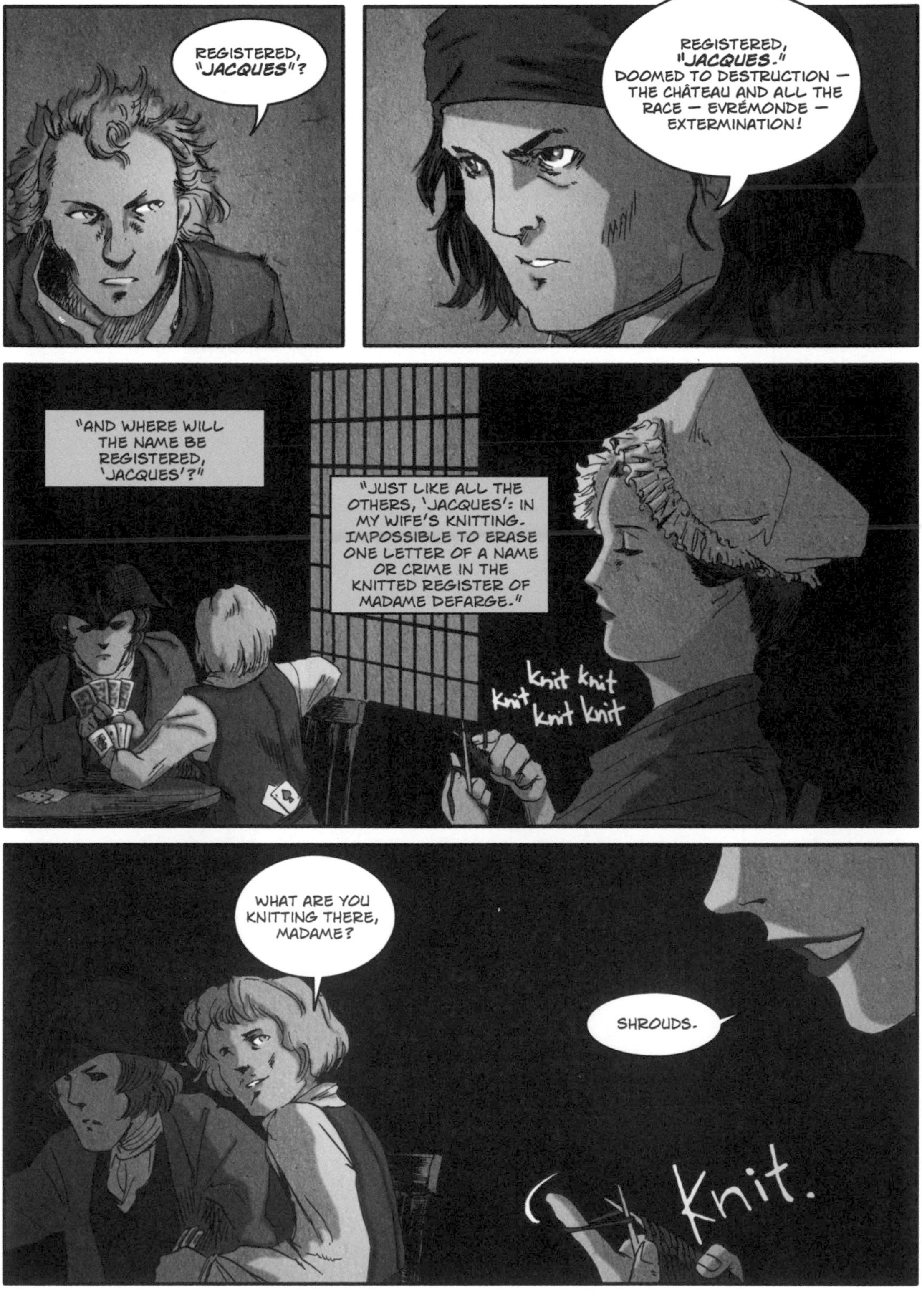
REGISTERED, "JACQUES"?
REGISTERED, "JACQUES." DOOMED TO DESTRUCTION — THE CHÂTEAU AND ALL THE RACE — EVRÉMONDE — EXTERMINATION!
"AND WHERE WILL THE NAME BE REGISTERED, 'JACQUES'?"
"JUST LIKE ALL THE OTHERS, 'JACQUES': IN MY WIFE'S KNITTING. IMPOSSIBLE TO ERASE ONE LETTER OF A NAME OR CRIME IN THE KNITTED REGISTER OF MADAME DEFARGE."
knit knit knit knit knit
WHAT ARE YOU KNITTING THERE, MADAME?
SHROUDS.
Knit.

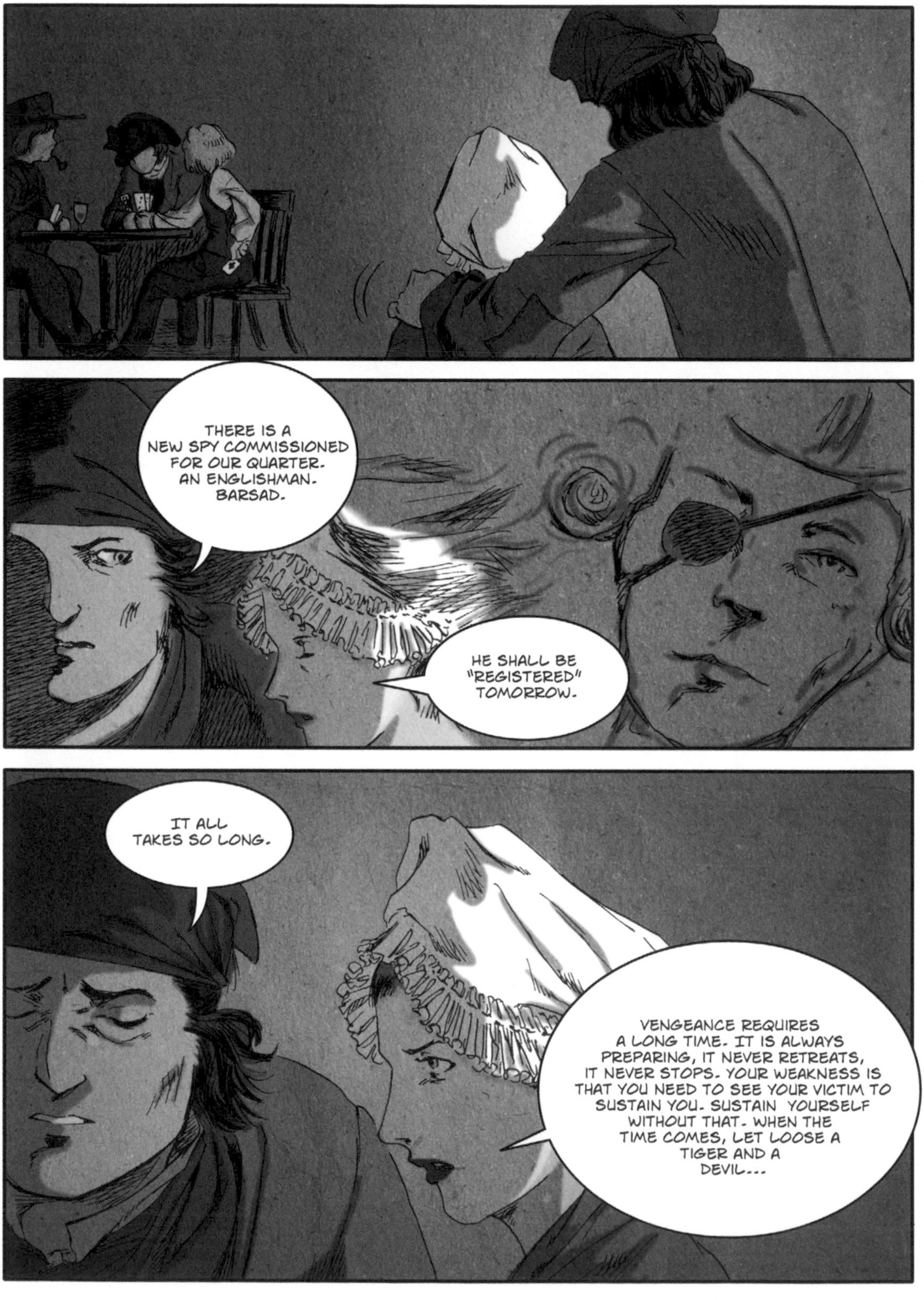
THERE IS A NEW SPY COMMISSIONED FOR OUR QUARTER. AN ENGLISHMAN. BARSAD.
HE SHALL BE "REGISTERED" TOMORROW.
IT ALL TAKES SO LONG.
VENGEANCE REQUIRES A LONG TIME. IT IS ALWAYS PREPARING, IT NEVER RETREATS, IT NEVER STOPS. YOUR WEAKNESS IS THAT YOU NEED TO SEE YOUR VICTIM TO SUSTAIN YOU. SUSTAIN YOURSELF WITHOUT THAT. WHEN THE TIME COMES, LET LOOSE A TIGER AND A DEVIL...

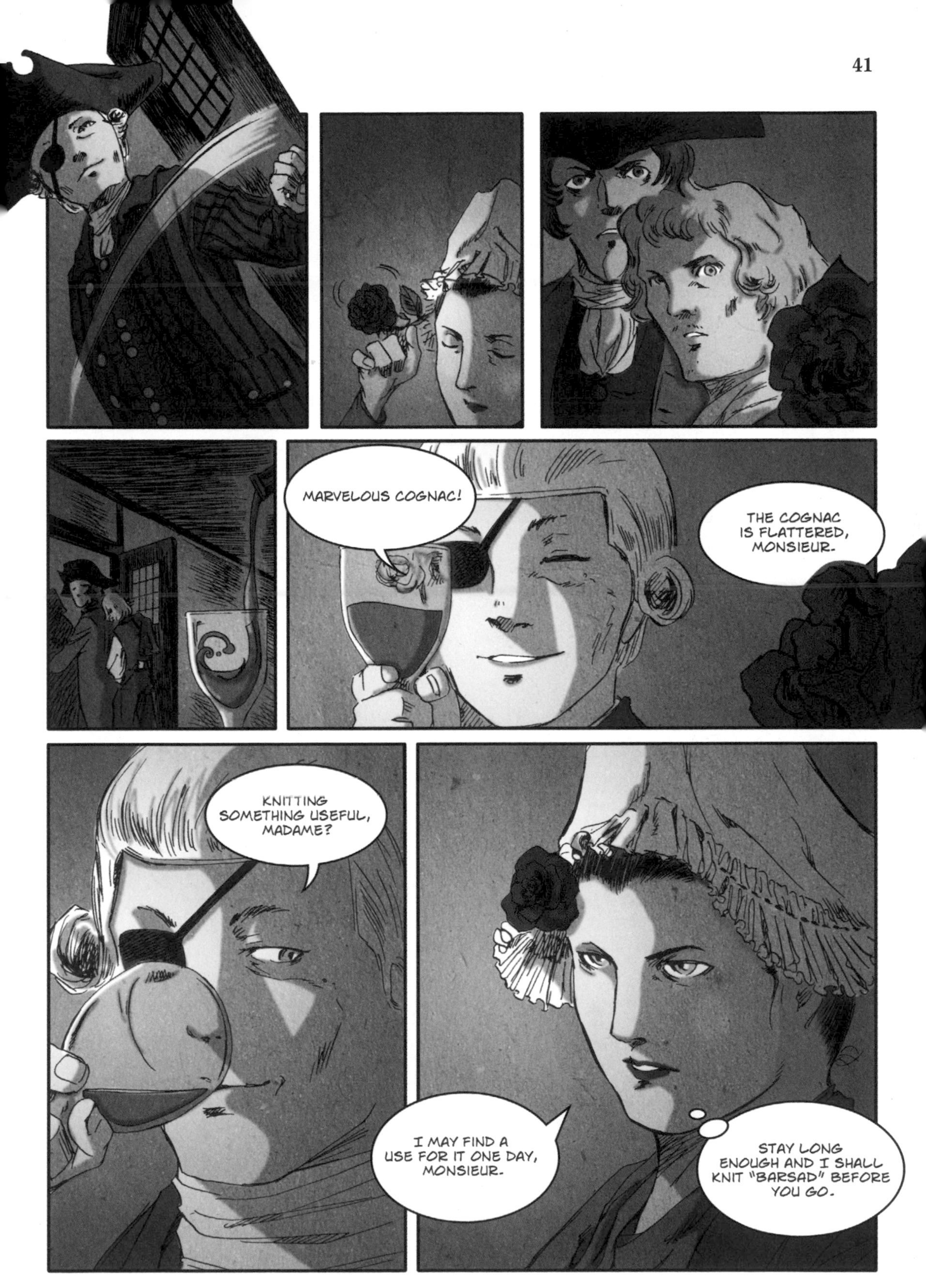
MARVELOUS COGNAC!
THE COGNAC IS FLATTERED, MONSIEUR.
KNITTING SOMETHING USEFUL, MADAME?
I MAY FIND A USE FOR IT ONE DAY, MONSIEUR.
STAY LONG ENOUGH AND I SHALL KNIT "BARSAD" BEFORE YOU GO.

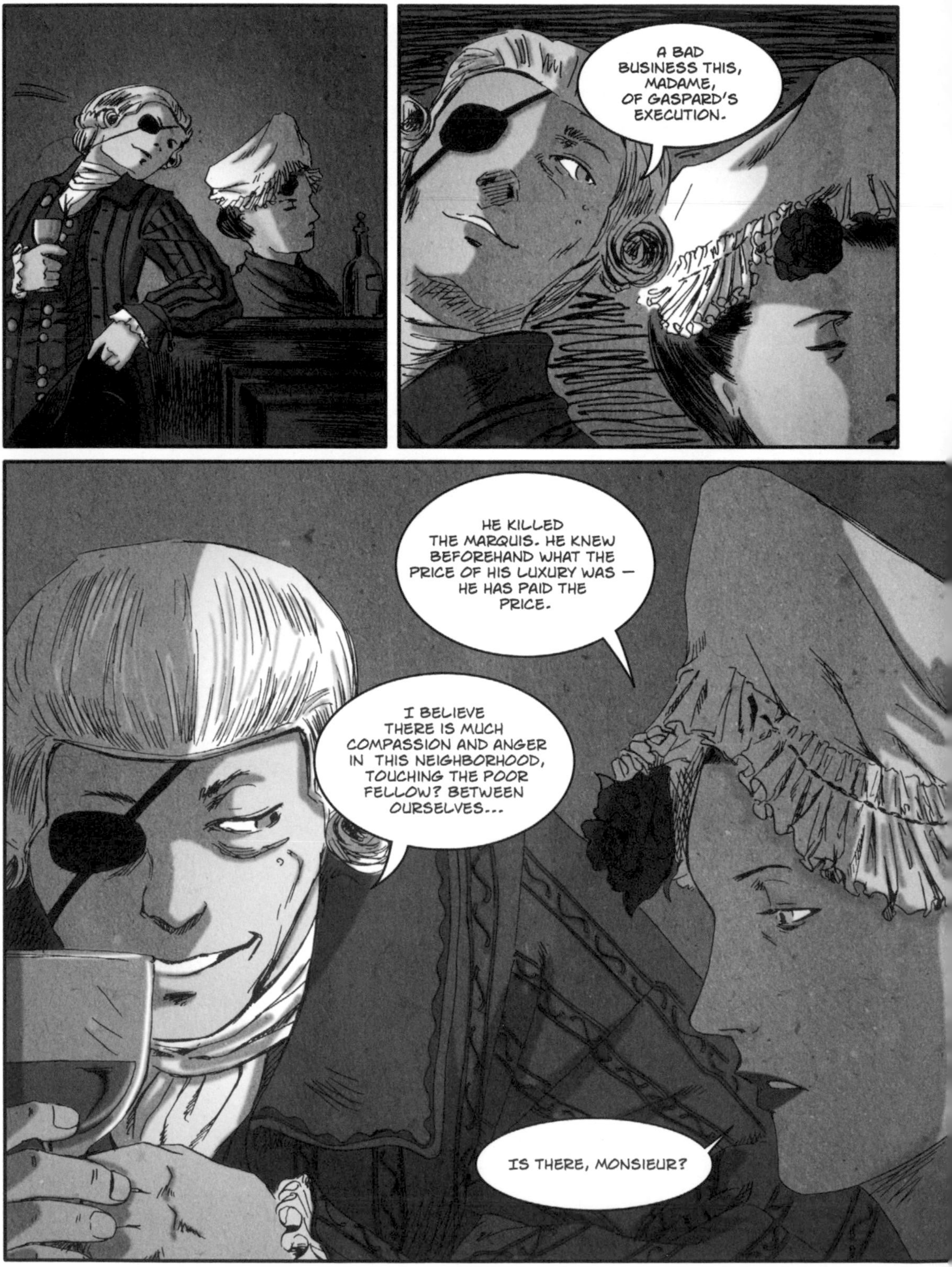
A BAD BUSINESS THIS, MADAME, OF GASPARD'S EXECUTION.
HE KILLED THE MARQUIS. HE KNEW BEFOREHAND WHAT THE PRICE OF HIS LUXURY WAS — HE HAS PAID THE PRICE.
I BELIEVE THERE IS MUCH COMPASSION AND ANGER IN THIS NEIGHBORHOOD, TOUCHING THE POOR FELLOW? BETWEEN OURSELVES...
IS THERE, MONSIEUR?

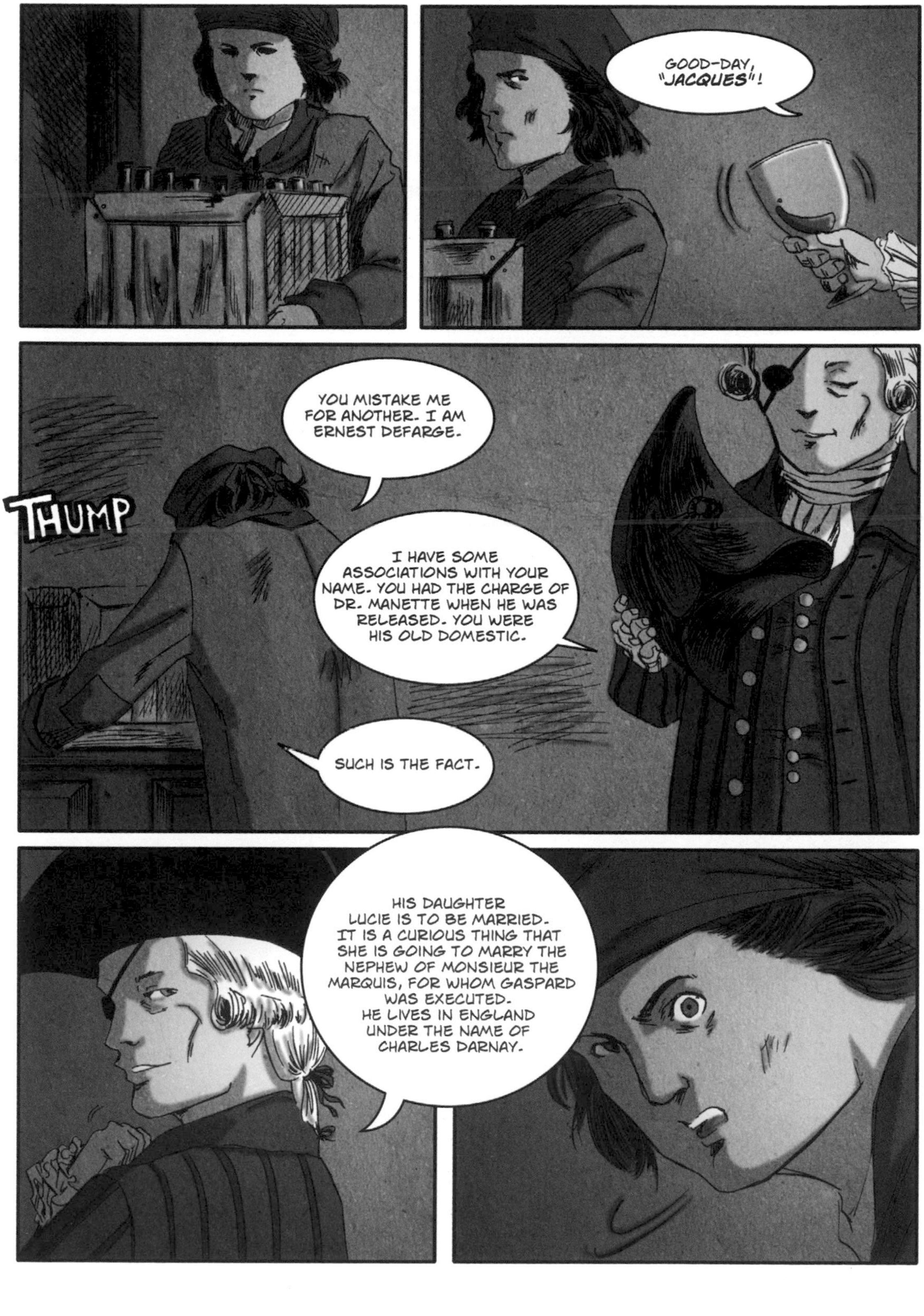
GOOD-DAY, "JACQUES"!
YOU MISTAKE ME FOR ANOTHER. I AM ERNEST DEFARGE.
THUMP
I HAVE SOME ASSOCIATIONS WITH YOUR NAME. YOU HAD THE CHARGE OF DR. MANETTE WHEN HE WAS RELEASED. YOU WERE HIS OLD DOMESTIC.
SUCH IS THE FACT.
HIS DAUGHTER LUCIE IS TO BE MARRIED. IT IS A CURIOUS THING THAT SHE IS GOING TO MARRY THE NEPHEW OF MONSIEUR THE MARQUIS, FOR WHOM GASPARD WAS EXECUTED. HE LIVES IN ENGLAND UNDER THE NAME OF CHARLES DARNAY.

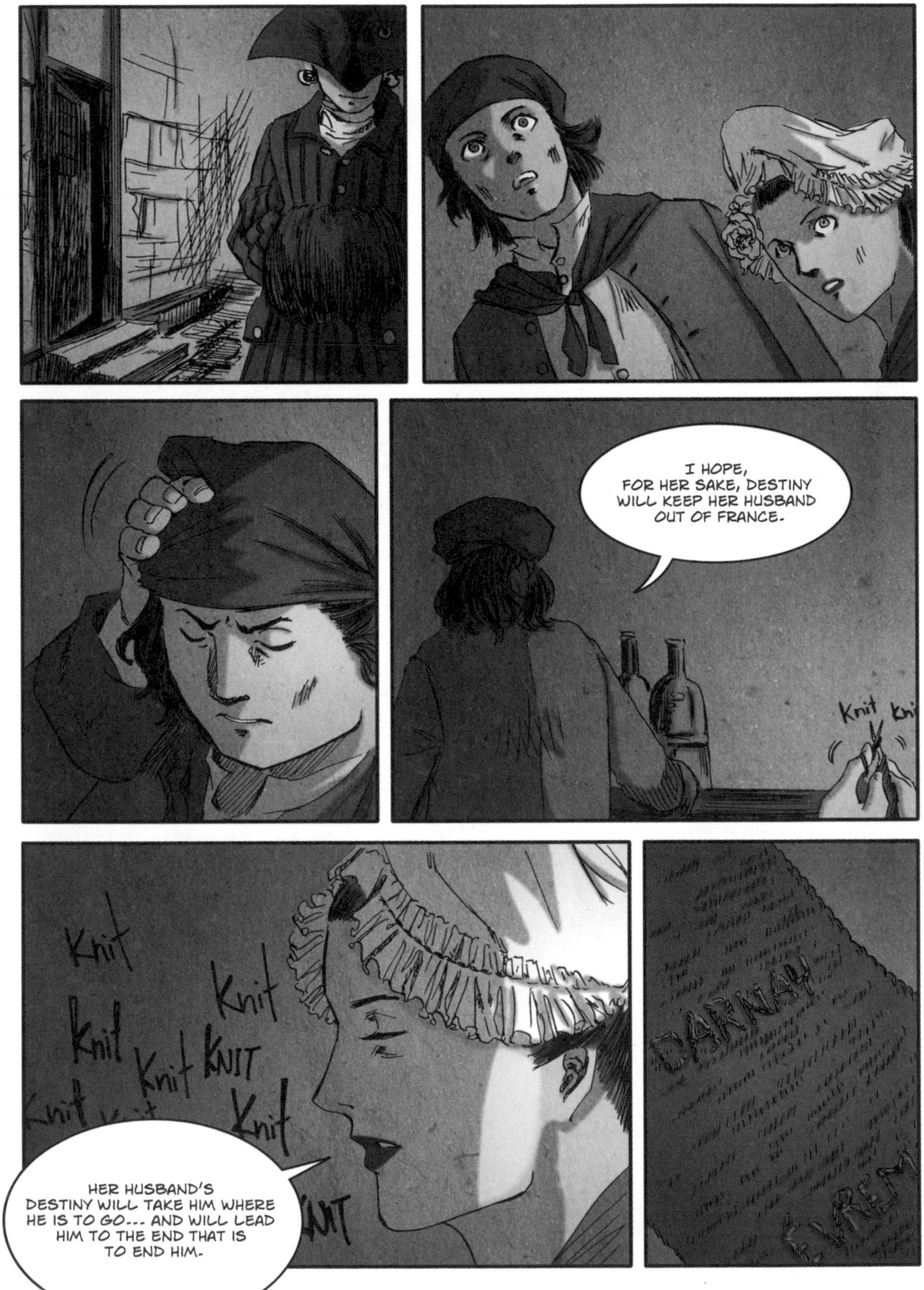
I HOPE, FOR HER SAKE, DESTINY WILL KEEP HER HUSBAND OUT OF FRANCE.
Knit Kni
Knit Knit Knit Knit KNIT Knit Knit KNIT
HER HUSBAND'S DESTINY WILL TAKE HIM WHERE HE IS TO GO... AND WILL LEAD HIM TO THE END THAT IS TO END HIM.
DARNAY
EVREM

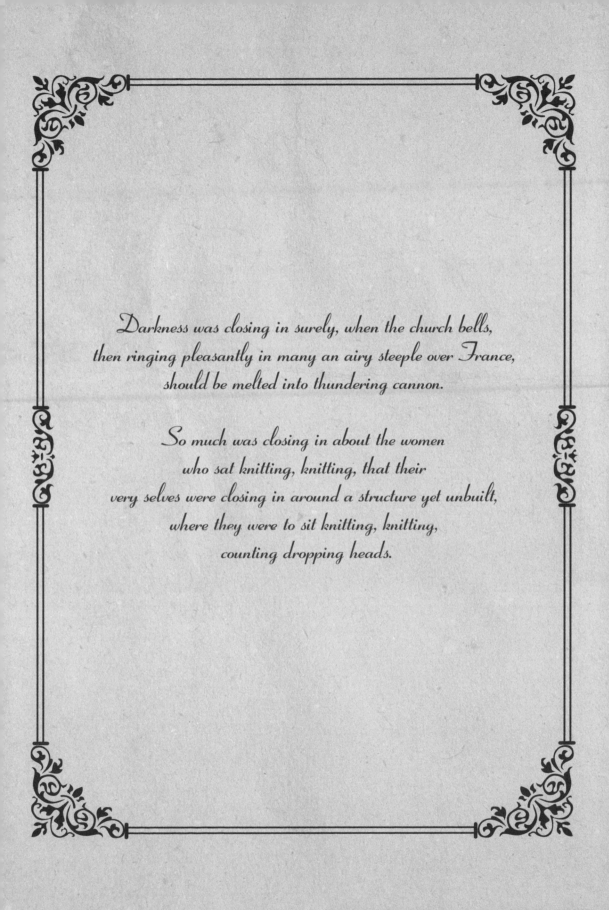

Darkness was closing in surely, when the church bells,
then ringing pleasantly in many an airy steeple over France,
should be melted into thundering cannon.

So much was closing in about the women
who sat knitting, knitting, that their
very selves were closing in around a structure yet unbuilt,
where they were to sit knitting, knitting,
counting dropping heads.

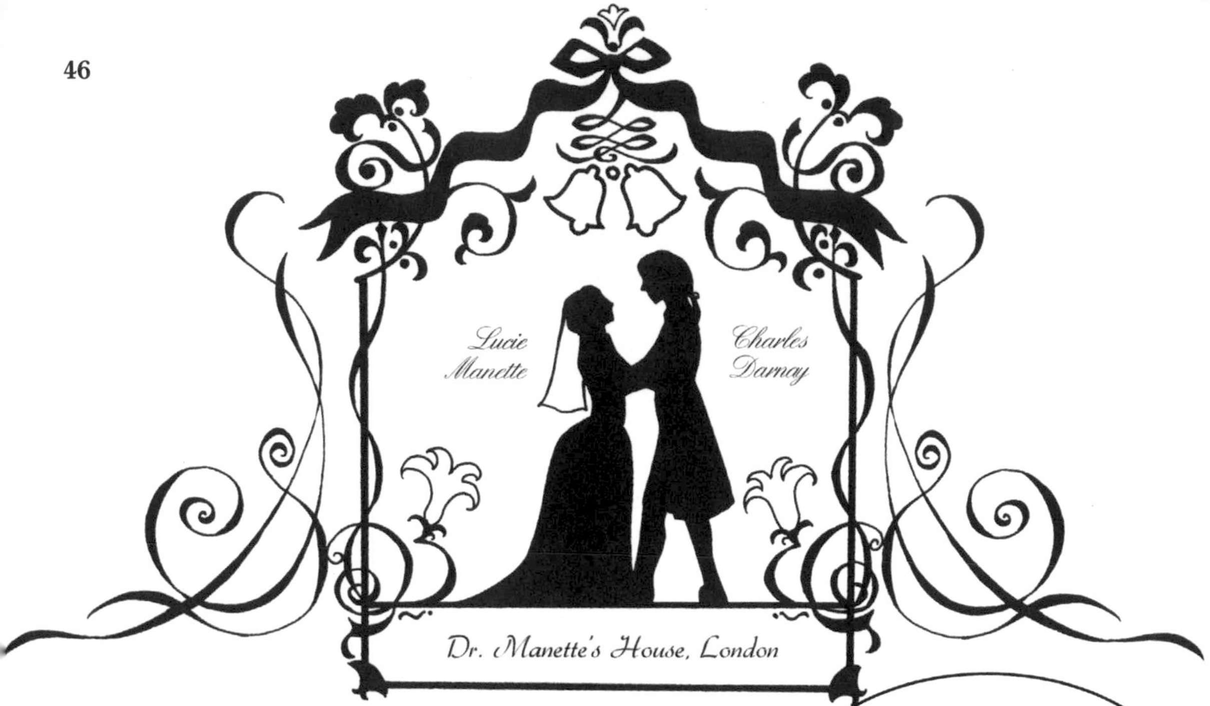
Lucie
Manette
Charles
Darnay
Dr. Manette's House, London

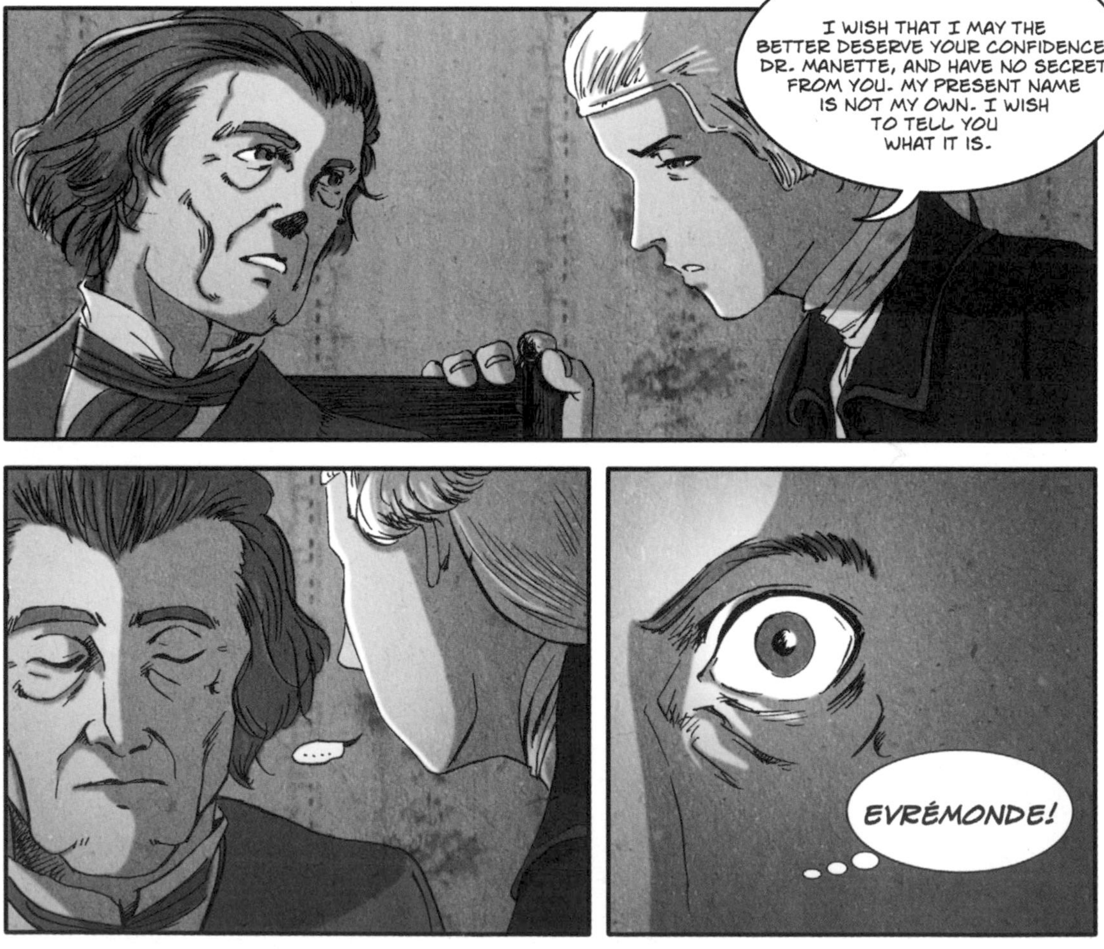
I WISH THAT I MAY THE BETTER DESERVE YOUR CONFIDENCE, DR. MANETTE, AND HAVE NO SECRET FROM YOU. MY PRESENT NAME IS NOT MY OWN. I WISH TO TELL YOU WHAT IT IS.
....
EVRÉMONDE!

That night, Mr. Lorry pays Dr. Manette a visit...

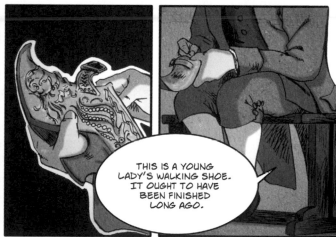

THIS IS A YOUNG LADY'S WALKING SHOE. IT OUGHT TO HAVE BEEN FINISHED LONG AGO.

DOCTOR, DO YOU KNOW ME? THIS IS NOT YOUR PROPER OCCUPATION...

DOCTOR!

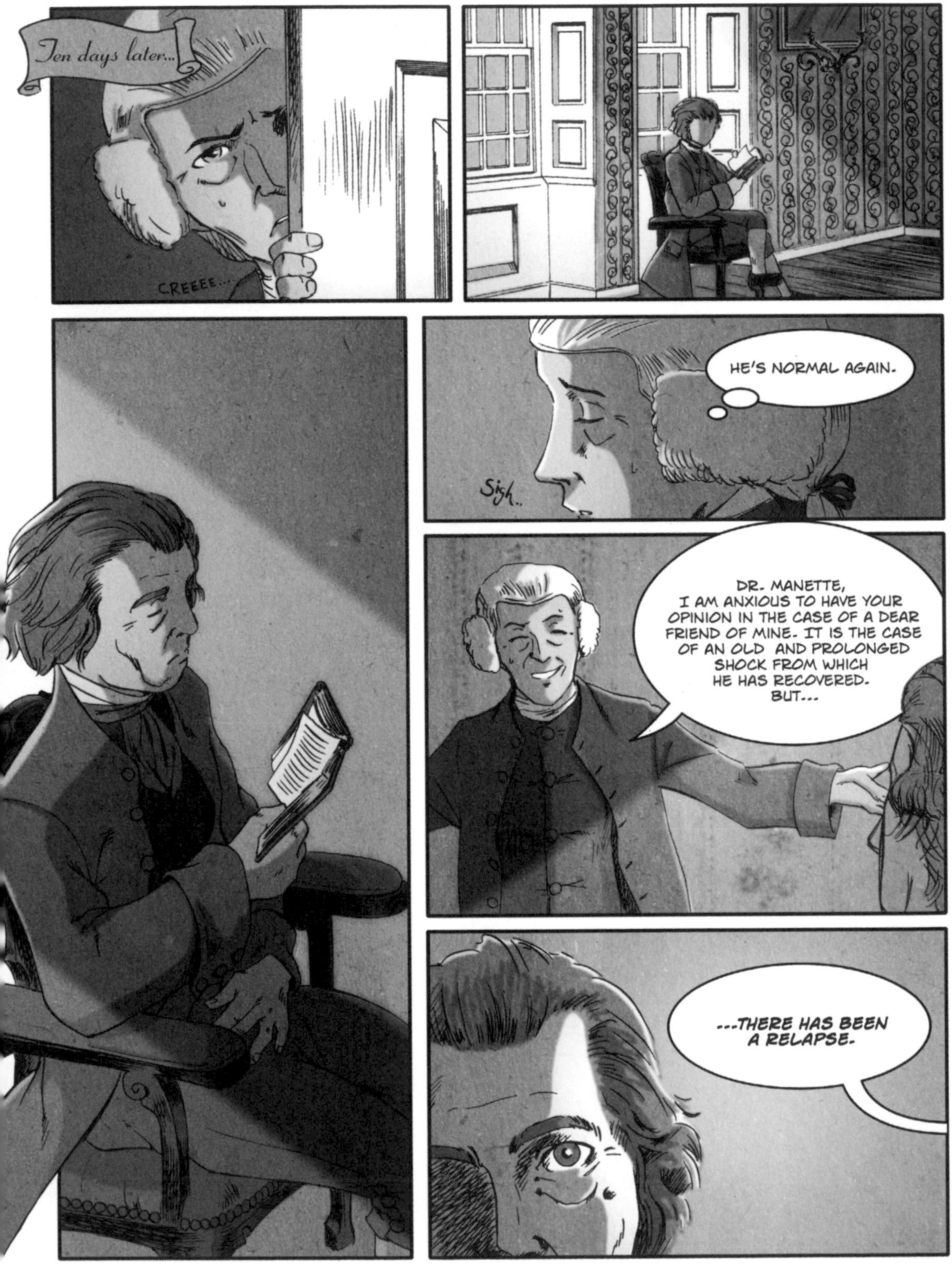
Ten days later...
CREEEE...
HE'S NORMAL AGAIN.
Sigh..
DR. MANETTE, I AM ANXIOUS TO HAVE YOUR OPINION IN THE CASE OF A DEAR FRIEND OF MINE. IT IS THE CASE OF AN OLD AND PROLONGED SHOCK FROM WHICH HE HAS RECOVERED. BUT...
...THERE HAS BEEN A RELAPSE.

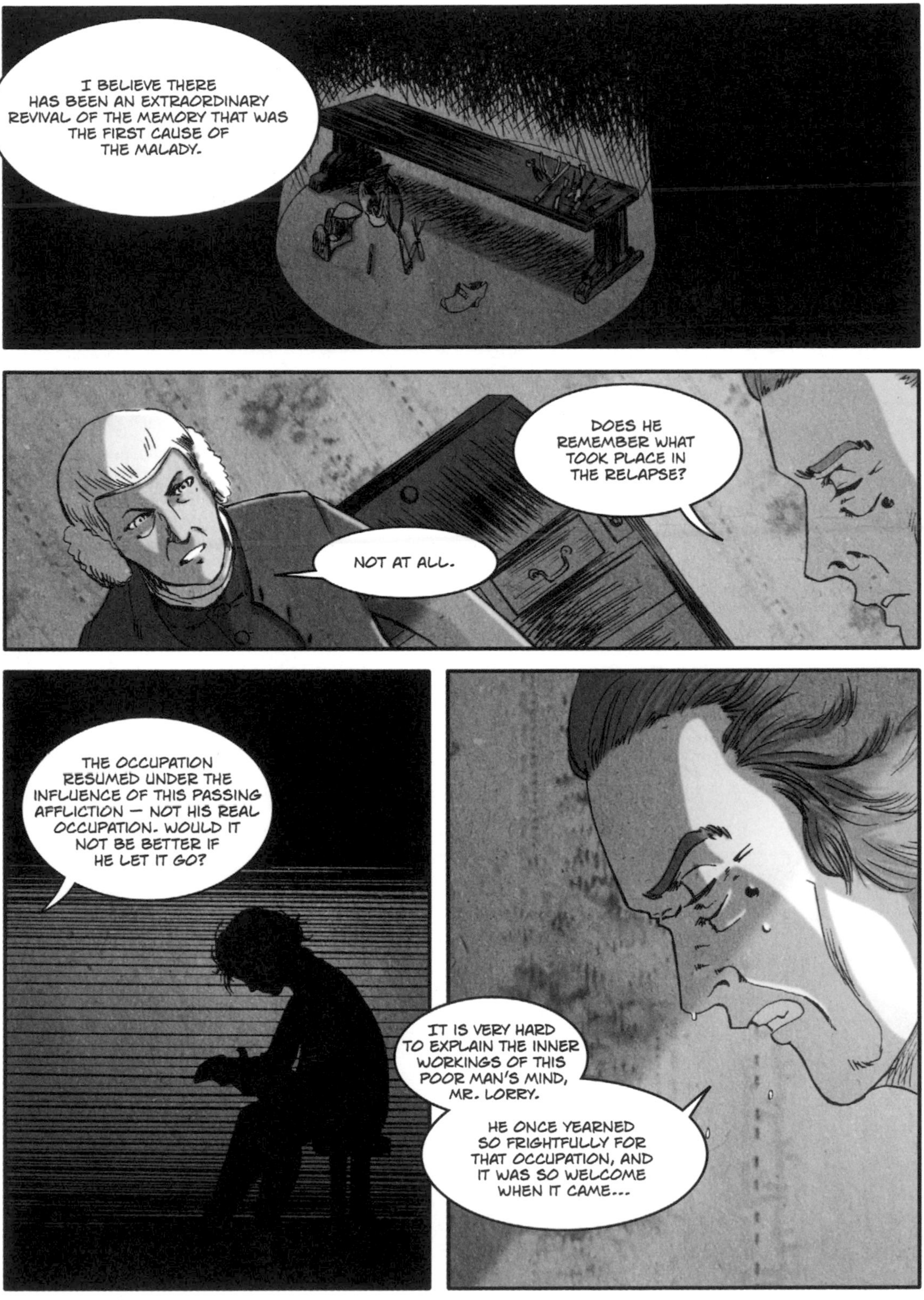
I BELIEVE THERE HAS BEEN AN EXTRAORDINARY REVIVAL OF THE MEMORY THAT WAS THE FIRST CAUSE OF THE MALADY.
DOES HE REMEMBER WHAT TOOK PLACE IN THE RELAPSE?
NOT AT ALL.
THE OCCUPATION RESUMED UNDER THE INFLUENCE OF THIS PASSING AFFLICTION — NOT HIS REAL OCCUPATION. WOULD IT NOT BE BETTER IF HE LET IT GO?
IT IS VERY HARD TO EXPLAIN THE INNER WORKINGS OF THIS POOR MAN'S MIND, MR. LORRY.
HE ONCE YEARNED SO FRIGHTFULLY FOR THAT OCCUPATION, AND IT WAS SO WELCOME WHEN IT CAME...

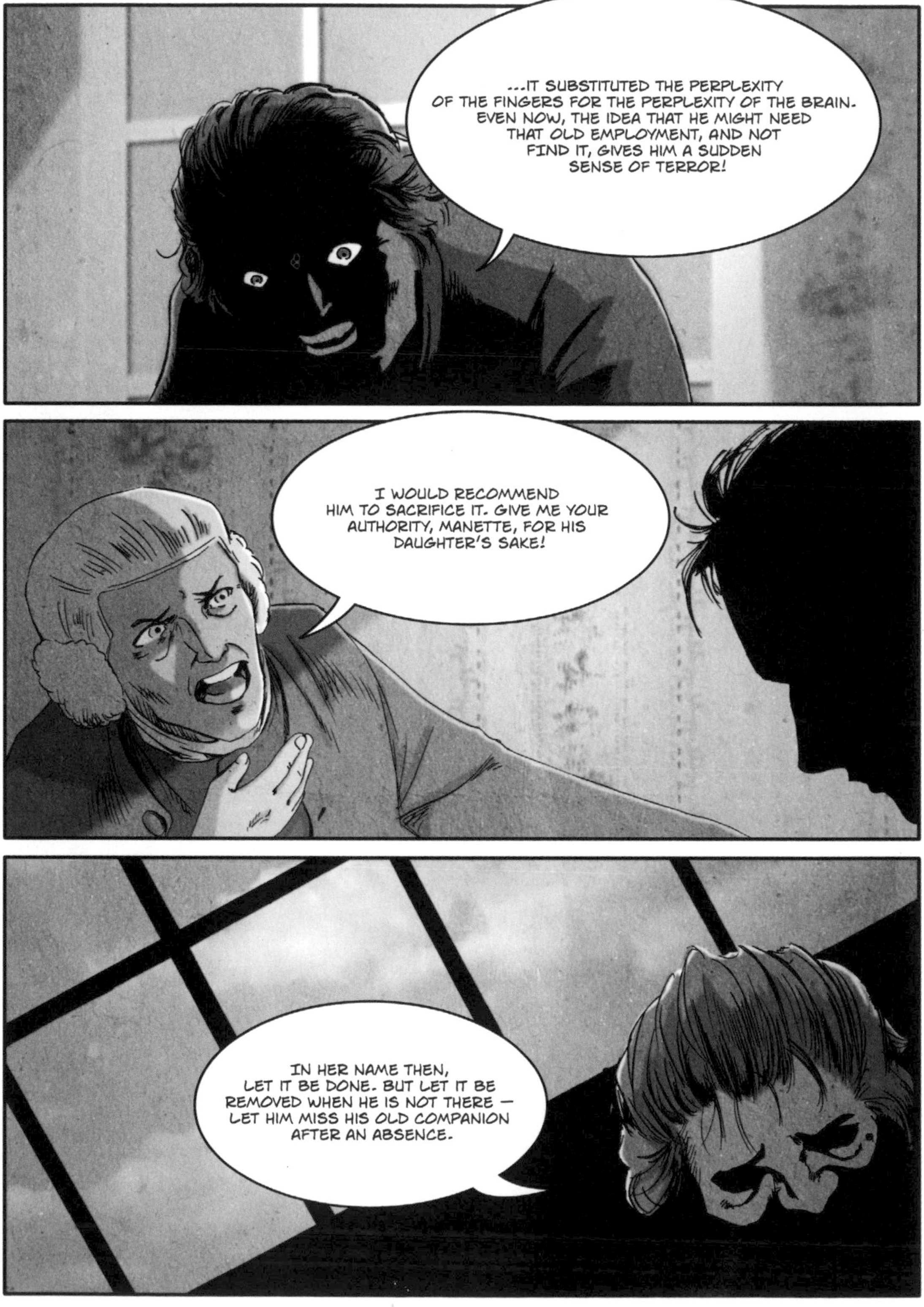
...IT SUBSTITUTED THE PERPLEXITY OF THE FINGERS FOR THE PERPLEXITY OF THE BRAIN. EVEN NOW, THE IDEA THAT HE MIGHT NEED THAT OLD EMPLOYMENT, AND NOT FIND IT, GIVES HIM A SUDDEN SENSE OF TERROR!
I WOULD RECOMMEND HIM TO SACRIFICE IT. GIVE ME YOUR AUTHORITY, MANETTE, FOR HIS DAUGHTER'S SAKE!
IN HER NAME THEN, LET IT BE DONE. BUT LET IT BE REMOVED WHEN HE IS NOT THERE — LET HIM MISS HIS OLD COMPANION AFTER AN ABSENCE.

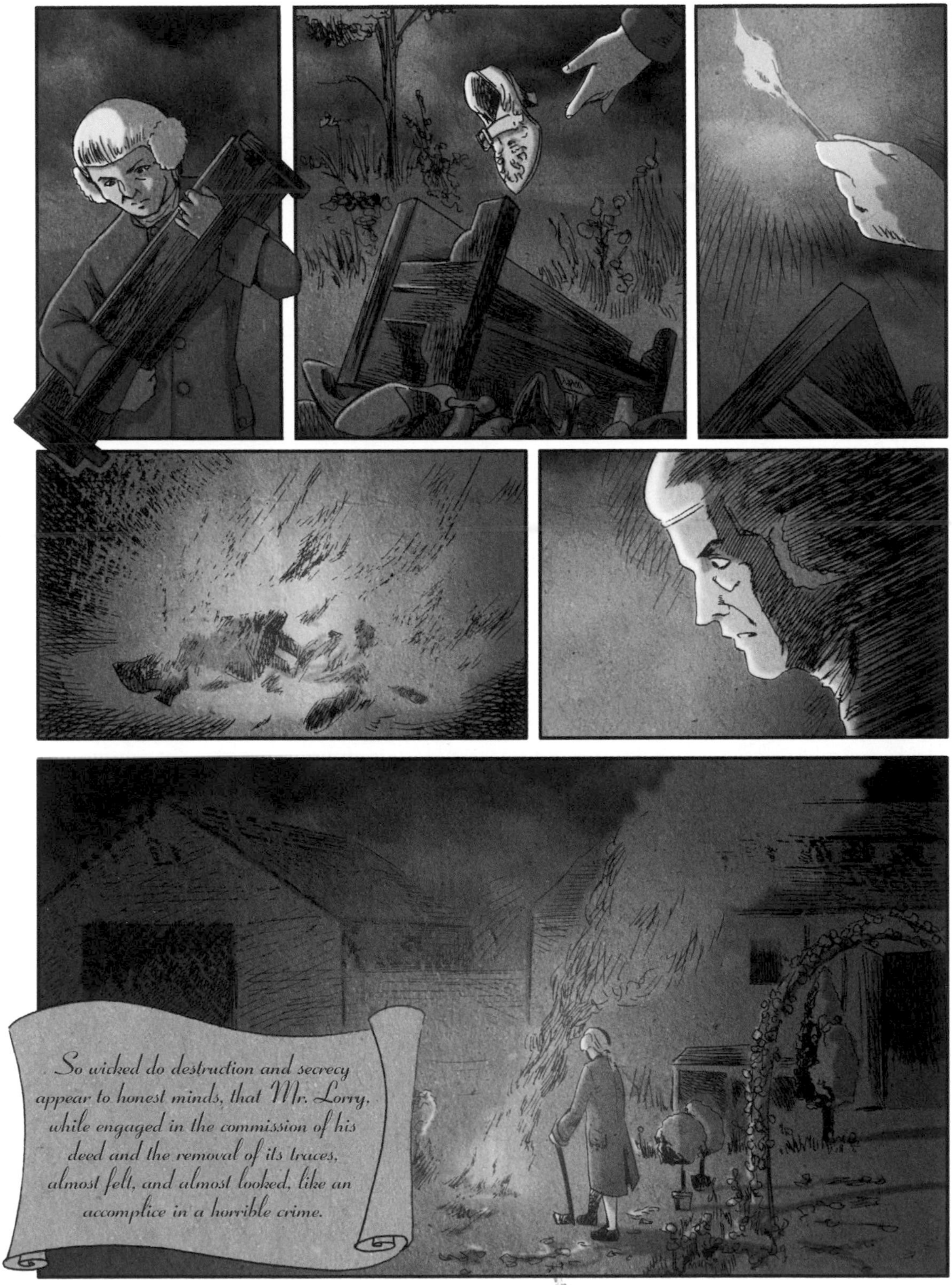
So wicked do destruction and secrecy appear to honest minds, that Mr. Lorry, while engaged in the commission of his deed and the removal of its traces, almost felt, and almost looked, like an accomplice in a horrible crime.

Headlong, mad, and dangerous footsteps, footsteps not easily clean again if once stained red, the footsteps raging in far off Saint-Antoine…

Muskets were being distributed — so were cartridges, powder, and ball, bars of iron and wood, knives, axes, pikes…

People who could lay hold of nothing else, set themselves with bleeding hands to force stones and bricks out of their places in walls…

Every pulse and heart in Saint-Antoine was on high-fever strain and at high-fever heat…

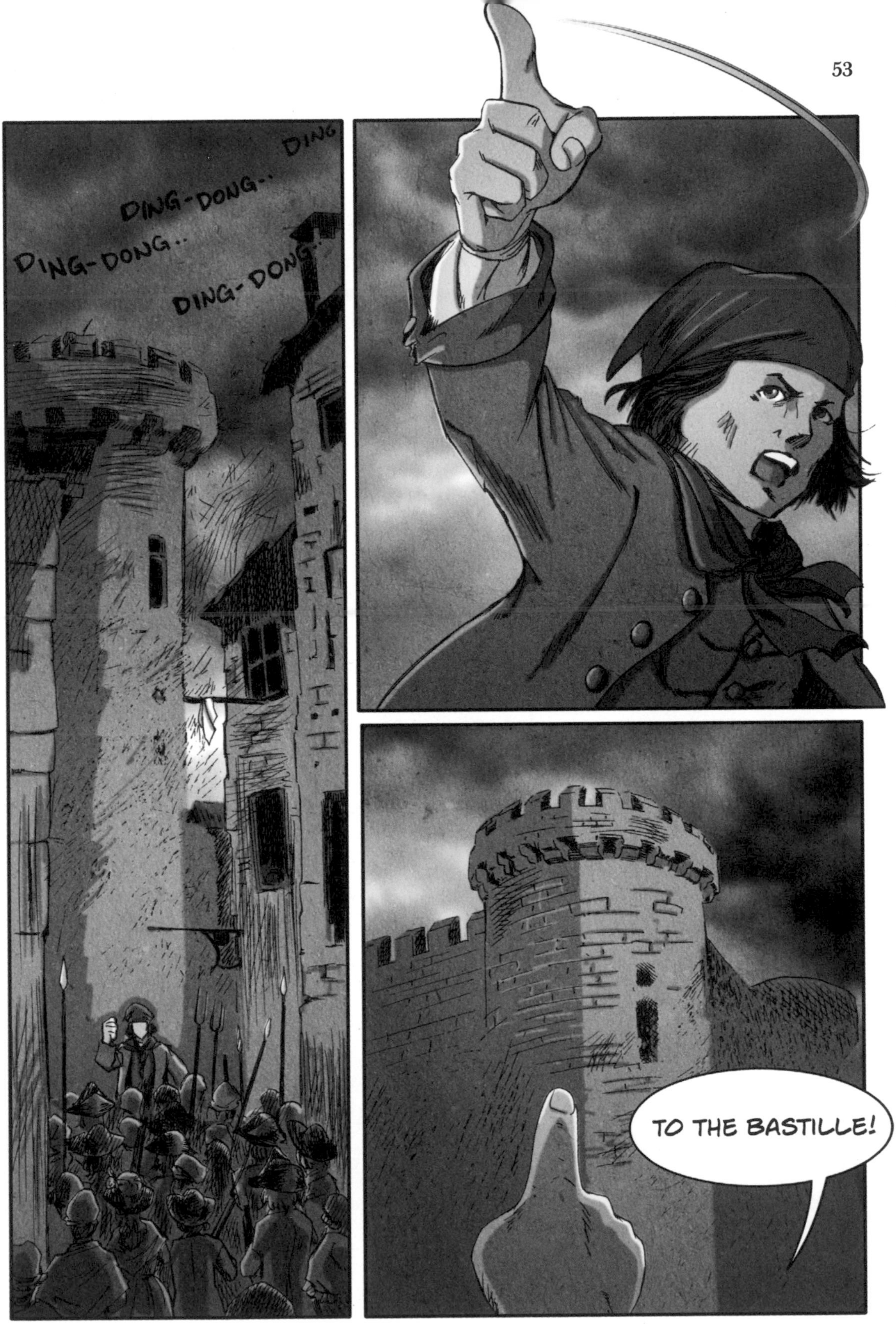
DING-DONG..
DING-DONG..
DING-DONG..
DING
TO THE BASTILLE!

With a roar that sounded
as if all the breath in France had been shaped
into the detested word, the living sea rose,
wave on wave, depth on depth,
and overflowed the city to that point.
Alarm bells ringing, drums beating,
the sea raging and thundering on its new beach,
the attack began...

THE PRISONERS!

SECRET CELLS!

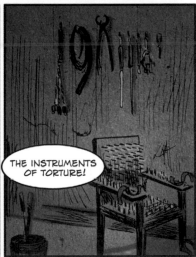

THE INSTRUMENTS OF TORTURE!

TO ME, WOMEN!

WE CAN KILL AS WELL AS THE MEN WHEN THE PLACE IS TAKEN!

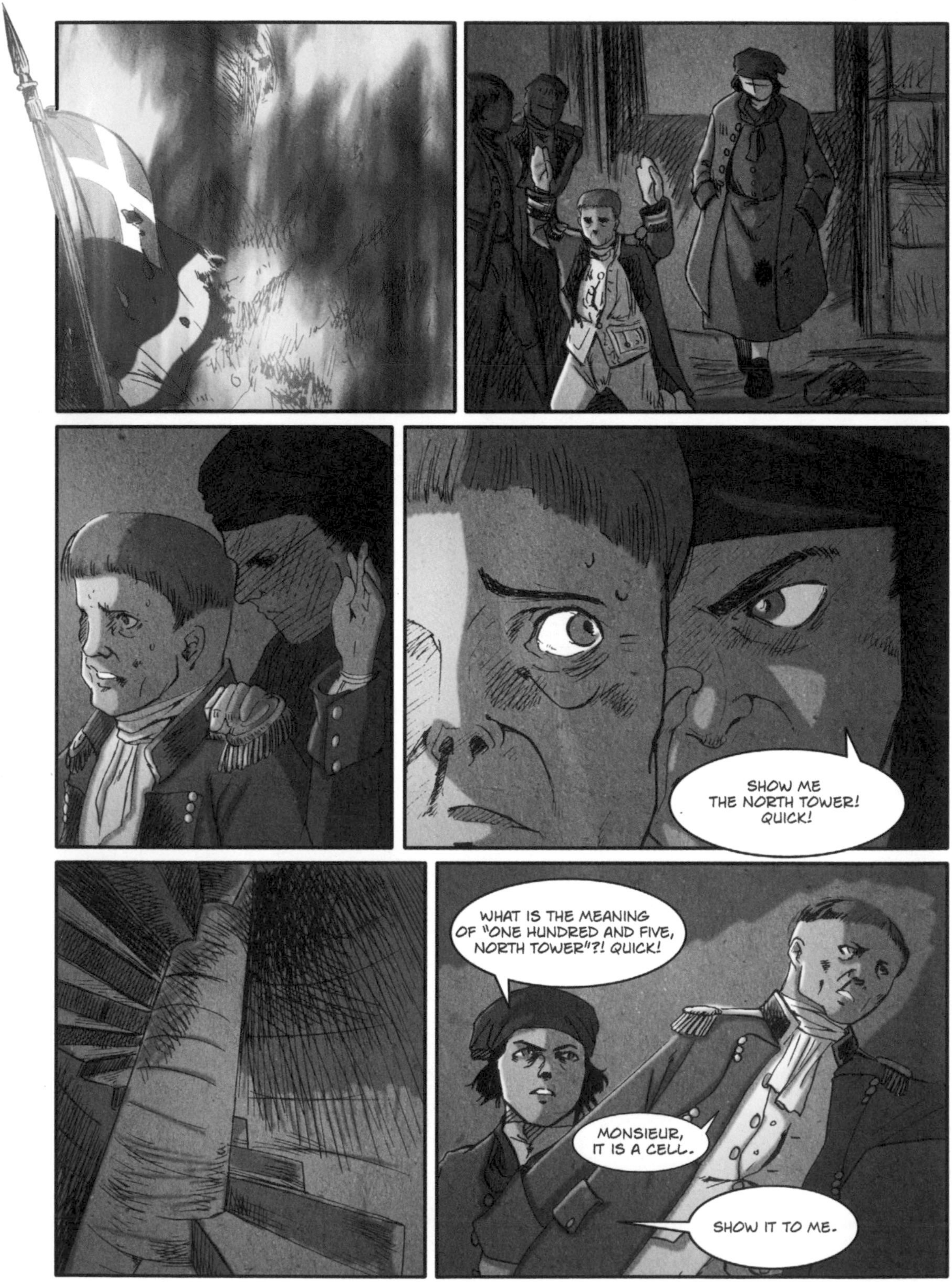
SHOW ME
THE NORTH TOWER!
QUICK!
WHAT IS THE MEANING
OF "ONE HUNDRED AND FIVE,
NORTH TOWER"?! QUICK!
MONSIEUR,
IT IS A CELL.
SHOW IT TO ME.

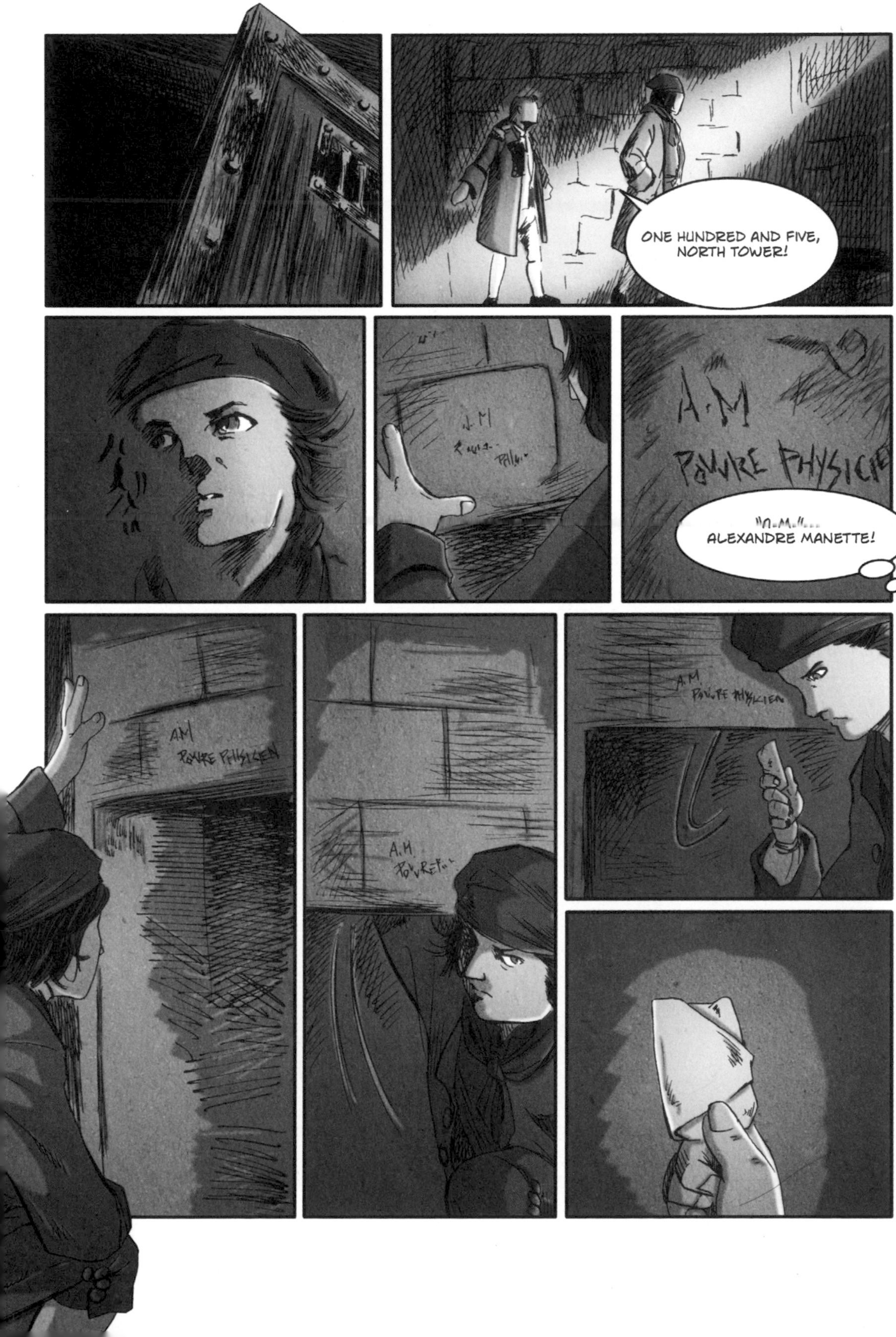
ONE HUNDRED AND FIVE, NORTH TOWER!
"A.M."...
ALEXANDRE MANETTE!

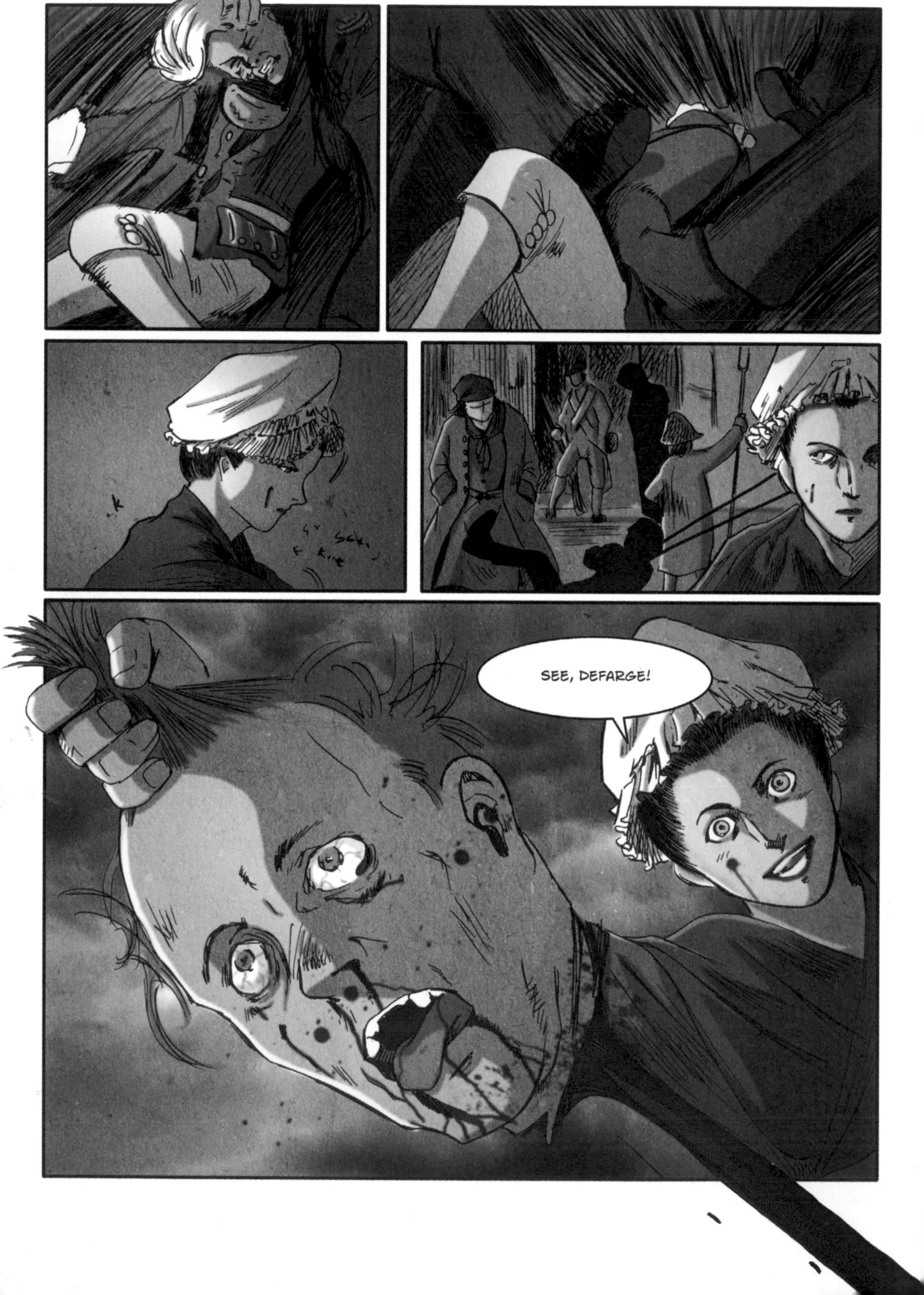
SEE, DEFARGE!

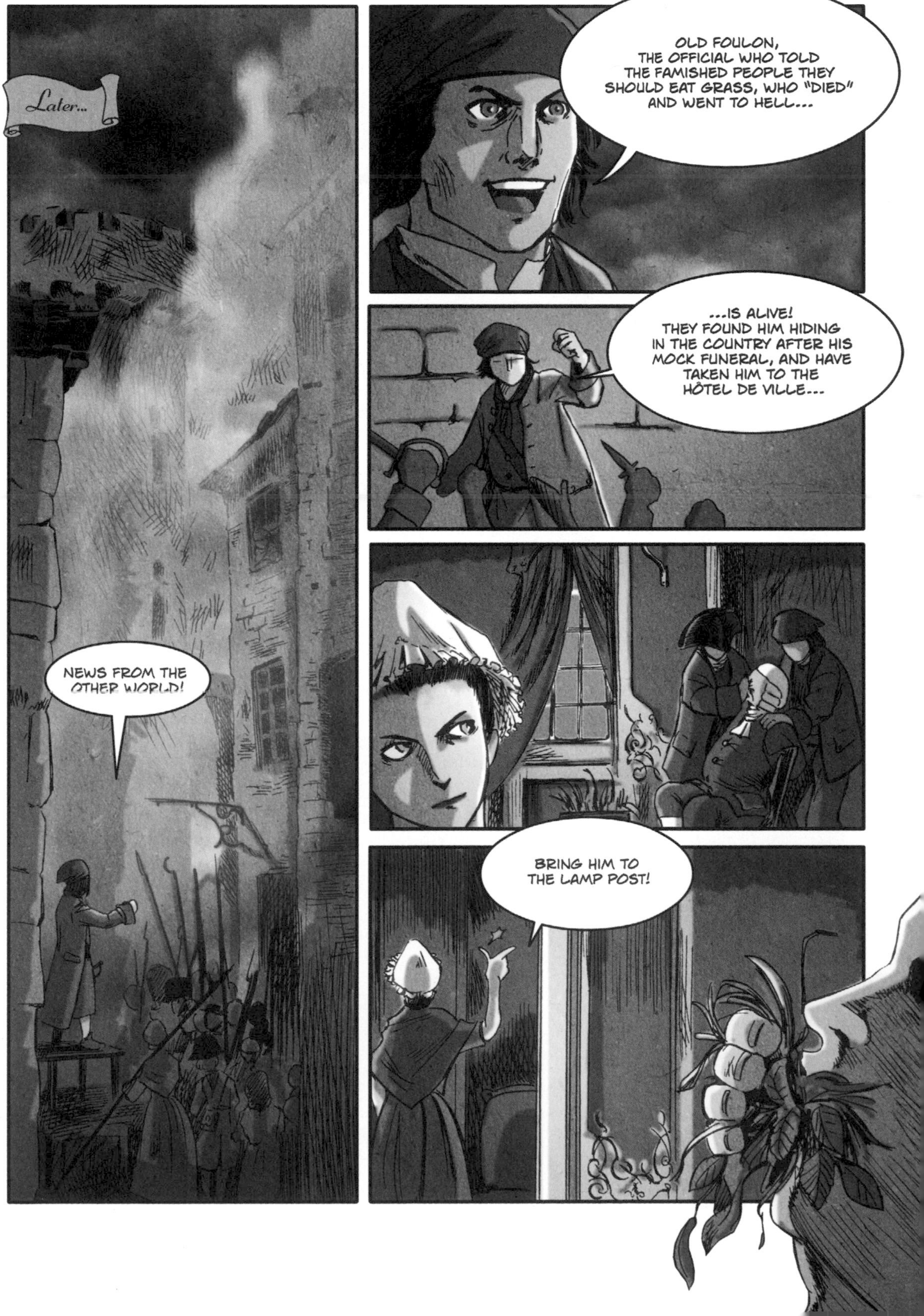
Later...
NEWS FROM THE OTHER WORLD!
OLD FOULON, THE OFFICIAL WHO TOLD THE FAMISHED PEOPLE THEY SHOULD EAT GRASS, WHO "DIED" AND WENT TO HELL...
...IS ALIVE! THEY FOUND HIM HIDING IN THE COUNTRY AFTER HIS MOCK FUNERAL, AND HAVE TAKEN HIM TO THE HÔTEL DE VILLE...
BRING HIM TO THE LAMP POST!

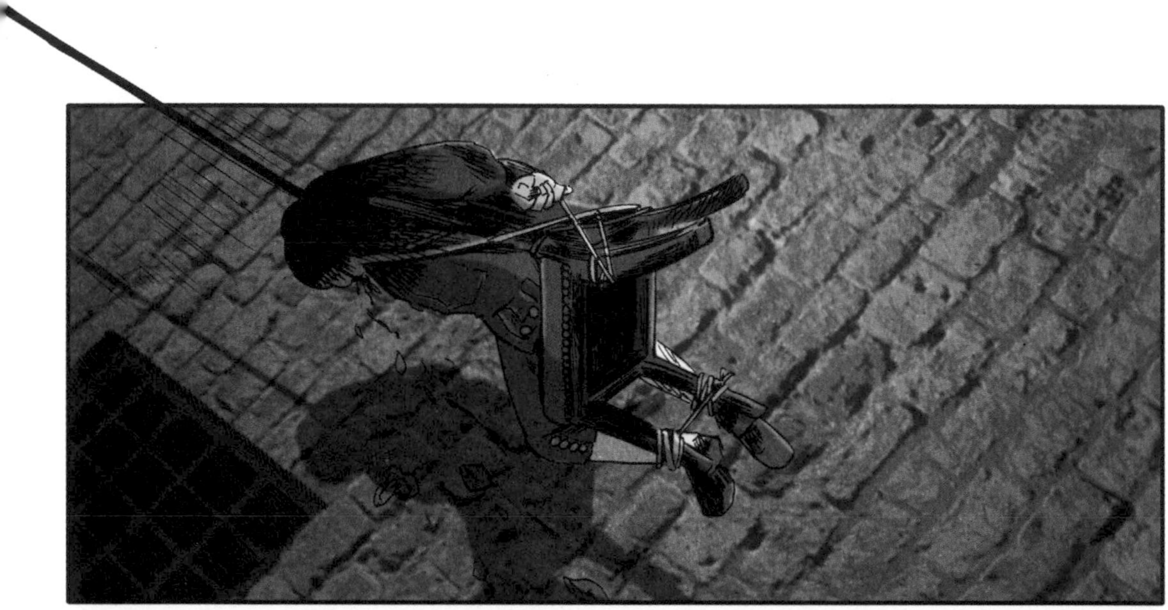

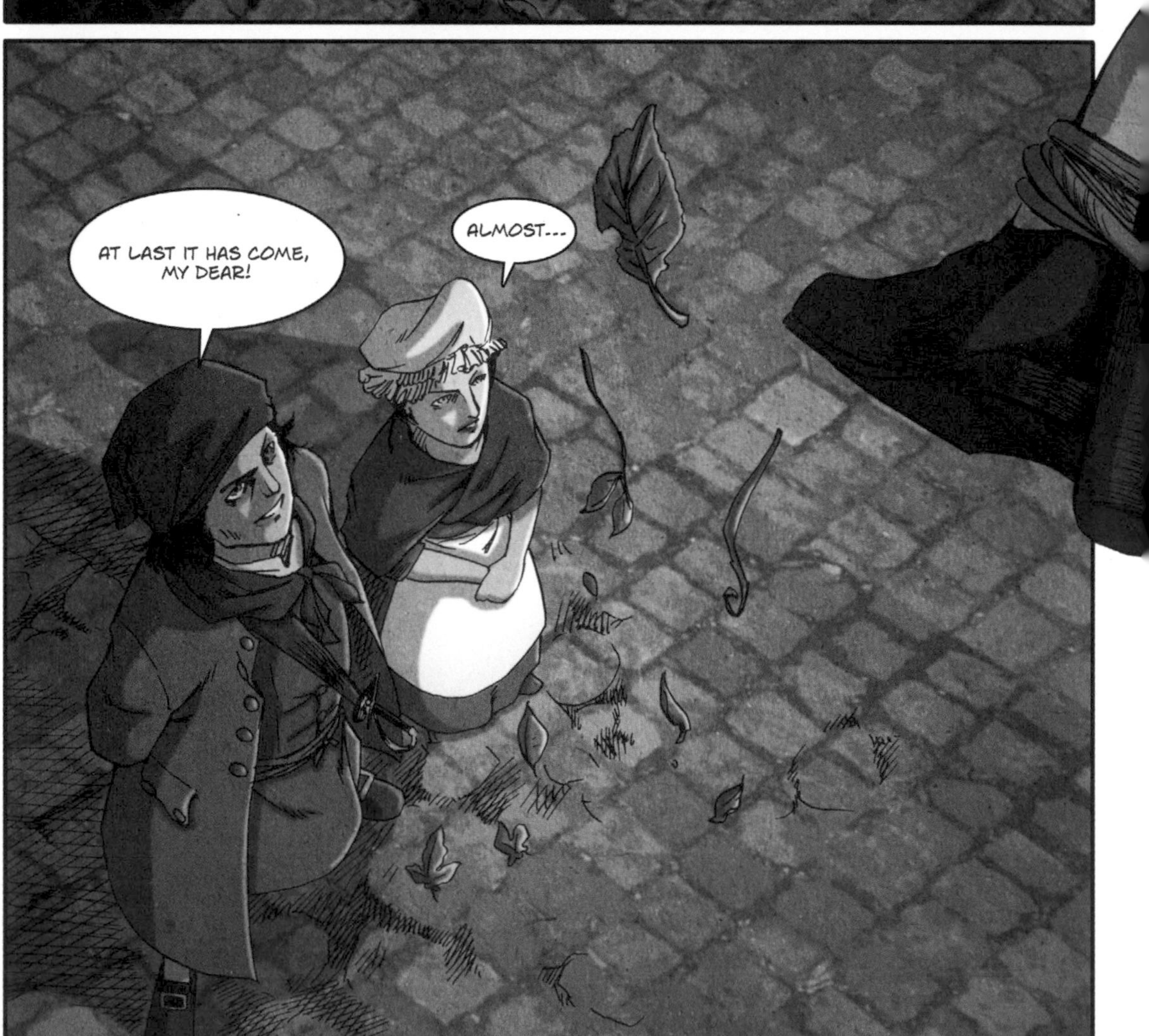
AT LAST IT HAS COME, MY DEAR!
ALMOST...

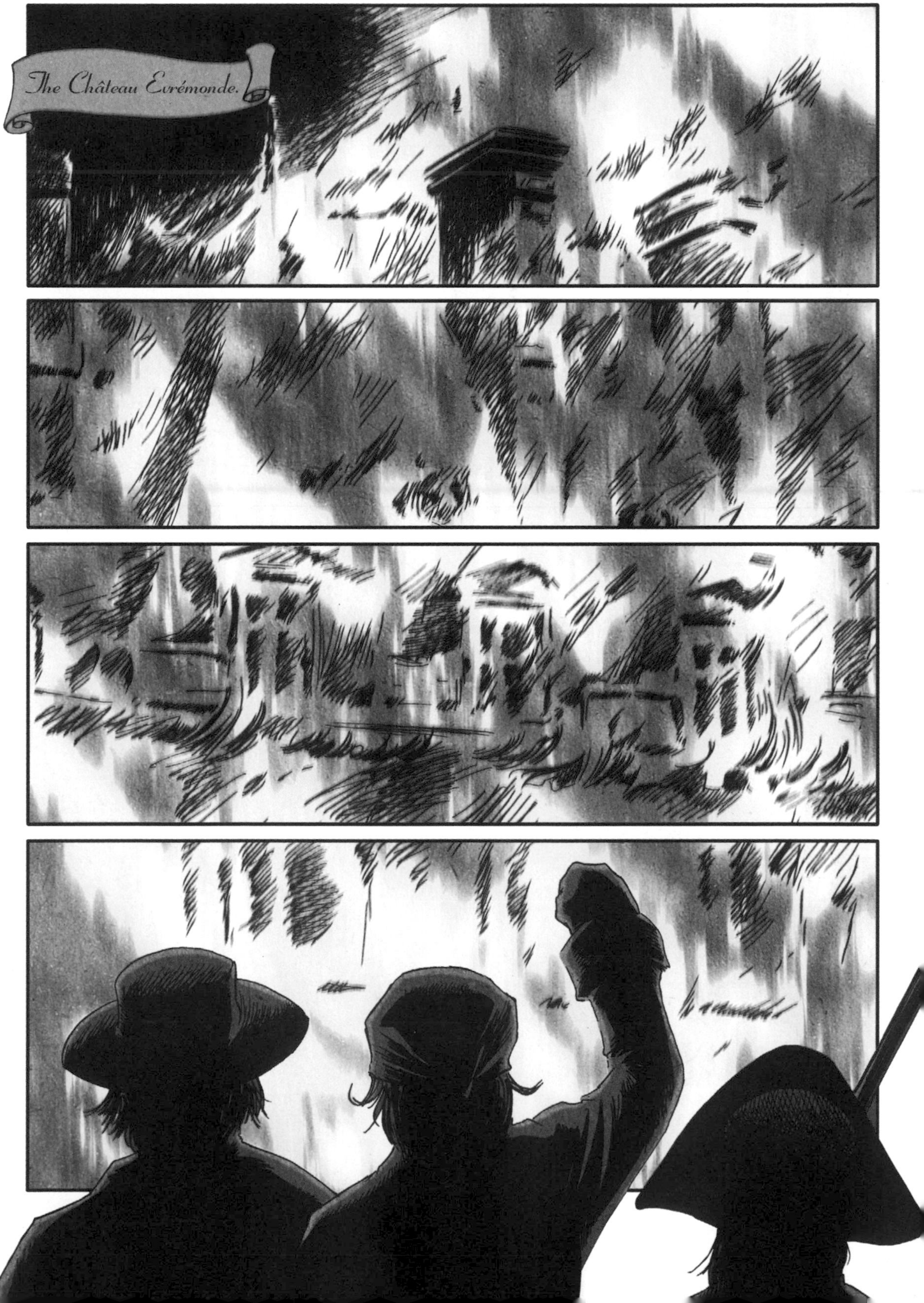
The Château Evrémonde.

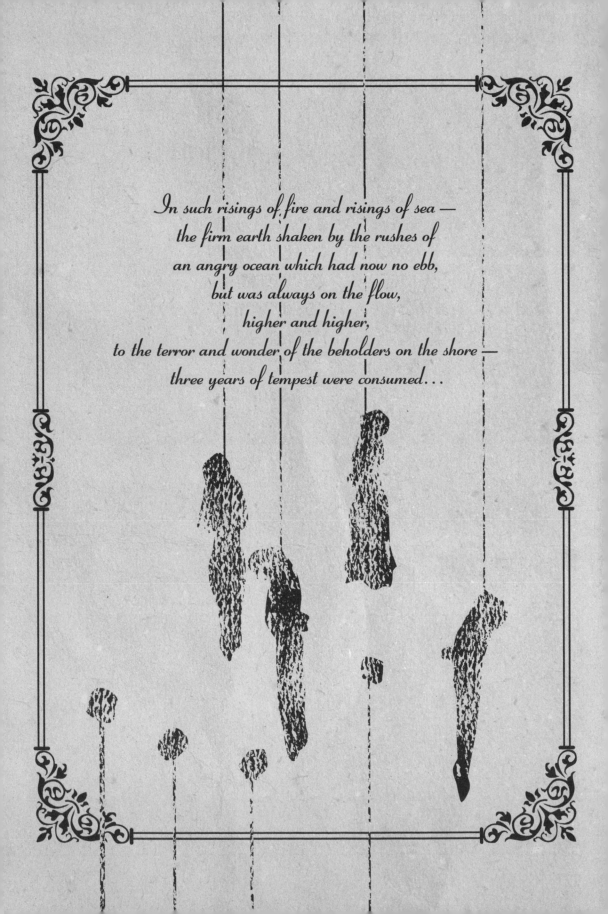

In such risings of fire and risings of sea —
the firm earth shaken by the rushes of
an angry ocean which had now no ebb,
but was always on the flow,
higher and higher,
to the terror and wonder of the beholders on the shore —
three years of tempest were consumed...

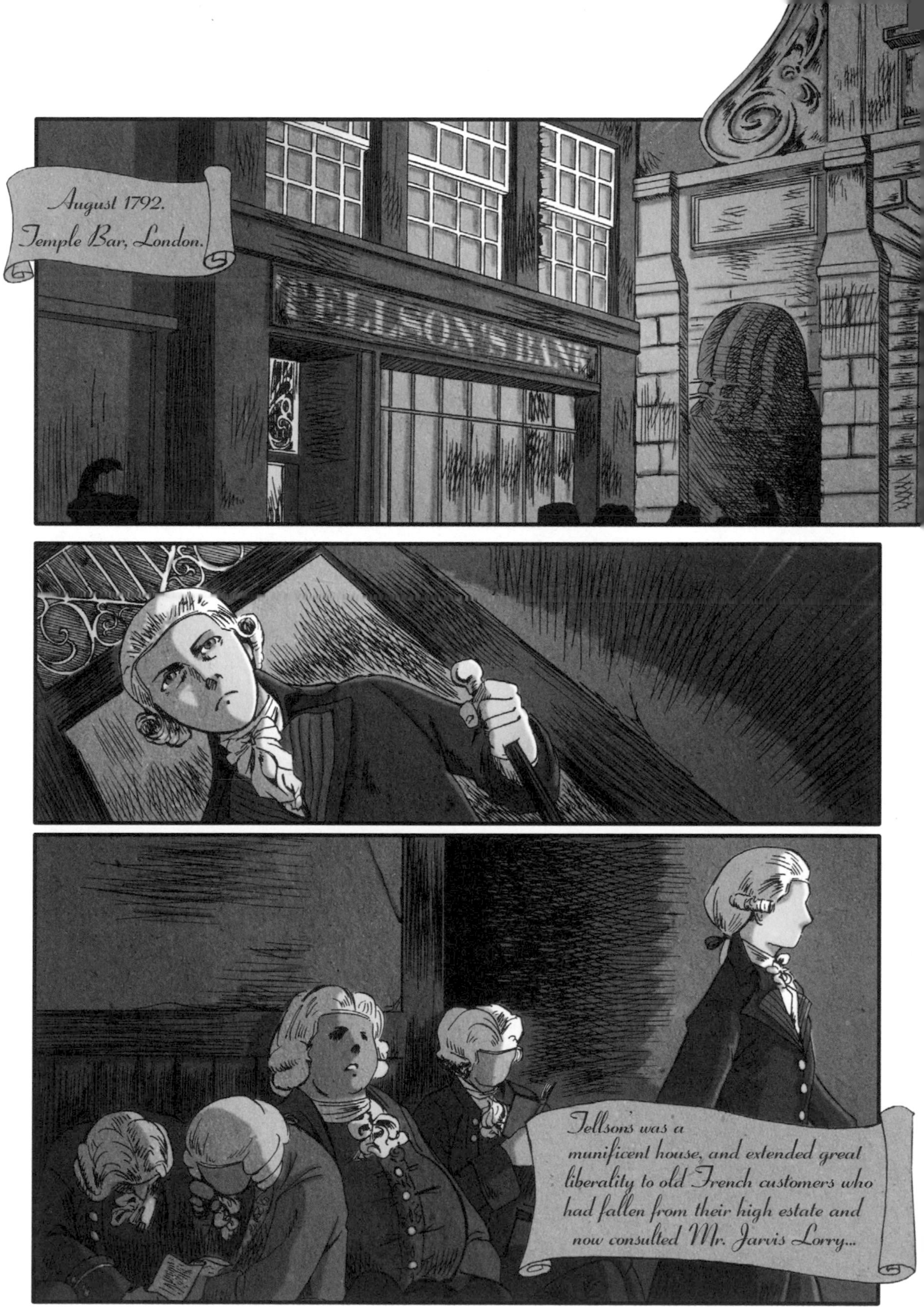
August 1792.
Temple Bar, London.
Tellson's was a munificent house, and extended great liberality to old French customers who had fallen from their high estate and now consulted Mr. Jarvis Lorry...

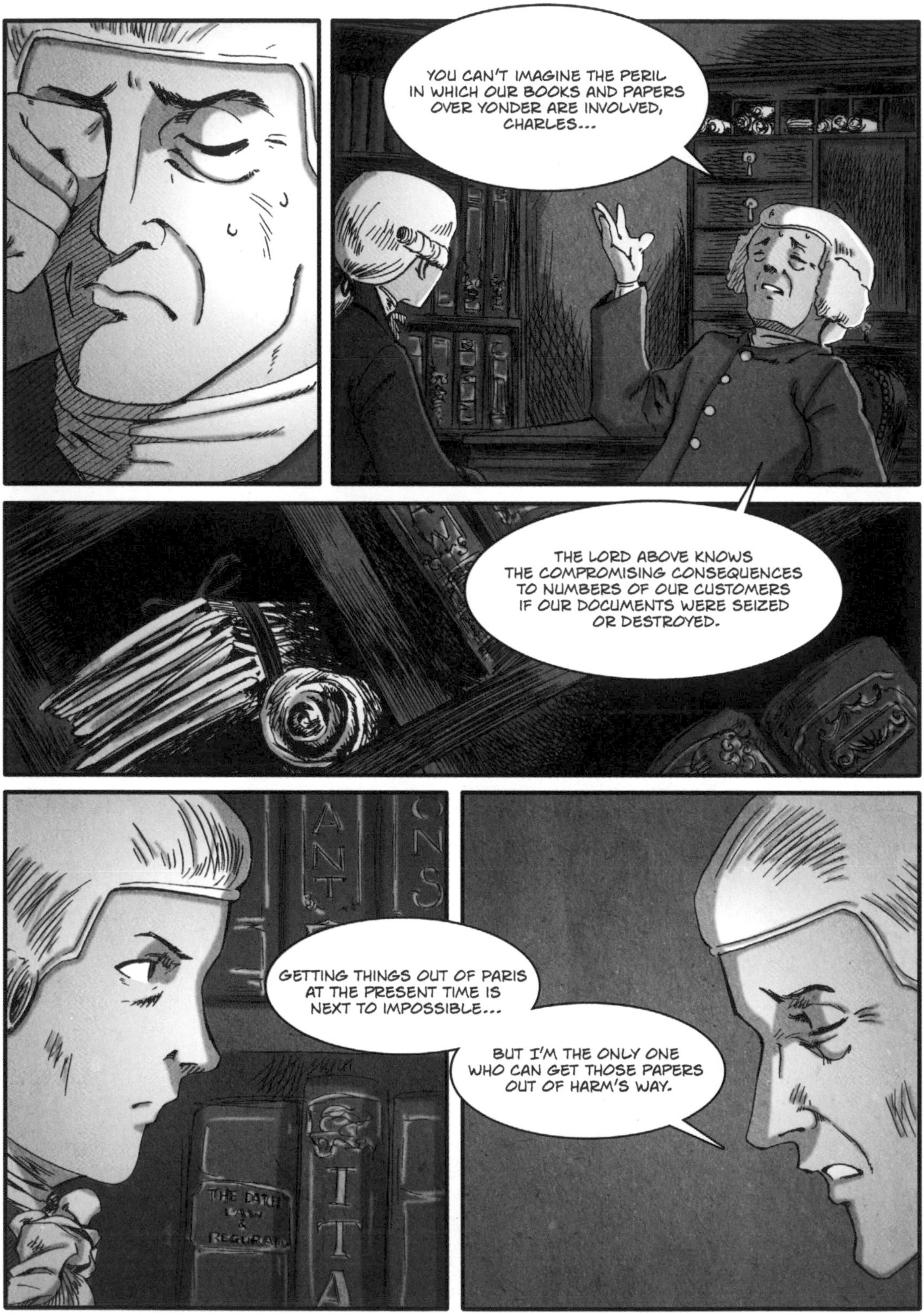
YOU CAN'T IMAGINE THE PERIL IN WHICH OUR BOOKS AND PAPERS OVER YONDER ARE INVOLVED, CHARLES...
THE LORD ABOVE KNOWS THE COMPROMISING CONSEQUENCES TO NUMBERS OF OUR CUSTOMERS IF OUR DOCUMENTS WERE SEIZED OR DESTROYED.
GETTING THINGS OUT OF PARIS AT THE PRESENT TIME IS NEXT TO IMPOSSIBLE...
BUT I'M THE ONLY ONE WHO CAN GET THOSE PAPERS OUT OF HARM'S WAY.

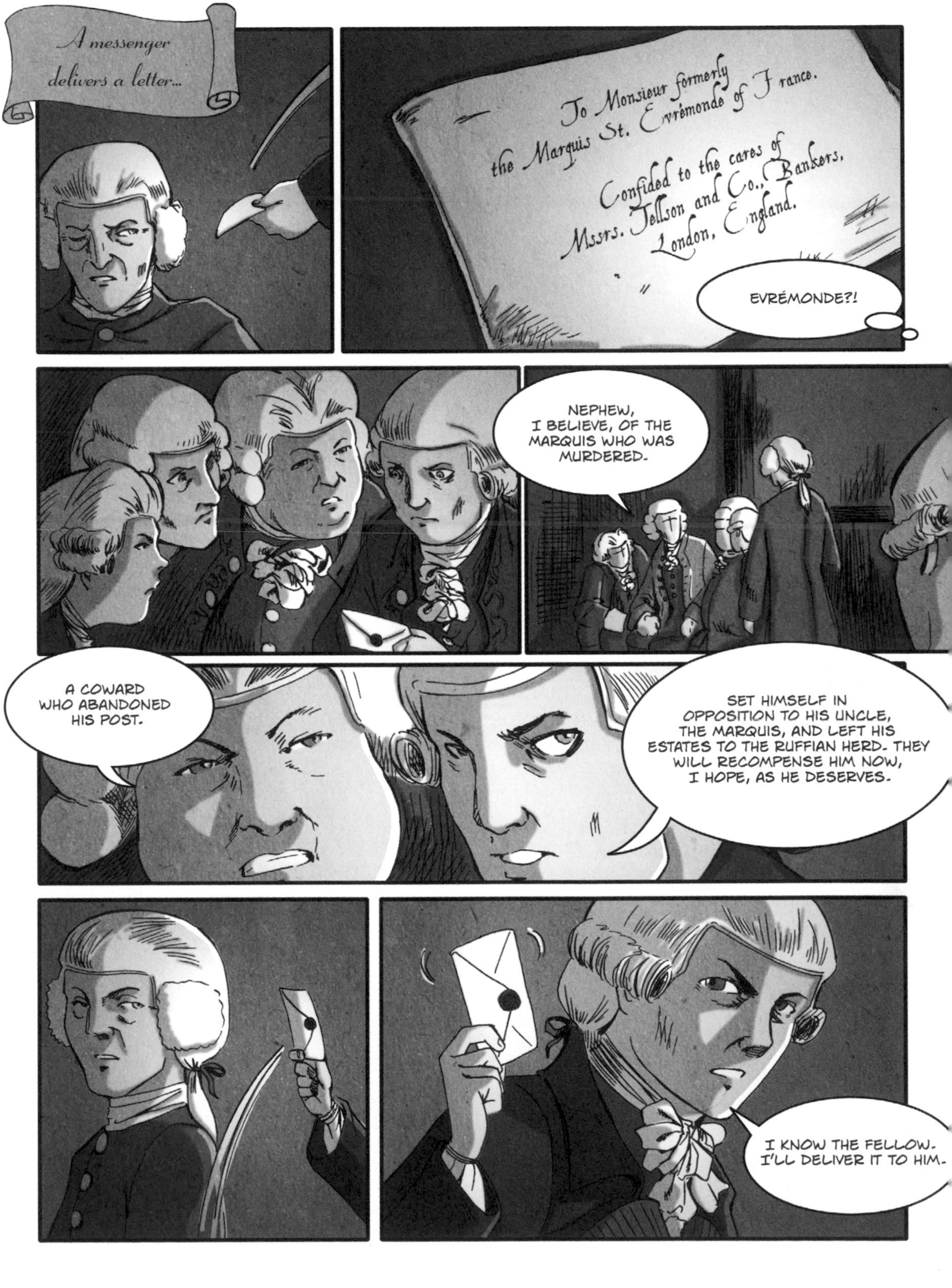
A messenger delivers a letter...
To Monsieur formerly
the Marquis St. Evrémonde of France.
Confided to the cares of
Mssrs. Tellson and Co., Bankers,
London, England.
EVRÉMONDE?!
NEPHEW, I BELIEVE, OF THE MARQUIS WHO WAS MURDERED.
A COWARD WHO ABANDONED HIS POST.
SET HIMSELF IN OPPOSITION TO HIS UNCLE, THE MARQUIS, AND LEFT HIS ESTATES TO THE RUFFIAN HERD. THEY WILL RECOMPENSE HIM NOW, I HOPE, AS HE DESERVES.
I KNOW THE FELLOW. I'LL DELIVER IT TO HIM.

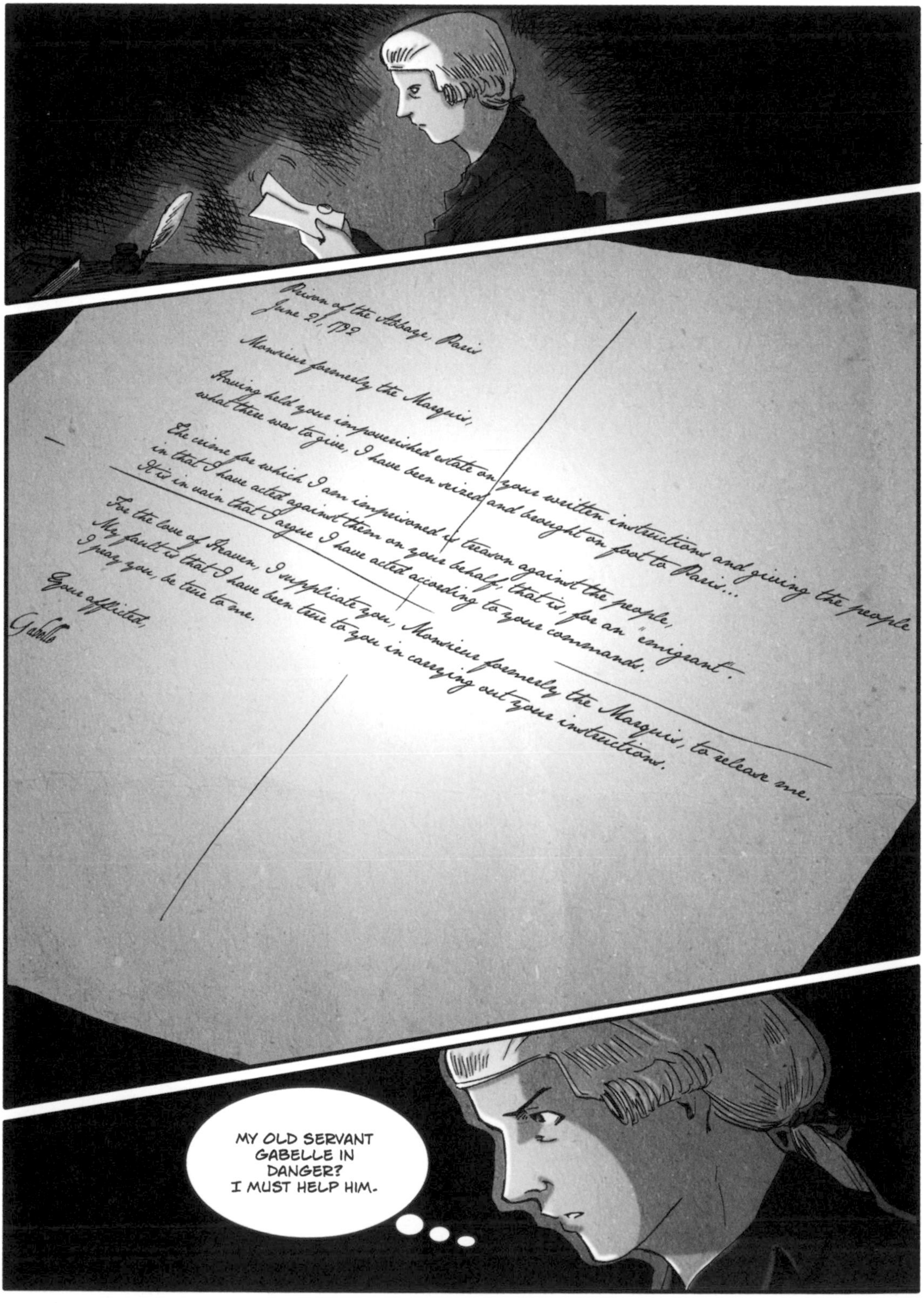
Prison of the Abbaye, Paris
June 21, 1792
Monsieur formerly the Marquis,
Having held your impoverished estate on your written instructions and giving the people what there was to give, I have been seized and brought on foot to Paris...
The crime for which I am imprisoned is treason against the people, in that I have acted against them on your behalf; that is, for an "emigrant".
It is in vain that I argue I have acted according to your commands.
For the love of Heaven, I supplicate you, Monsieur formerly the Marquis, to release me.
My fault is that I have been true to you in carrying out your instructions.
I pray you, be true to me.
Your afflicted,
Gabelle
MY OLD SERVANT GABELLE IN DANGER? I MUST HELP HIM.

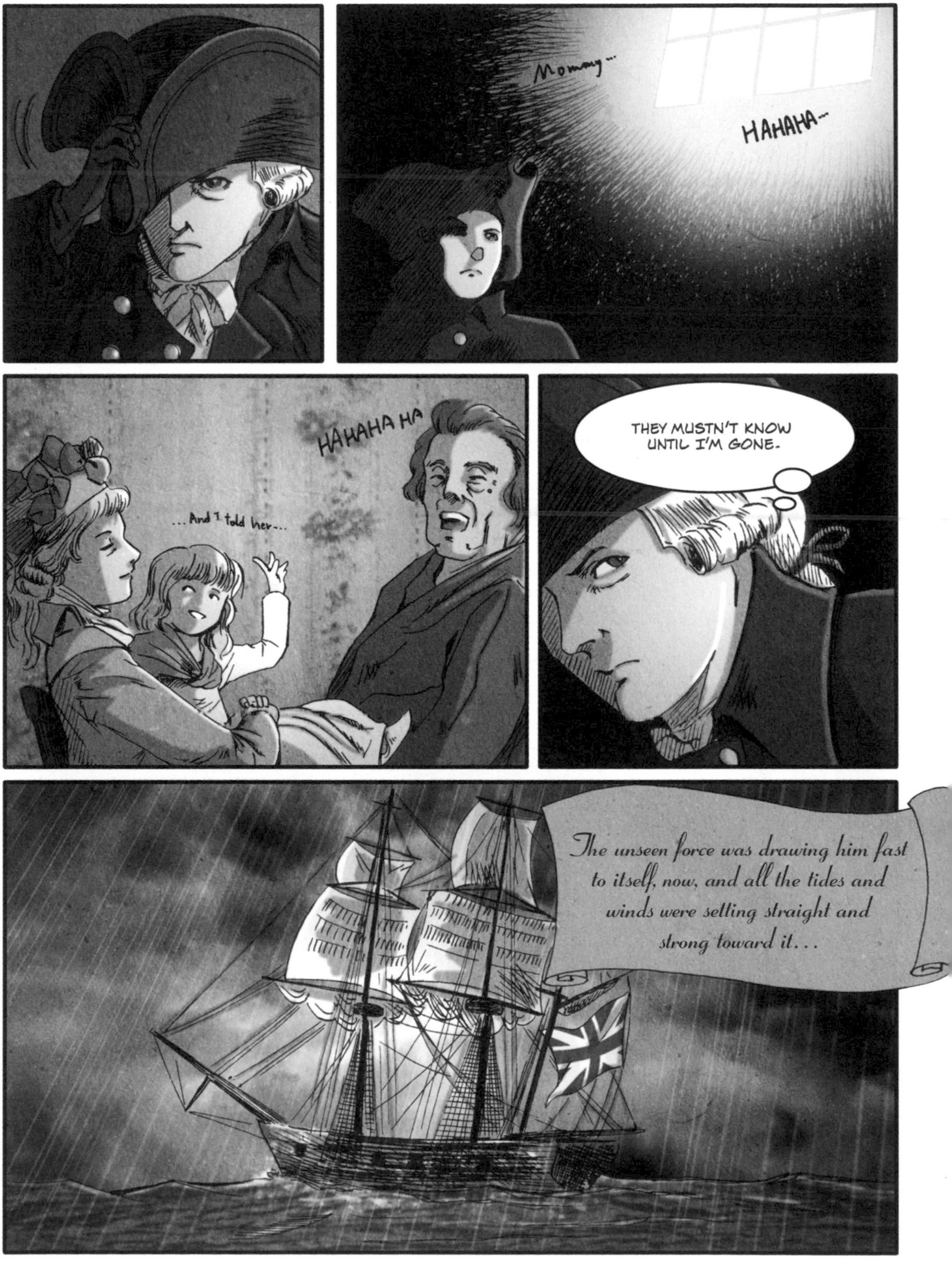
Mommy...
HAHAHA...
HAHAHA HA
...And I told her...
THEY MUSTN'T KNOW UNTIL I'M GONE.
The unseen force was drawing him fast to itself, now, and all the tides and winds were setting straight and strong toward it...

BOOK THE THIRD
The Track of a Storm

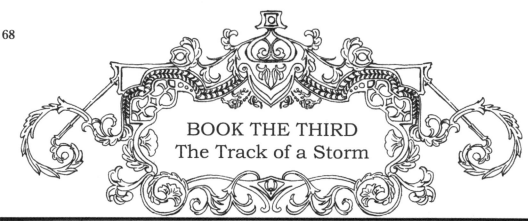

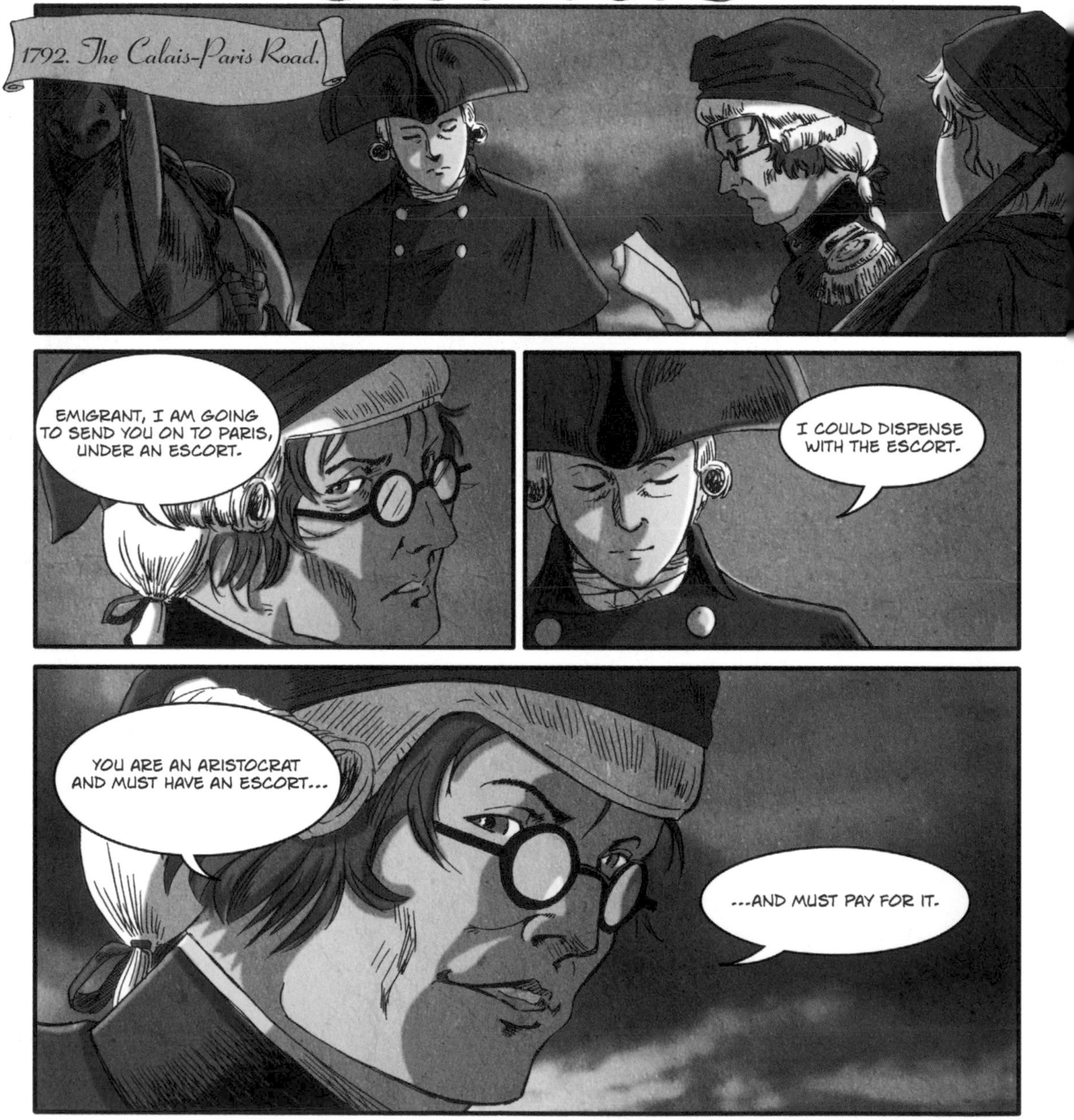
1792. The Calais-Paris Road.
EMIGRANT, I AM GOING TO SEND YOU ON TO PARIS, UNDER AN ESCORT.
I COULD DISPENSE WITH THE ESCORT.
YOU ARE AN ARISTOCRAT AND MUST HAVE AN ESCORT...
...AND MUST PAY FOR IT.

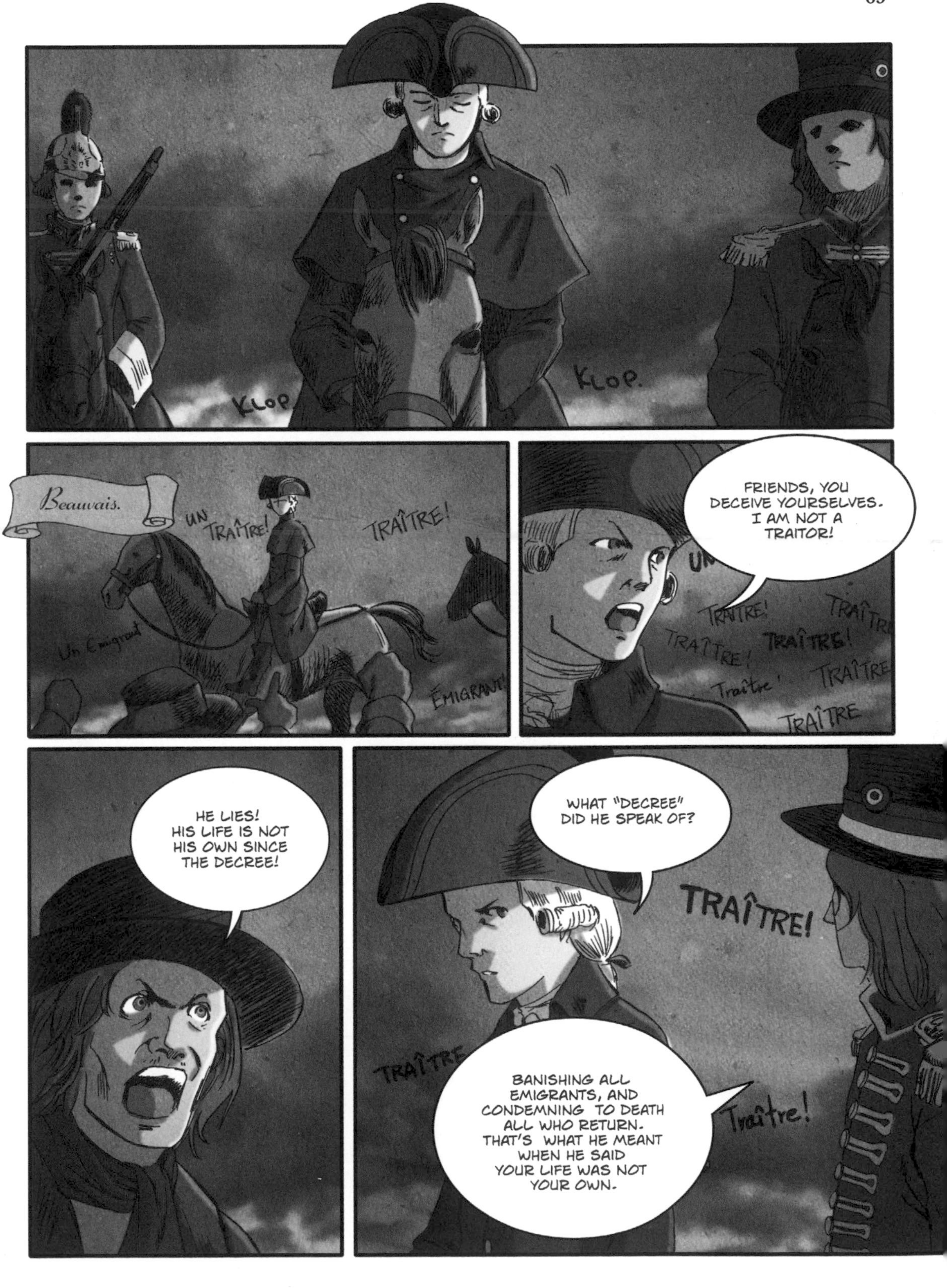
KLOP.
KLOP.
Beauvais.
UN TRAÎTRE!
TRAÎTRE!
Un Emigrant
ÉMIGRANT!
FRIENDS, YOU DECEIVE YOURSELVES. I AM NOT A TRAITOR!
TRAÎTRE!
TRAÎTRE!
TRAÎTRE!
Traître!
TRAÎTRE
HE LIES! HIS LIFE IS NOT HIS OWN SINCE THE DECREE!
WHAT "DECREE" DID HE SPEAK OF?
TRAÎTRE!
TRAÎTRE
BANISHING ALL EMIGRANTS, AND CONDEMNING TO DEATH ALL WHO RETURN. THAT'S WHAT HE MEANT WHEN HE SAID YOUR LIFE WAS NOT YOUR OWN.
Traître!

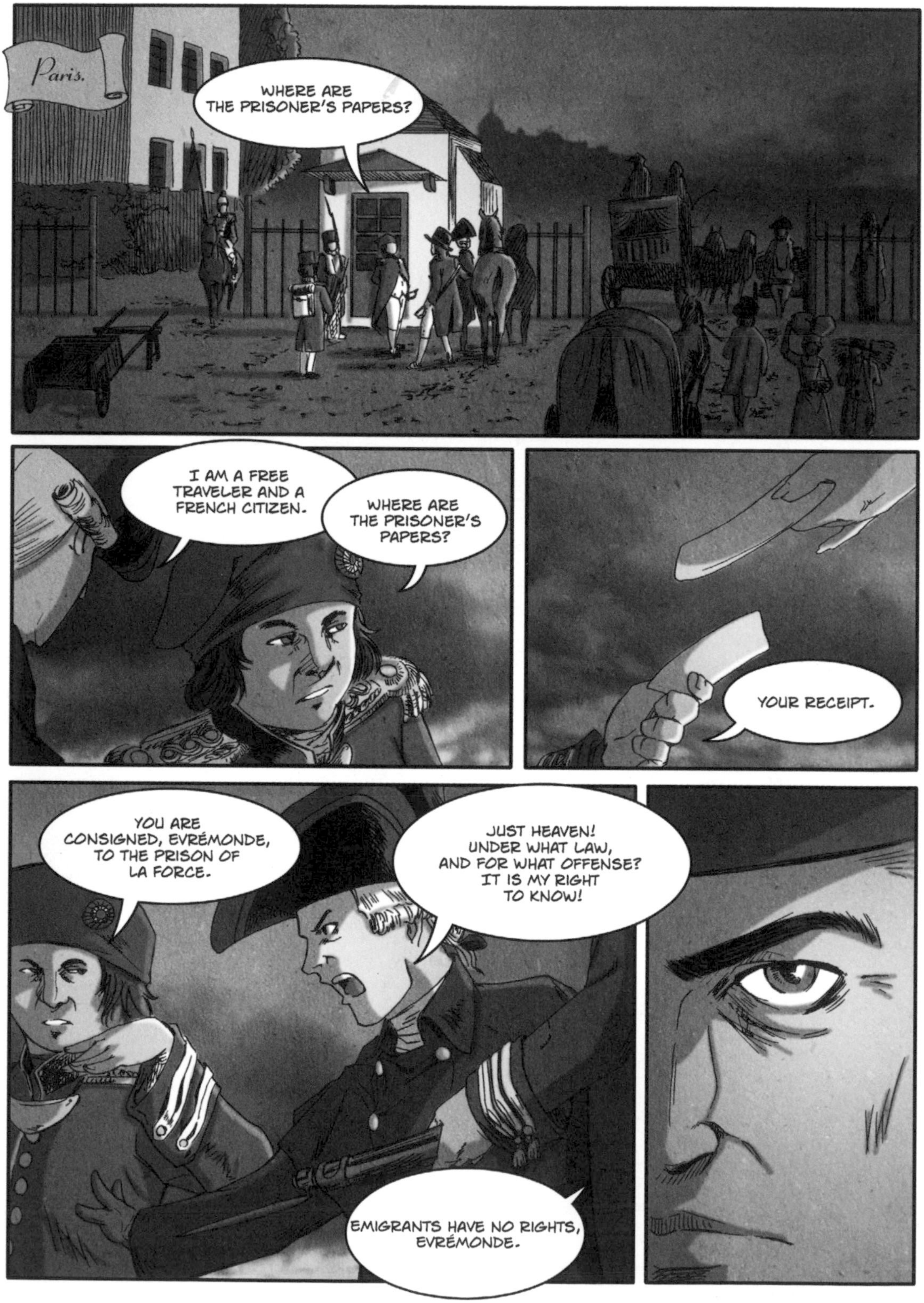
Paris.
WHERE ARE THE PRISONER'S PAPERS?
I AM A FREE TRAVELER AND A FRENCH CITIZEN.
WHERE ARE THE PRISONER'S PAPERS?
YOUR RECEIPT.
YOU ARE CONSIGNED, EVRÉMONDE, TO THE PRISON OF LA FORCE.
JUST HEAVEN! UNDER WHAT LAW, AND FOR WHAT OFFENSE? IT IS MY RIGHT TO KNOW!
EMIGRANTS HAVE NO RIGHTS, EVRÉMONDE.

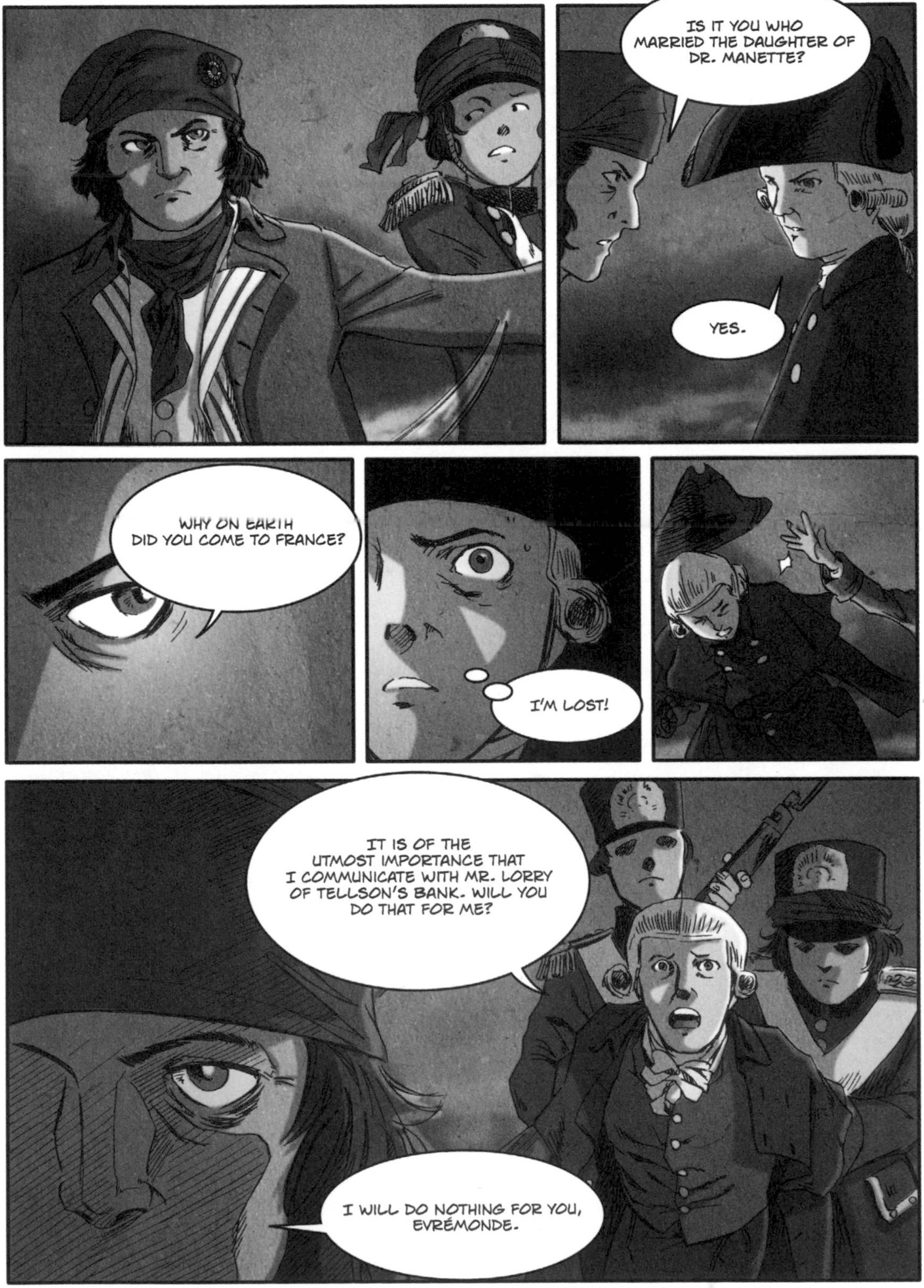
IS IT YOU WHO MARRIED THE DAUGHTER OF DR. MANETTE?
YES.
WHY ON EARTH DID YOU COME TO FRANCE?
I'M LOST!
IT IS OF THE UTMOST IMPORTANCE THAT I COMMUNICATE WITH MR. LORRY OF TELLSON'S BANK. WILL YOU DO THAT FOR ME?
I WILL DO NOTHING FOR YOU, EVRÉMONDE.

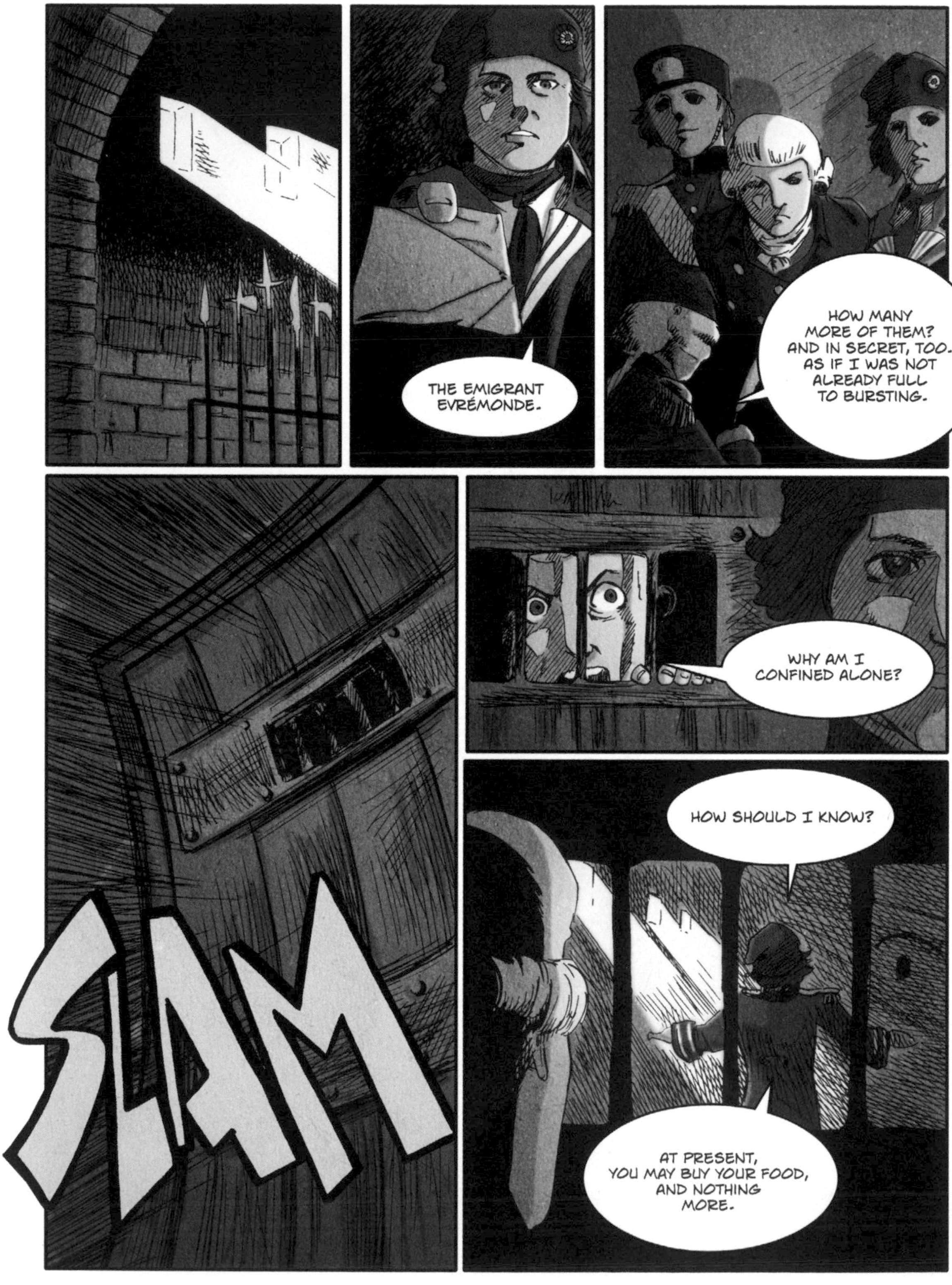
THE EMIGRANT EVRÉMONDE.
HOW MANY MORE OF THEM? AND IN SECRET, TOO. AS IF I WAS NOT ALREADY FULL TO BURSTING.
SLAM
WHY AM I CONFINED ALONE?
HOW SHOULD I KNOW?
AT PRESENT, YOU MAY BUY YOUR FOOD, AND NOTHING MORE.

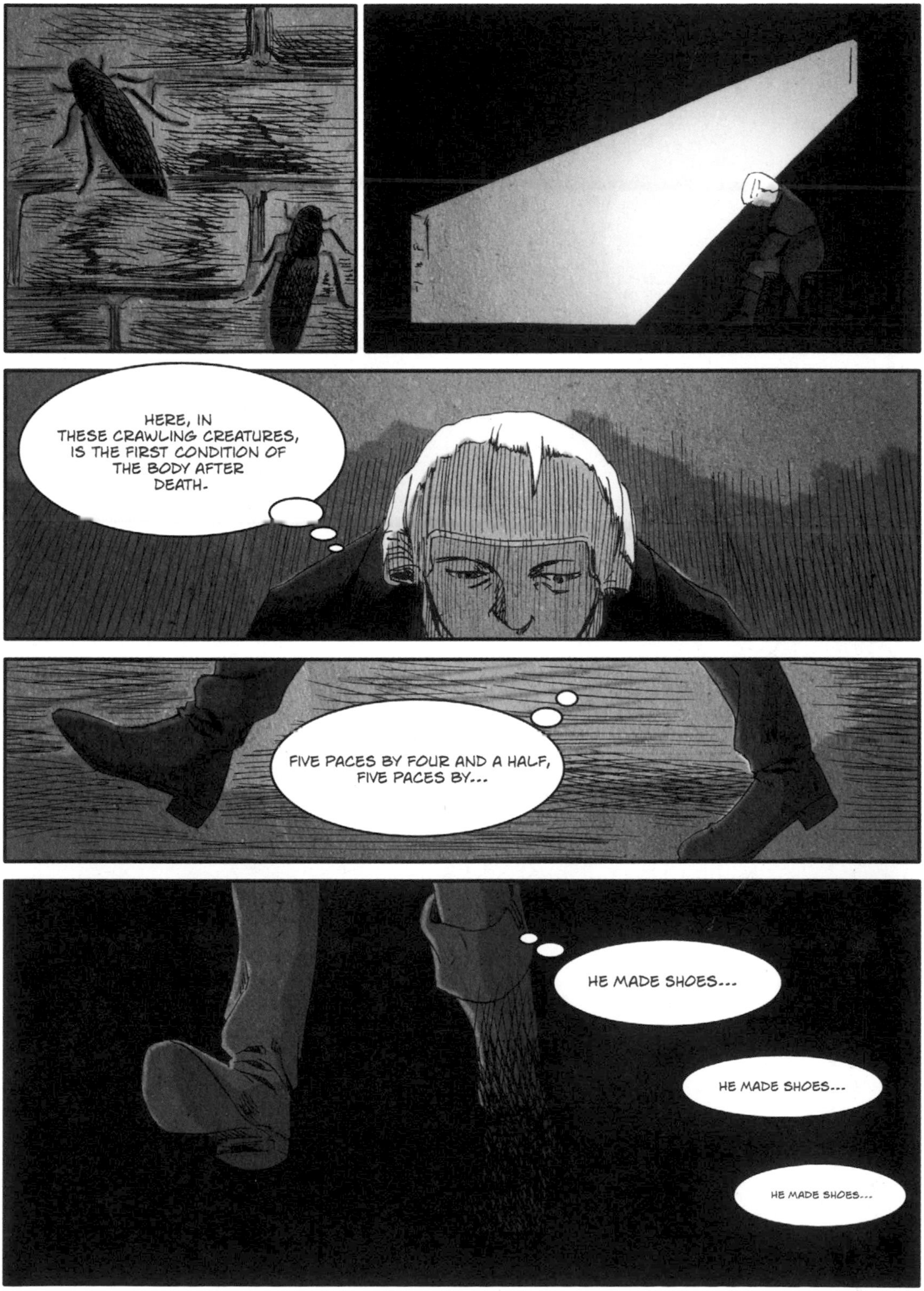
HERE, IN THESE CRAWLING CREATURES, IS THE FIRST CONDITION OF THE BODY AFTER DEATH.
FIVE PACES BY FOUR AND A HALF, FIVE PACES BY...
HE MADE SHOES...
HE MADE SHOES...
HE MADE SHOES...

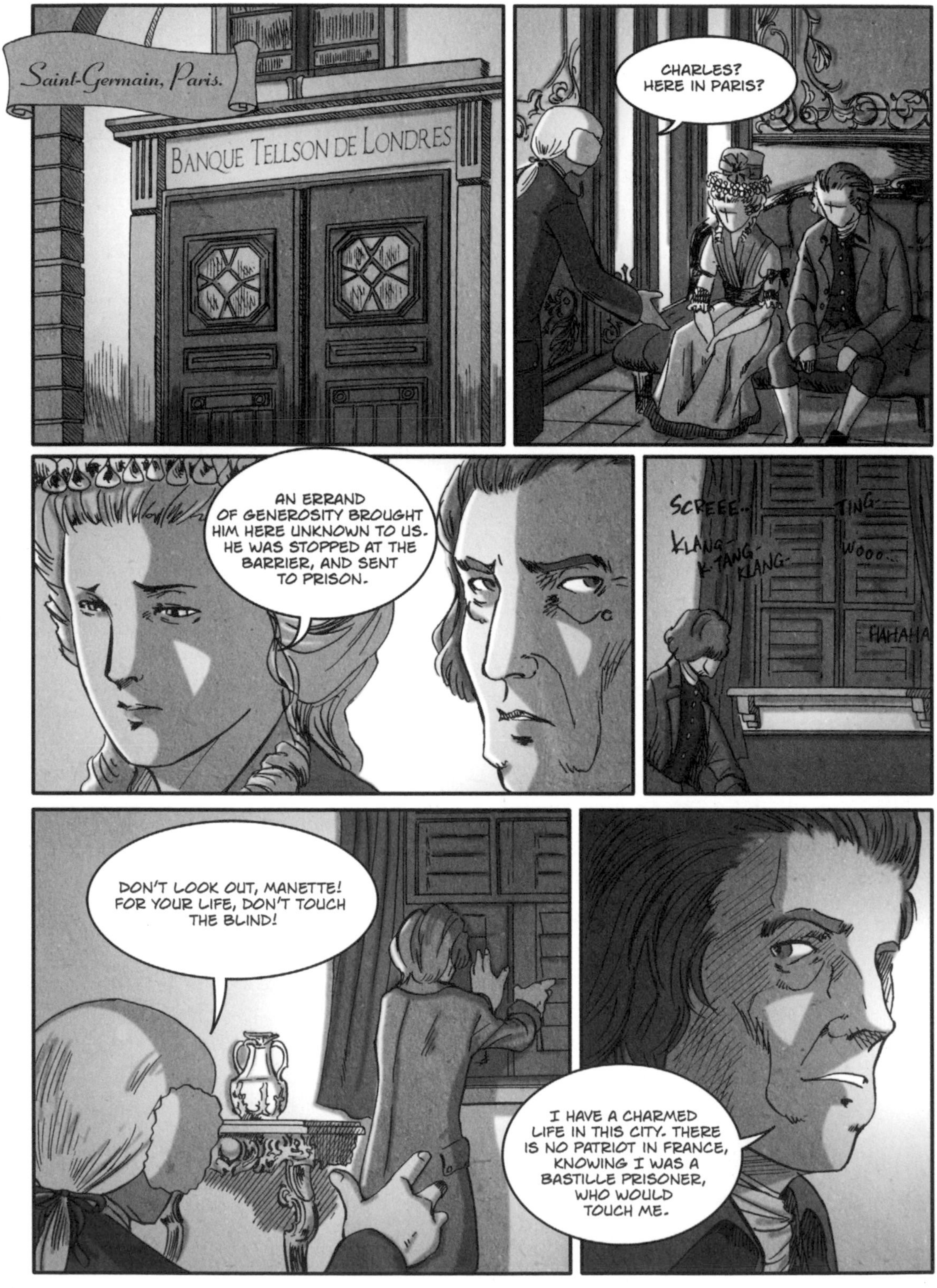
Saint-Germain, Paris.
BANQUE TELLSON DE LONDRES
CHARLES? HERE IN PARIS?
AN ERRAND OF GENEROSITY BROUGHT HIM HERE UNKNOWN TO US. HE WAS STOPPED AT THE BARRIER, AND SENT TO PRISON.
SCREEE...
TING-
KLANG-
K-TANG-
KLANG-
WOOO...
HAHAHA
DON'T LOOK OUT, MANETTE! FOR YOUR LIFE, DON'T TOUCH THE BLIND!
I HAVE A CHARMED LIFE IN THIS CITY. THERE IS NO PATRIOT IN FRANCE, KNOWING I WAS A BASTILLE PRISONER, WHO WOULD TOUCH ME.

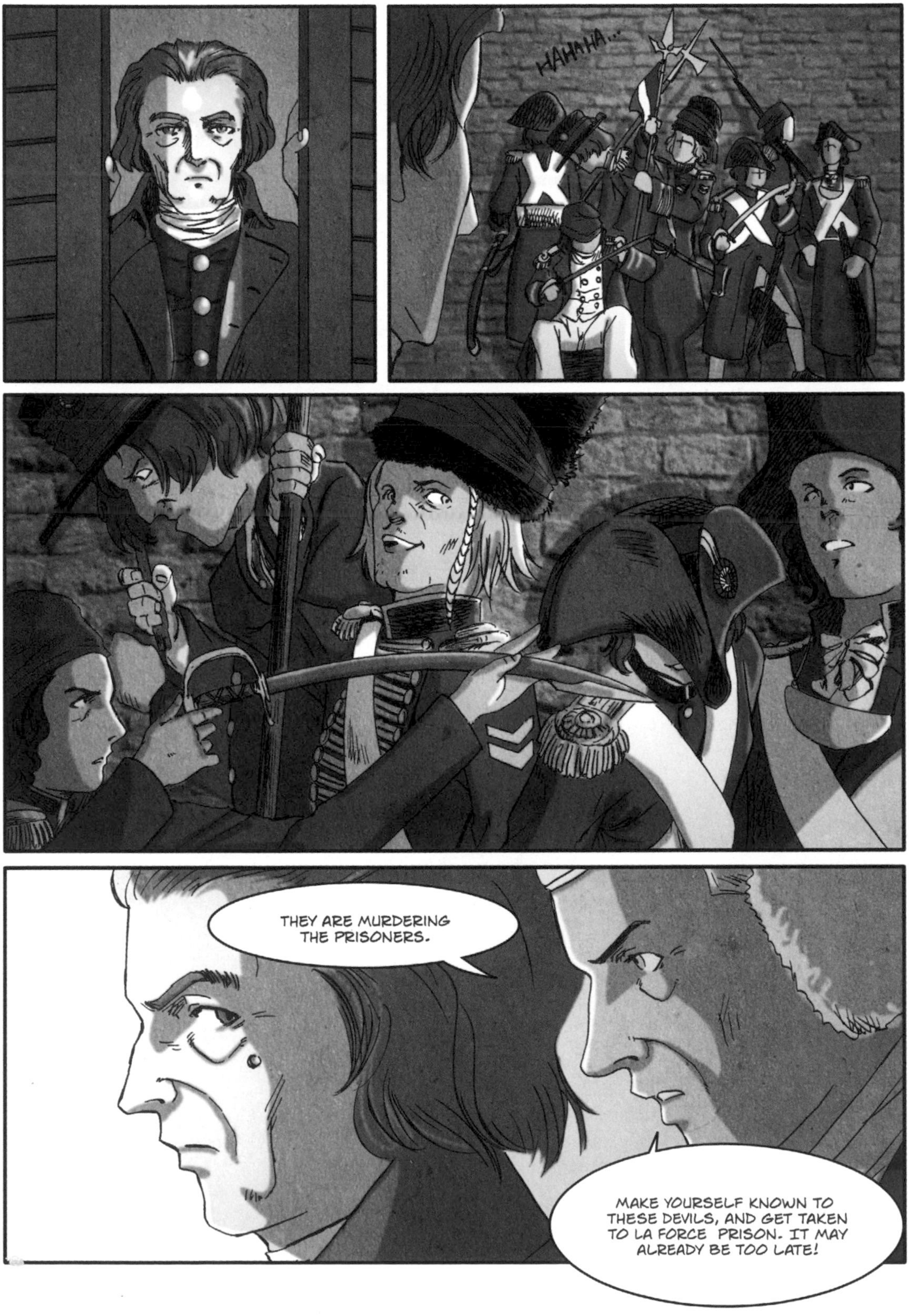
HAHAHA...
THEY ARE MURDERING THE PRISONERS.
MAKE YOURSELF KNOWN TO THESE DEVILS, AND GET TAKEN TO LA FORCE PRISON. IT MAY ALREADY BE TOO LATE!

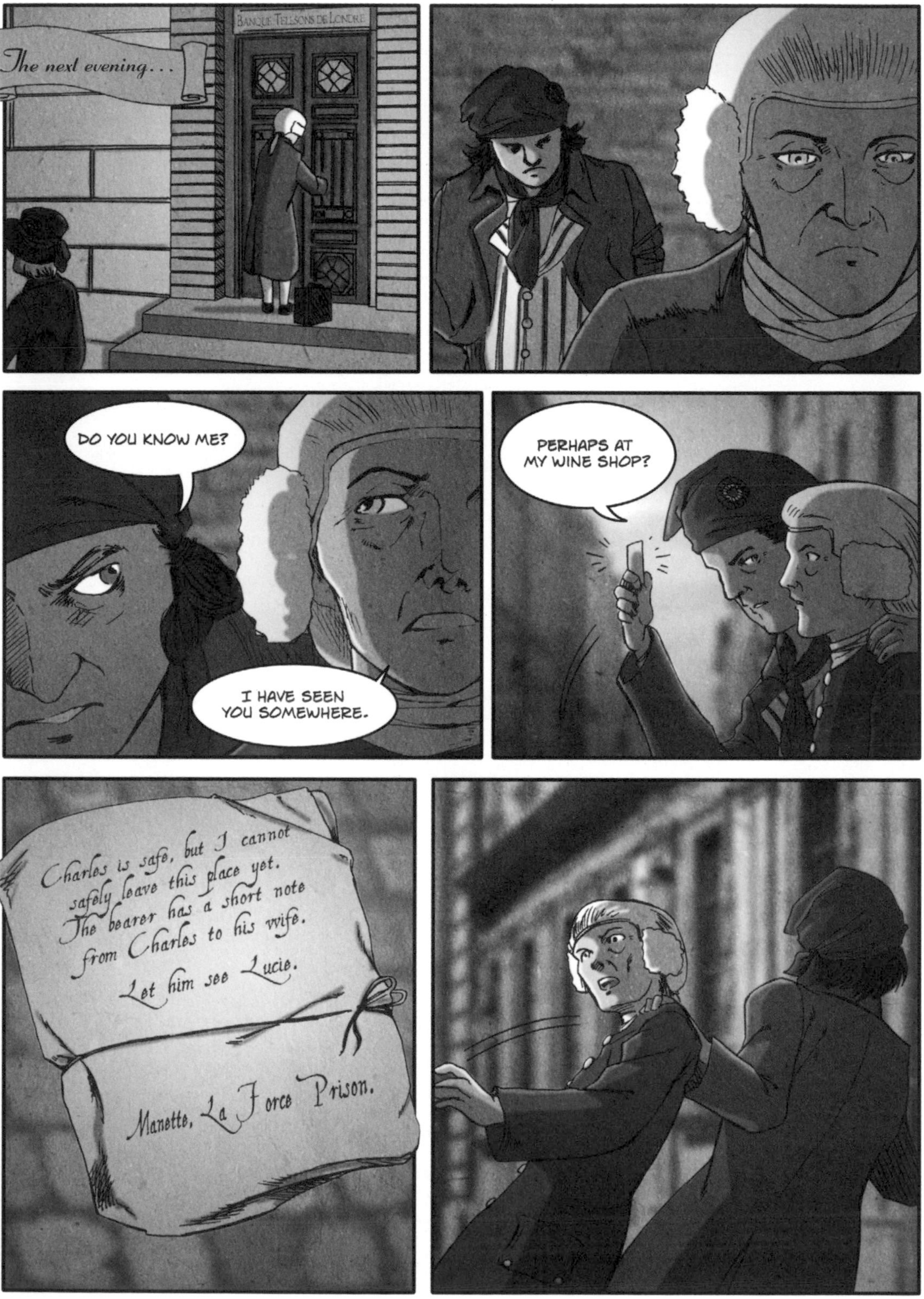
The next evening…
BANQUE TELLSONS DE LONDRE
DO YOU KNOW ME?
I HAVE SEEN YOU SOMEWHERE.
PERHAPS AT MY WINE SHOP?
Charles is safe, but I cannot safely leave this place yet. The bearer has a short note from Charles to his wife.
Let him see Lucie.
Manette, La Force Prison.

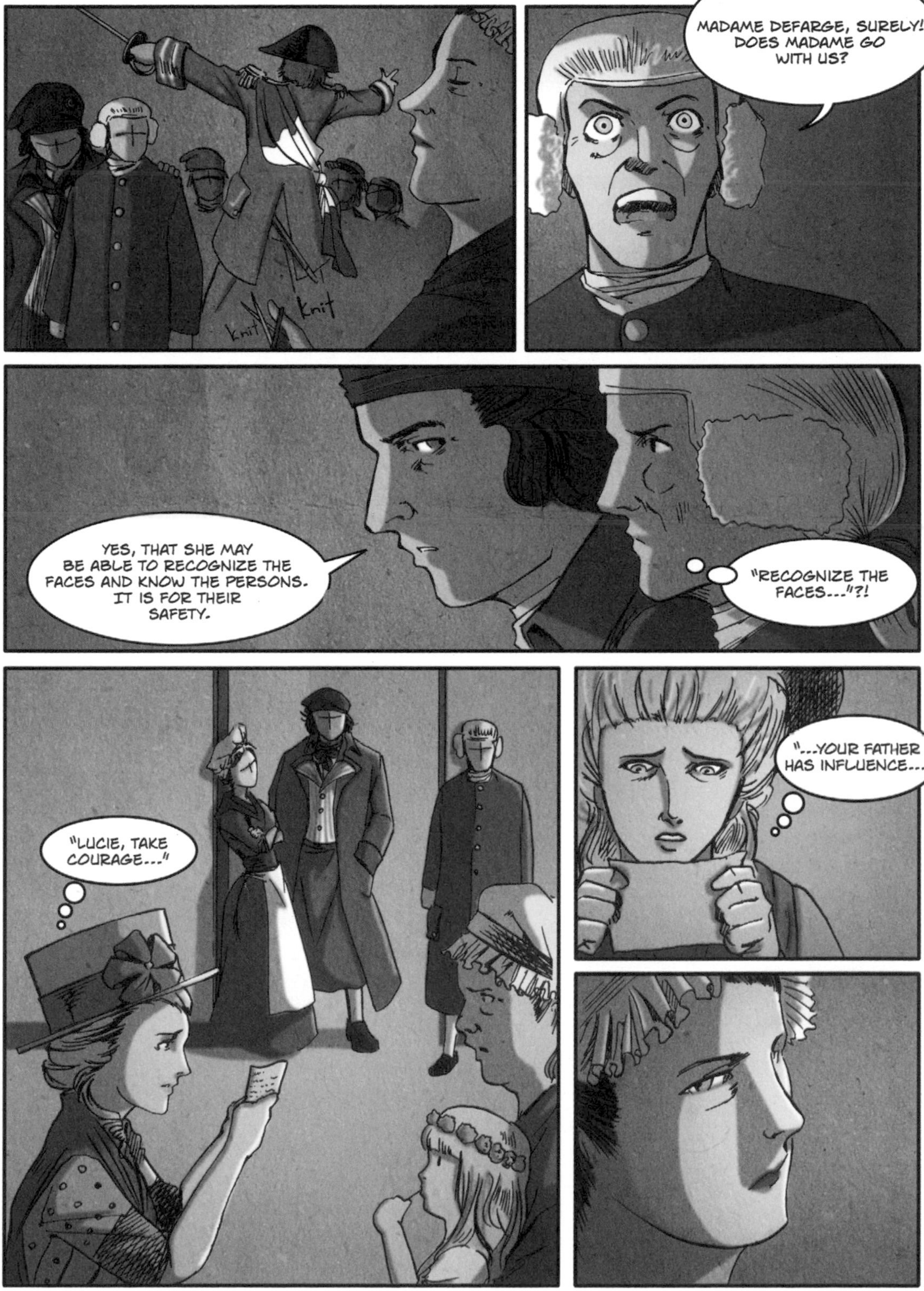
Knit
Knit
MADAME DEFARGE, SURELY! DOES MADAME GO WITH US?
YES, THAT SHE MAY BE ABLE TO RECOGNIZE THE FACES AND KNOW THE PERSONS. IT IS FOR THEIR SAFETY.
"RECOGNIZE THE FACES..."?!
"LUCIE, TAKE COURAGE..."
"...YOUR FATHER HAS INFLUENCE..."

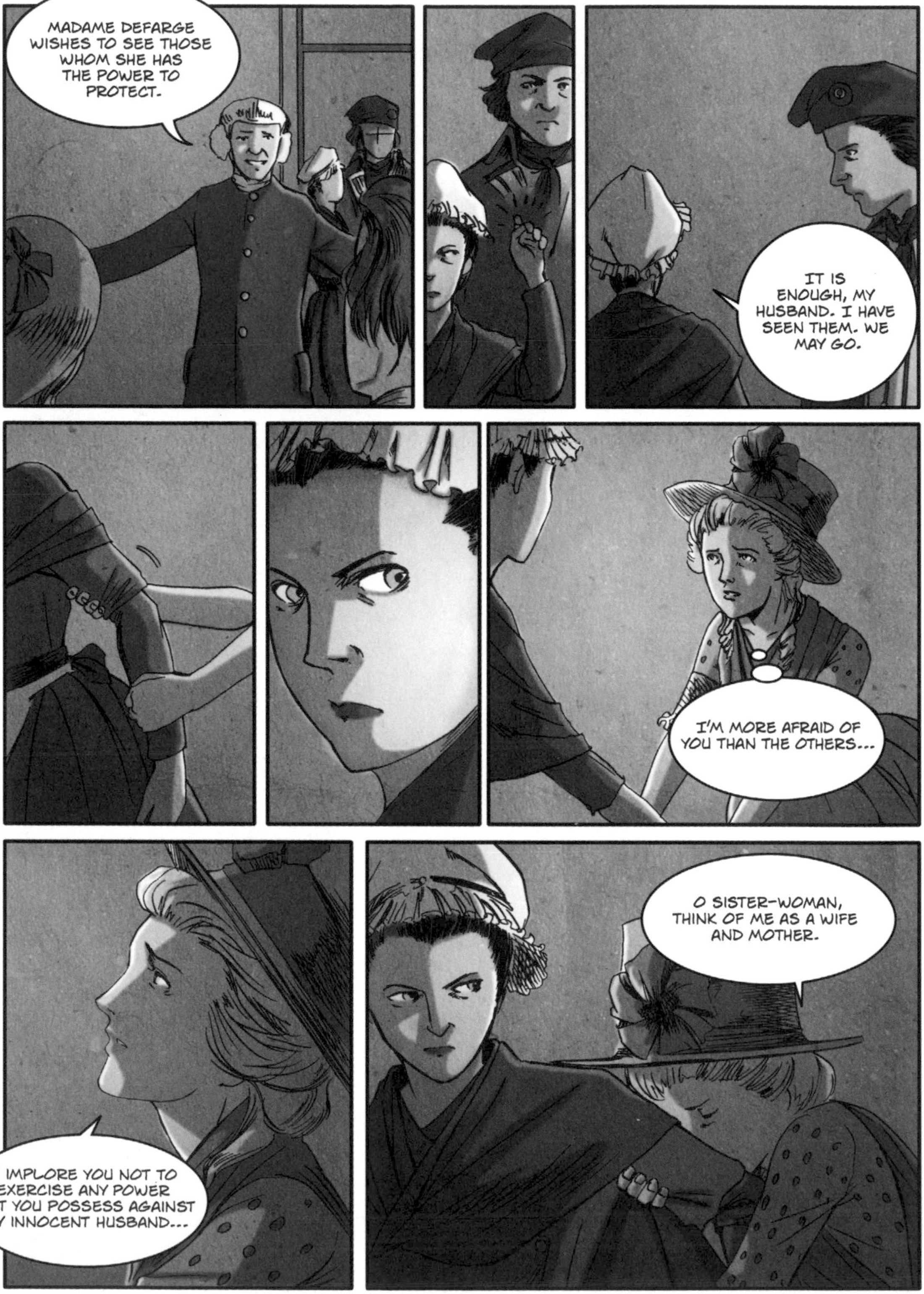
MADAME DEFARGE WISHES TO SEE THOSE WHOM SHE HAS THE POWER TO PROTECT.
IT IS ENOUGH, MY HUSBAND. I HAVE SEEN THEM. WE MAY GO.
I'M MORE AFRAID OF YOU THAN THE OTHERS...
I IMPLORE YOU NOT TO EXERCISE ANY POWER THAT YOU POSSESS AGAINST MY INNOCENT HUSBAND...
O SISTER-WOMAN, THINK OF ME AS A WIFE AND MOTHER.

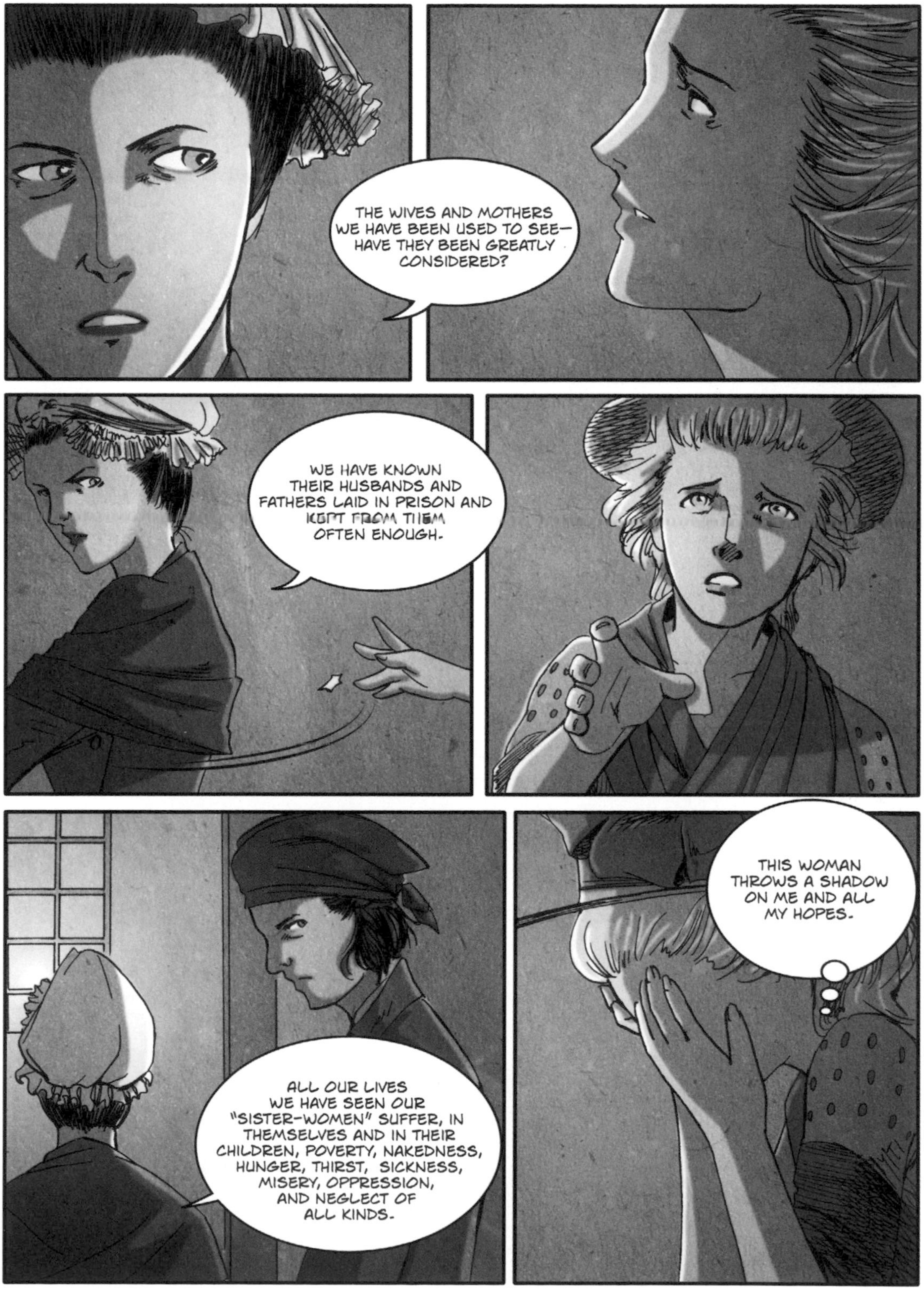
THE WIVES AND MOTHERS WE HAVE BEEN USED TO SEE— HAVE THEY BEEN GREATLY CONSIDERED?
WE HAVE KNOWN THEIR HUSBANDS AND FATHERS LAID IN PRISON AND KEPT FROM THEM OFTEN ENOUGH.
ALL OUR LIVES WE HAVE SEEN OUR "SISTER-WOMEN" SUFFER, IN THEMSELVES AND IN THEIR CHILDREN, POVERTY, NAKEDNESS, HUNGER, THIRST, SICKNESS, MISERY, OPPRESSION, AND NEGLECT OF ALL KINDS.
THIS WOMAN THROWS A SHADOW ON ME AND ALL MY HOPES.

There was no pause, no pity, no peace, no interval of relenting rest, no measurement of time. Hold of it was lost in the raging fever of a nation.

Now, breaking the unnatural silence of a whole city, the executioner showed the people the head of the king – and now, the head of his fair wife...

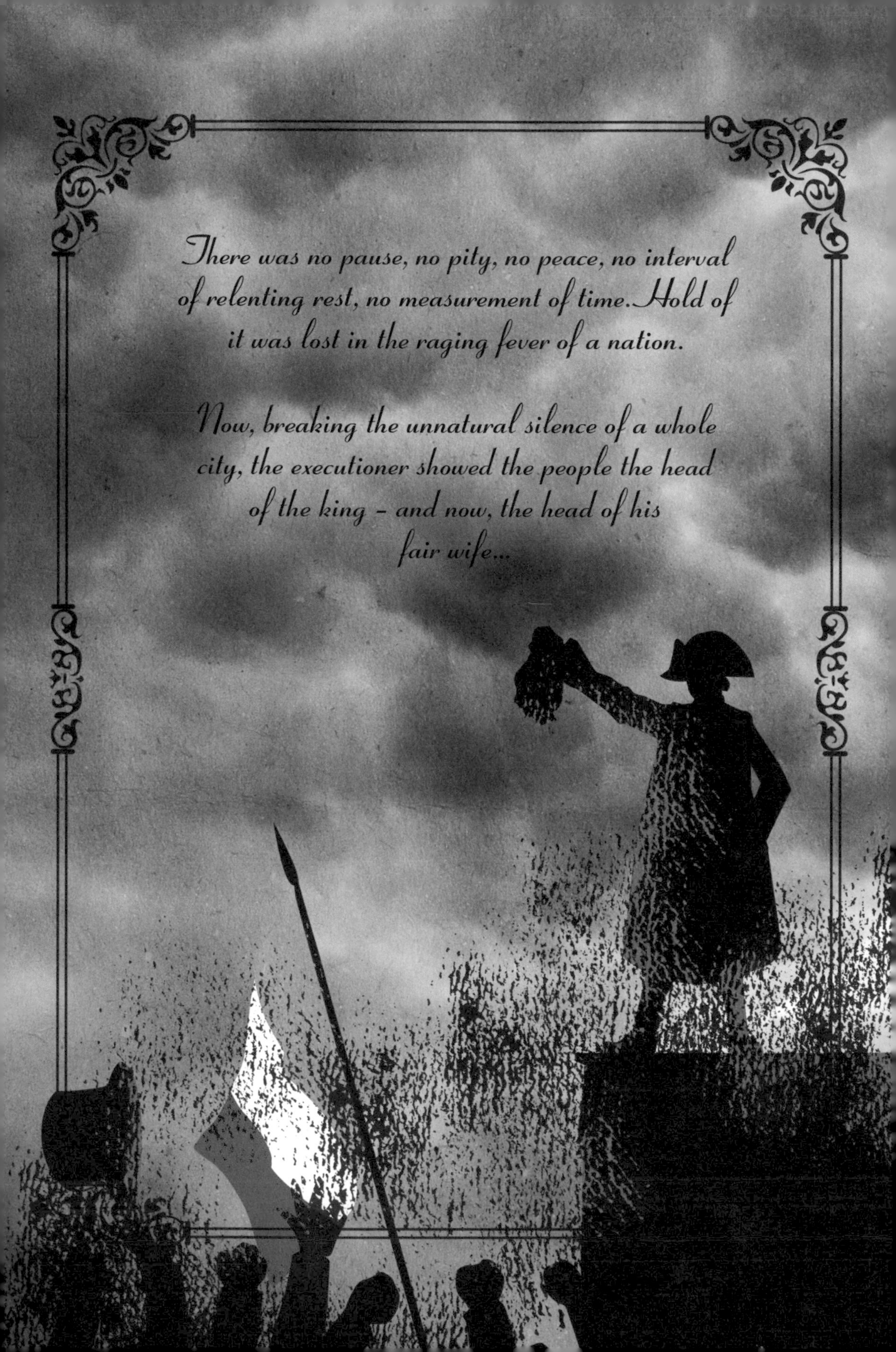

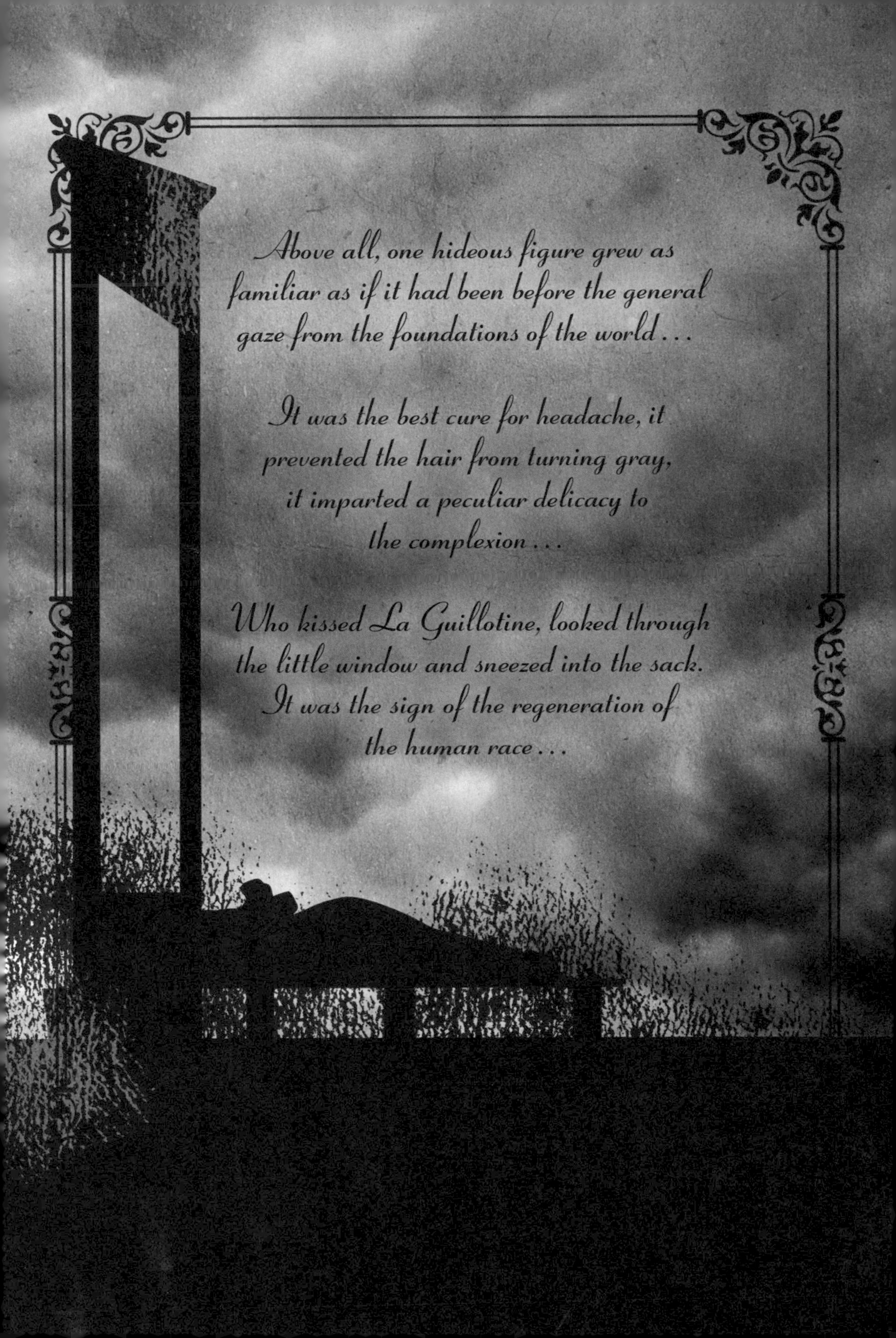

Above all, one hideous figure grew as familiar as if it had been before the general gaze from the foundations of the world . . .

It was the best cure for headache, it prevented the hair from turning gray, it imparted a peculiar delicacy to the complexion . . .

Who kissed La Guillotine, looked through the little window and sneezed into the sack. It was the sign of the regeneration of the human race . . .

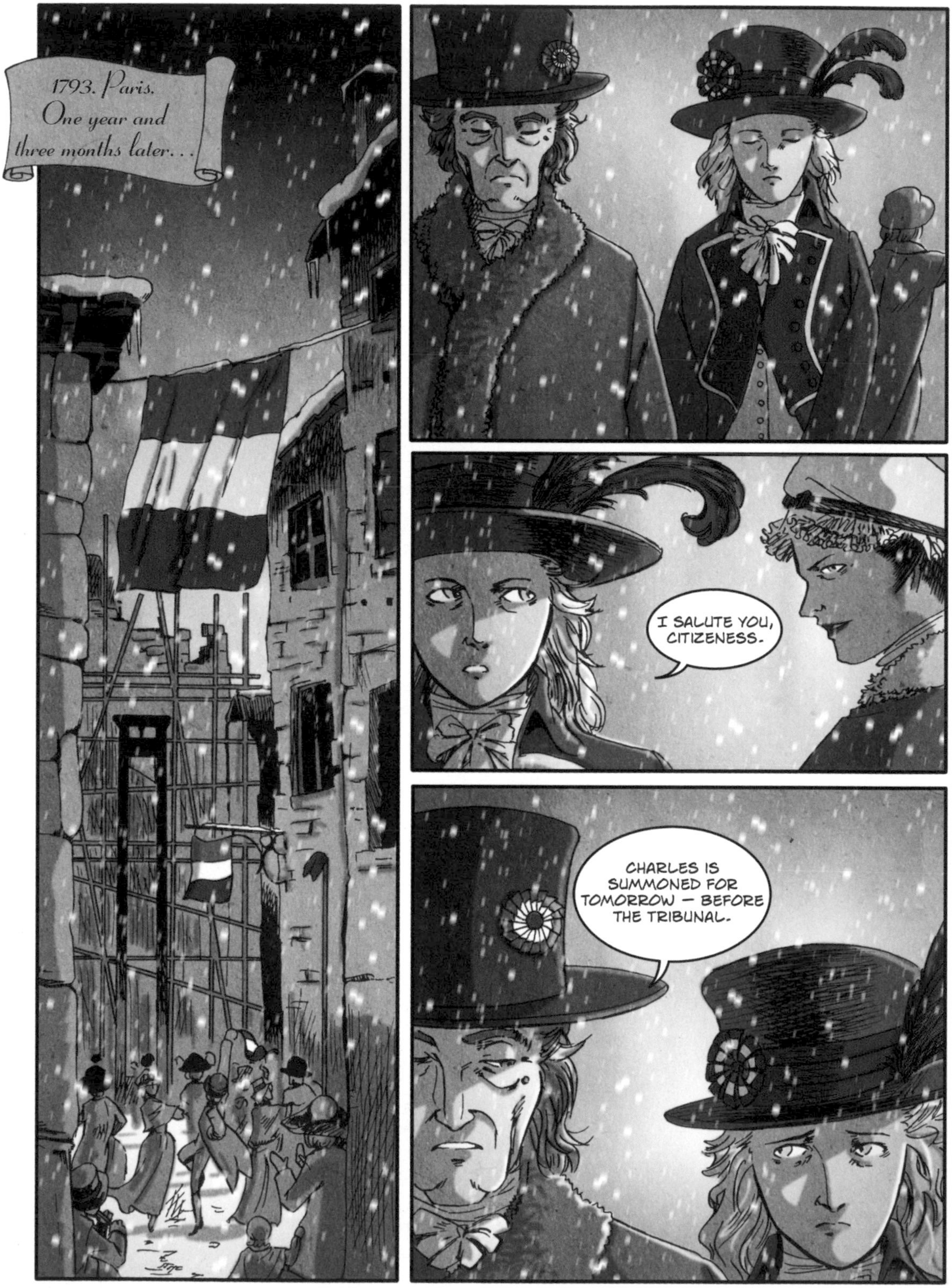
1793. Paris. One year and three months later...
I SALUTE YOU, CITIZENESS.
CHARLES IS SUMMONED FOR TOMORROW — BEFORE THE TRIBUNAL.

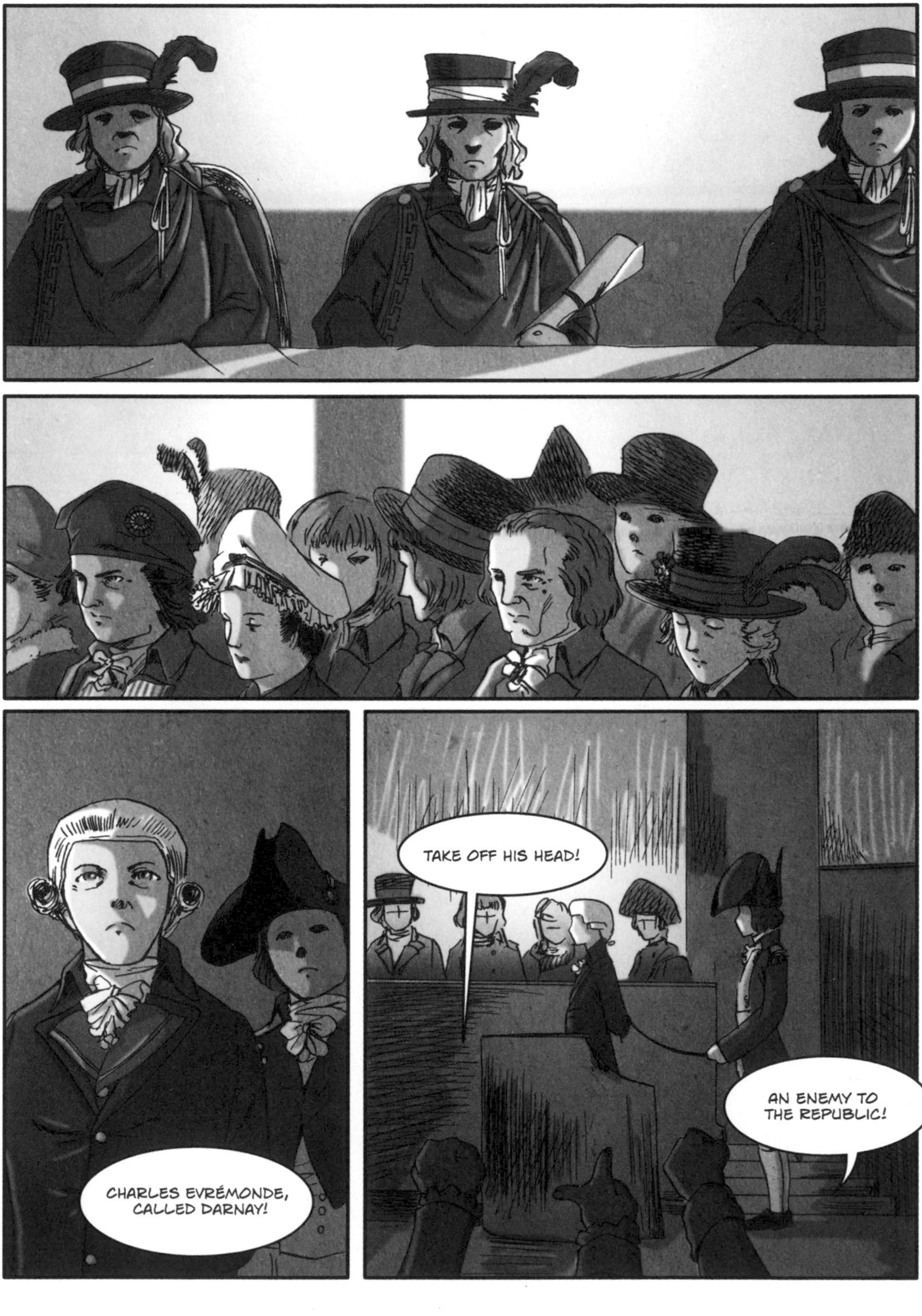
CHARLES EVRÉMONDE, CALLED DARNAY!
TAKE OFF HIS HEAD!
AN ENEMY TO THE REPUBLIC!

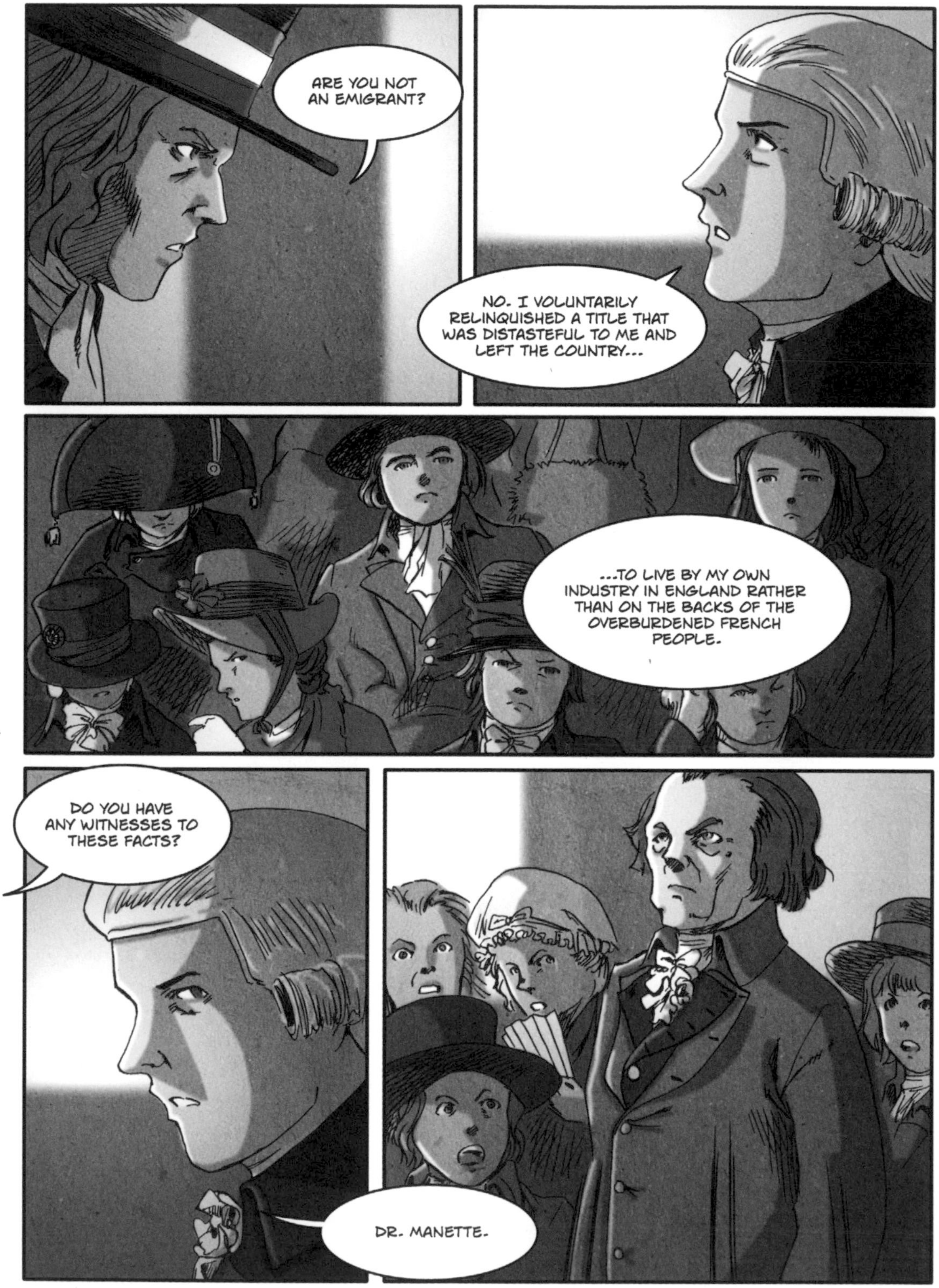
ARE YOU NOT AN EMIGRANT?
NO. I VOLUNTARILY RELINQUISHED A TITLE THAT WAS DISTASTEFUL TO ME AND LEFT THE COUNTRY...
...TO LIVE BY MY OWN INDUSTRY IN ENGLAND RATHER THAN ON THE BACKS OF THE OVERBURDENED FRENCH PEOPLE.
DO YOU HAVE ANY WITNESSES TO THESE FACTS?
DR. MANETTE.

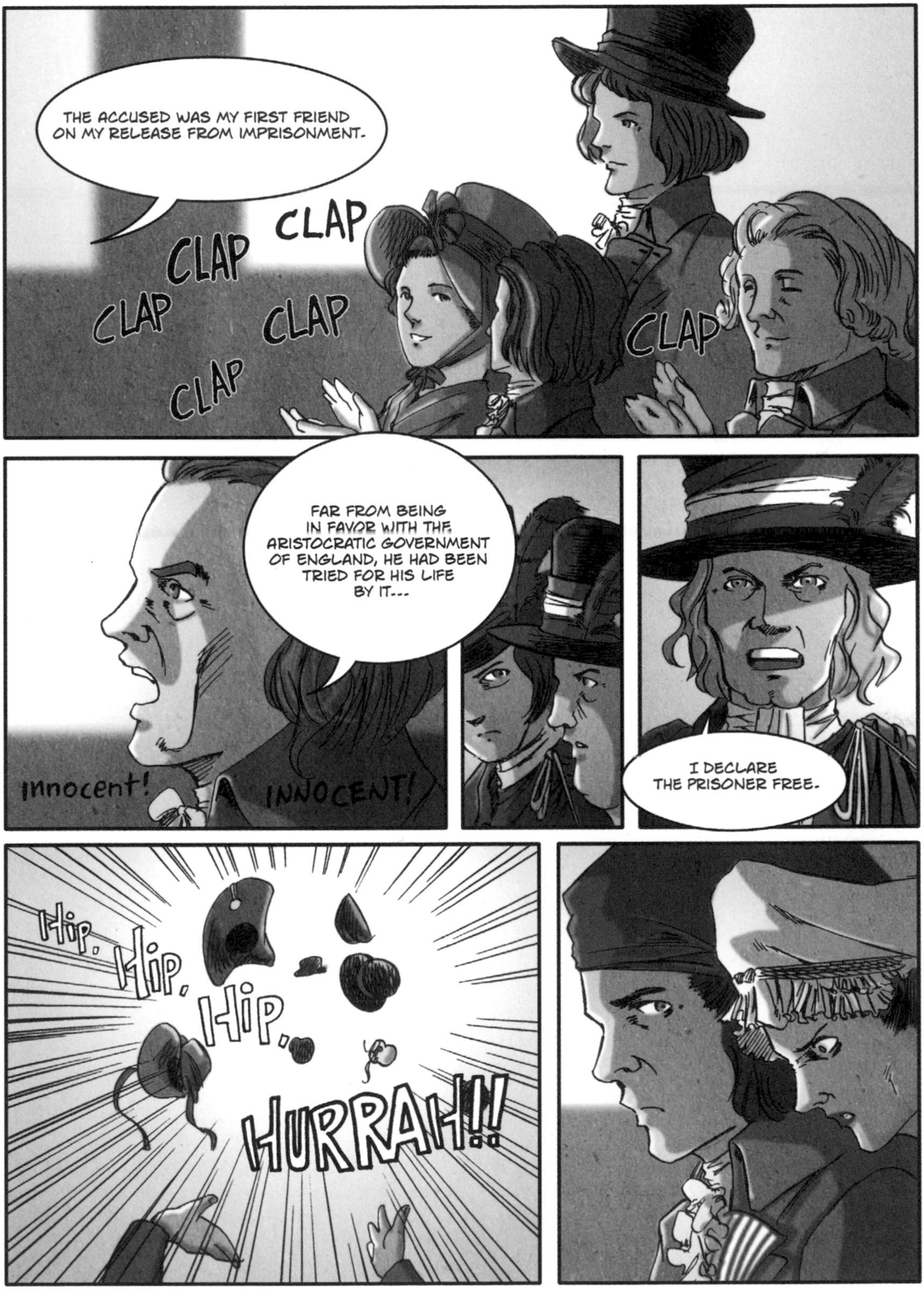
THE ACCUSED WAS MY FIRST FRIEND ON MY RELEASE FROM IMPRISONMENT.
CLAP
CLAP
CLAP
CLAP
CLAP
CLAP
FAR FROM BEING IN FAVOR WITH THE ARISTOCRATIC GOVERNMENT OF ENGLAND, HE HAD BEEN TRIED FOR HIS LIFE BY IT...
innocent!
INNOCENT!
I DECLARE THE PRISONER FREE.
Hip, Hip, Hip,
HURRAH!!

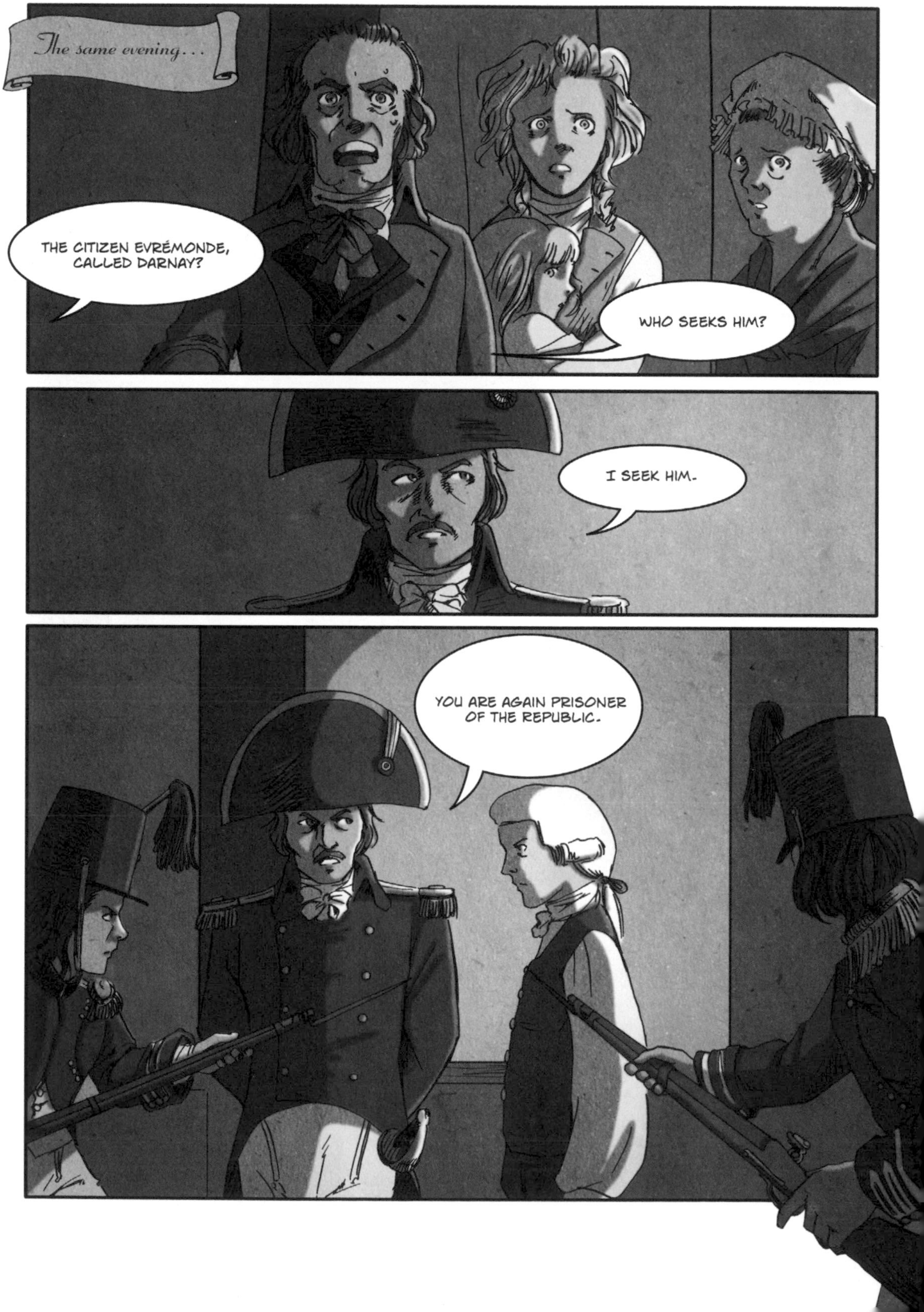
The same evening...
THE CITIZEN EVRÉMONDE, CALLED DARNAY?
WHO SEEKS HIM?
I SEEK HIM.
YOU ARE AGAIN PRISONER OF THE REPUBLIC.

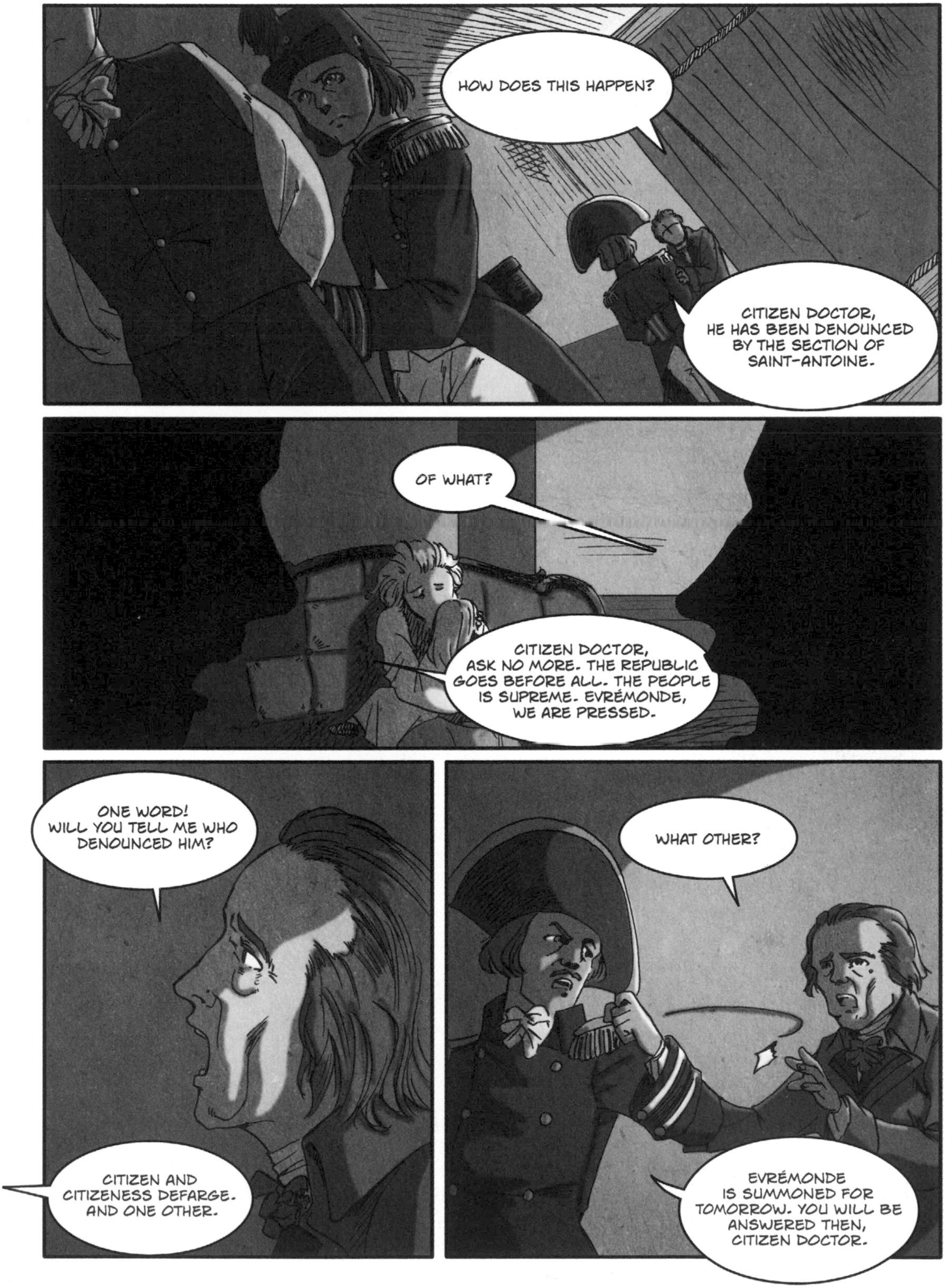
HOW DOES THIS HAPPEN?
CITIZEN DOCTOR, HE HAS BEEN DENOUNCED BY THE SECTION OF SAINT-ANTOINE.
OF WHAT?
CITIZEN DOCTOR, ASK NO MORE. THE REPUBLIC GOES BEFORE ALL. THE PEOPLE IS SUPREME. EVRÉMONDE, WE ARE PRESSED.
ONE WORD! WILL YOU TELL ME WHO DENOUNCED HIM?
CITIZEN AND CITIZENESS DEFARGE. AND ONE OTHER.
WHAT OTHER?
EVRÉMONDE IS SUMMONED FOR TOMORROW. YOU WILL BE ANSWERED THEN, CITIZEN DOCTOR.

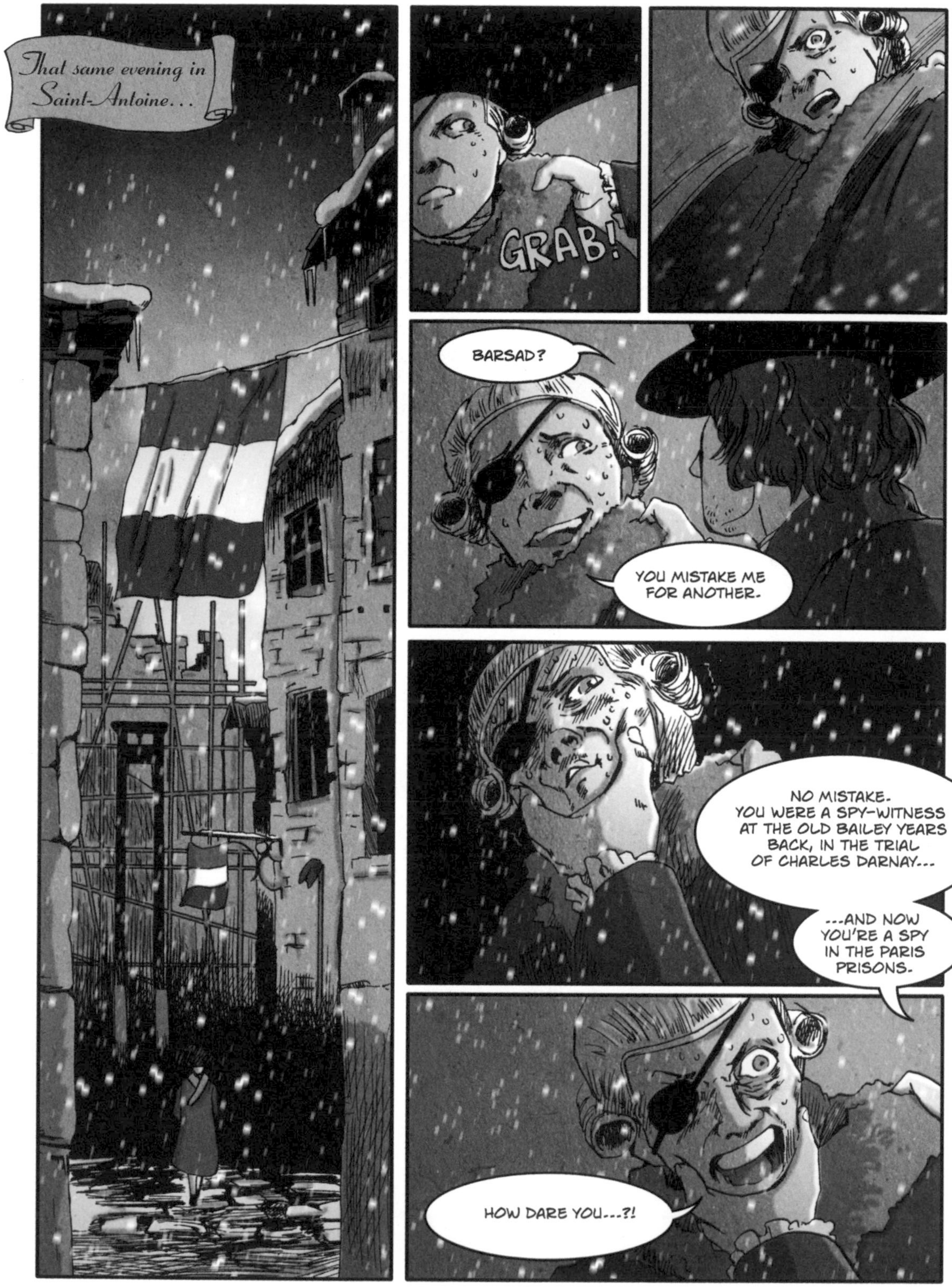
That same evening in Saint-Antoine...
GRAB!
BARSAD?
YOU MISTAKE ME FOR ANOTHER.
NO MISTAKE. YOU WERE A SPY-WITNESS AT THE OLD BAILEY YEARS BACK, IN THE TRIAL OF CHARLES DARNAY...
...AND NOW YOU'RE A SPY IN THE PARIS PRISONS.
HOW DARE YOU...?!

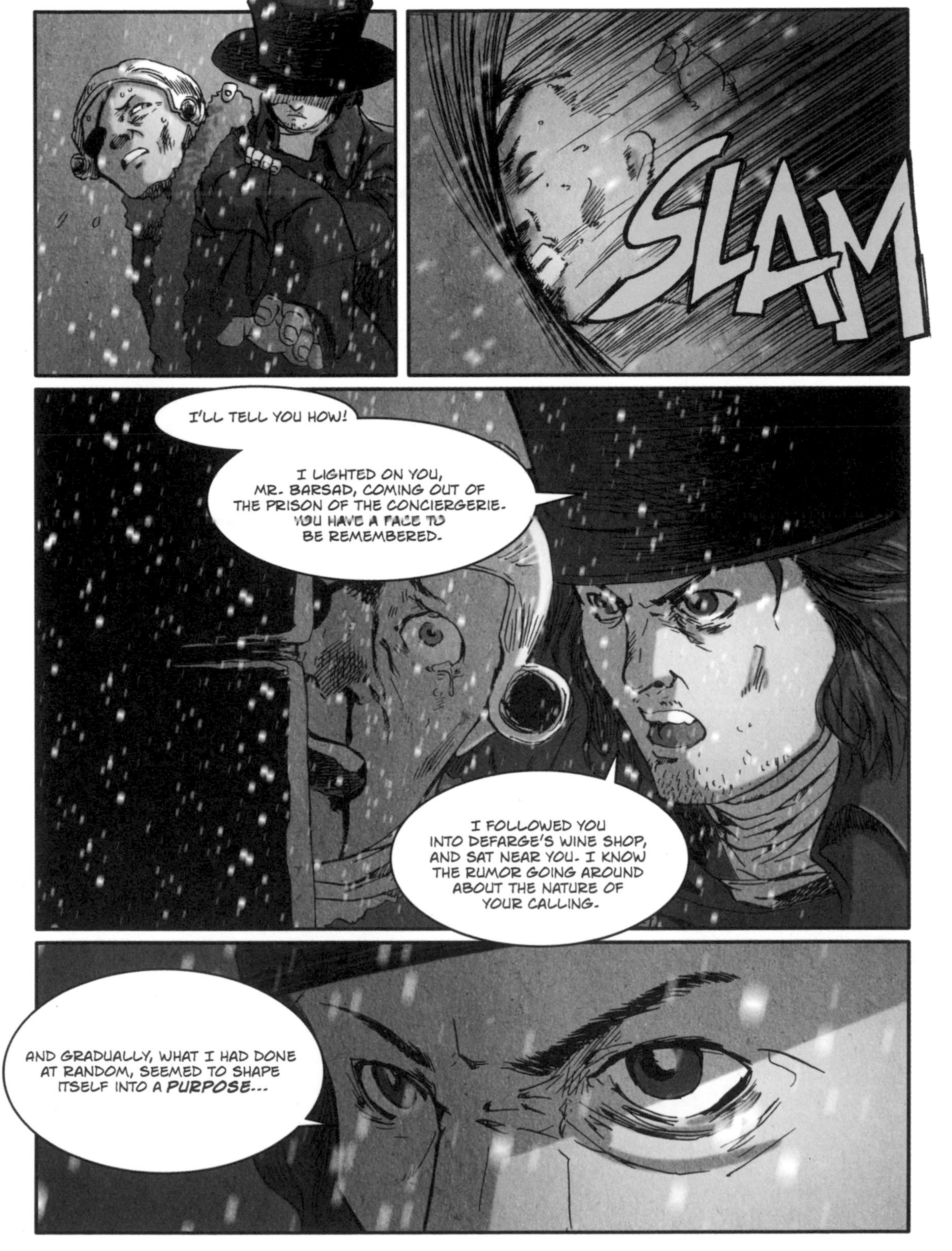
SLAM
I'LL TELL YOU HOW!
I LIGHTED ON YOU, MR. BARSAD, COMING OUT OF THE PRISON OF THE CONCIERGERIE. YOU HAVE A FACE TO BE REMEMBERED.
I FOLLOWED YOU INTO DEFARGE'S WINE SHOP, AND SAT NEAR YOU. I KNOW THE RUMOR GOING AROUND ABOUT THE NATURE OF YOUR CALLING.
AND GRADUALLY, WHAT I HAD DONE AT RANDOM, SEEMED TO SHAPE ITSELF INTO A PURPOSE...

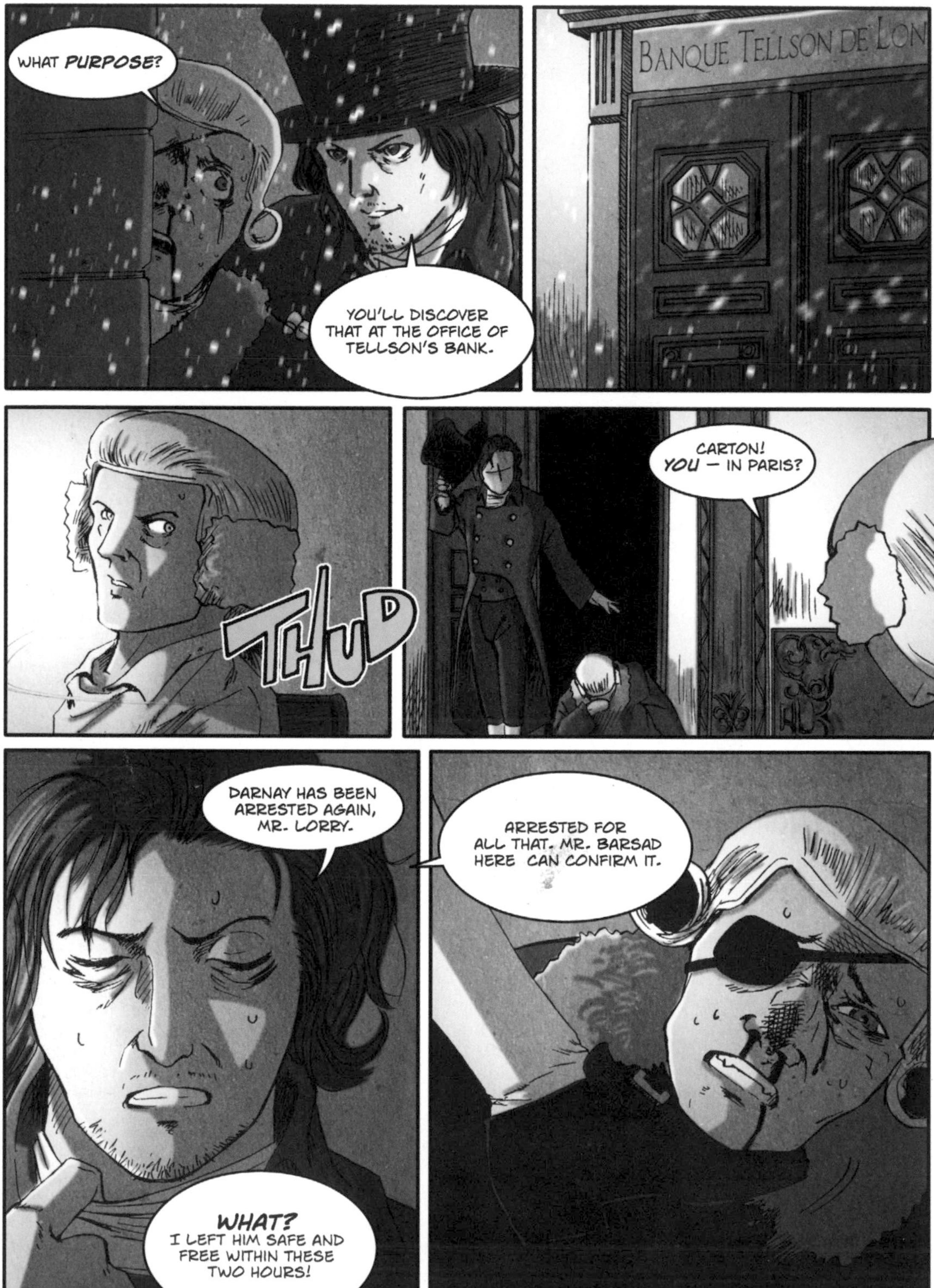
WHAT PURPOSE?
YOU'LL DISCOVER THAT AT THE OFFICE OF TELLSON'S BANK.
BANQUE TELLSON DE LON
THUD
CARTON! YOU — IN PARIS?
DARNAY HAS BEEN ARRESTED AGAIN, MR. LORRY.
WHAT? I LEFT HIM SAFE AND FREE WITHIN THESE TWO HOURS!
ARRESTED FOR ALL THAT. MR. BARSAD HERE CAN CONFIRM IT.

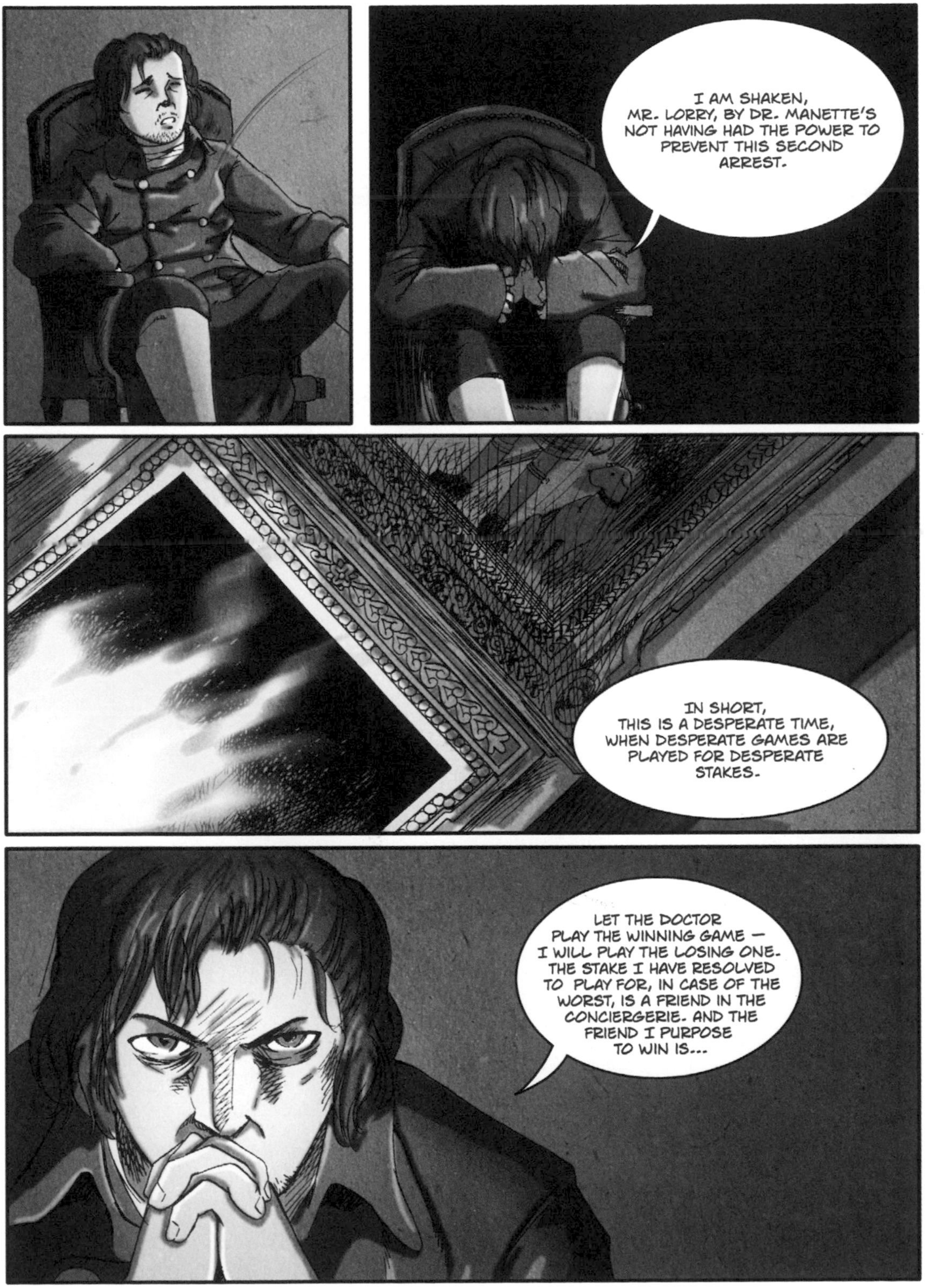
I AM SHAKEN, MR. LORRY, BY DR. MANETTE'S NOT HAVING HAD THE POWER TO PREVENT THIS SECOND ARREST.
IN SHORT, THIS IS A DESPERATE TIME, WHEN DESPERATE GAMES ARE PLAYED FOR DESPERATE STAKES.
LET THE DOCTOR PLAY THE WINNING GAME — I WILL PLAY THE LOSING ONE. THE STAKE I HAVE RESOLVED TO PLAY FOR, IN CASE OF THE WORST, IS A FRIEND IN THE CONCIERGERIE. AND THE FRIEND I PURPOSE TO WIN IS...

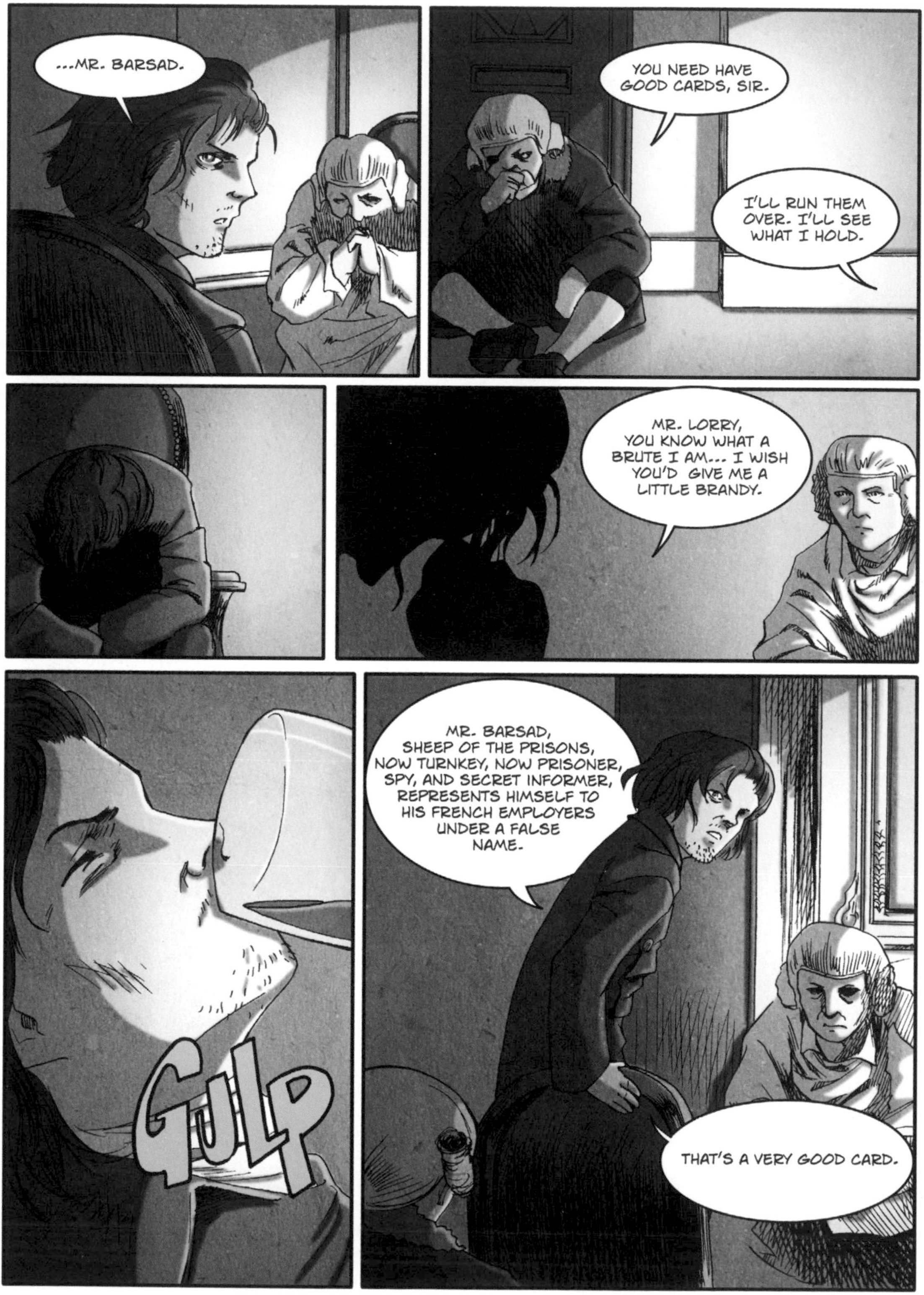
...MR. BARSAD.
YOU NEED HAVE GOOD CARDS, SIR.
I'LL RUN THEM OVER. I'LL SEE WHAT I HOLD.
MR. LORRY, YOU KNOW WHAT A BRUTE I AM... I WISH YOU'D GIVE ME A LITTLE BRANDY.
GULP
MR. BARSAD, SHEEP OF THE PRISONS, NOW TURNKEY, NOW PRISONER, SPY, AND SECRET INFORMER, REPRESENTS HIMSELF TO HIS FRENCH EMPLOYERS UNDER A FALSE NAME.
THAT'S A VERY GOOD CARD.

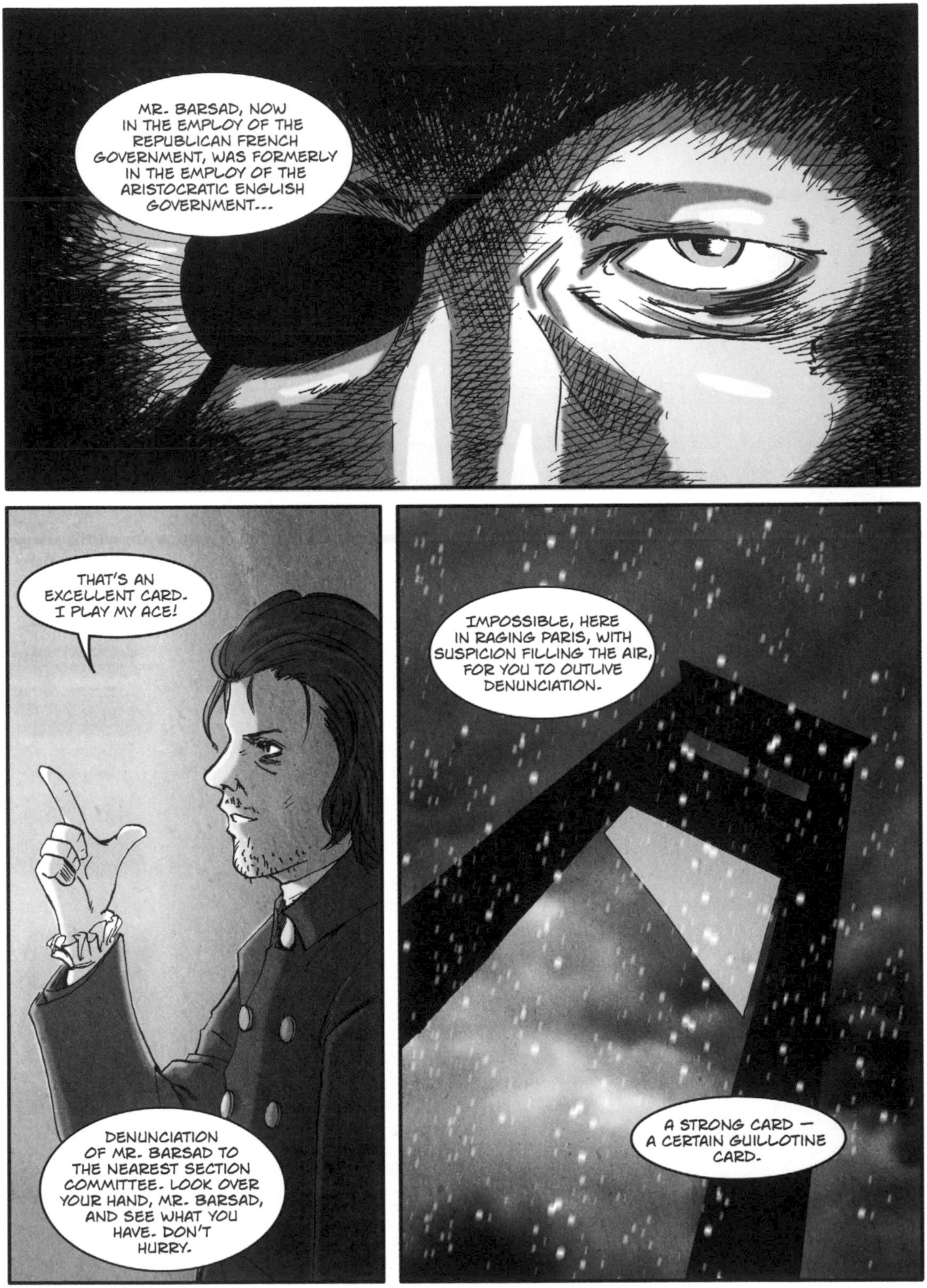
MR. BARSAD, NOW IN THE EMPLOY OF THE REPUBLICAN FRENCH GOVERNMENT, WAS FORMERLY IN THE EMPLOY OF THE ARISTOCRATIC ENGLISH GOVERNMENT...
THAT'S AN EXCELLENT CARD. I PLAY MY ACE!
DENUNCIATION OF MR. BARSAD TO THE NEAREST SECTION COMMITTEE. LOOK OVER YOUR HAND, MR. BARSAD, AND SEE WHAT YOU HAVE. DON'T HURRY.
IMPOSSIBLE, HERE IN RAGING PARIS, WITH SUSPICION FILLING THE AIR, FOR YOU TO OUTLIVE DENUNCIATION.
A STRONG CARD — A CERTAIN GUILLOTINE CARD.

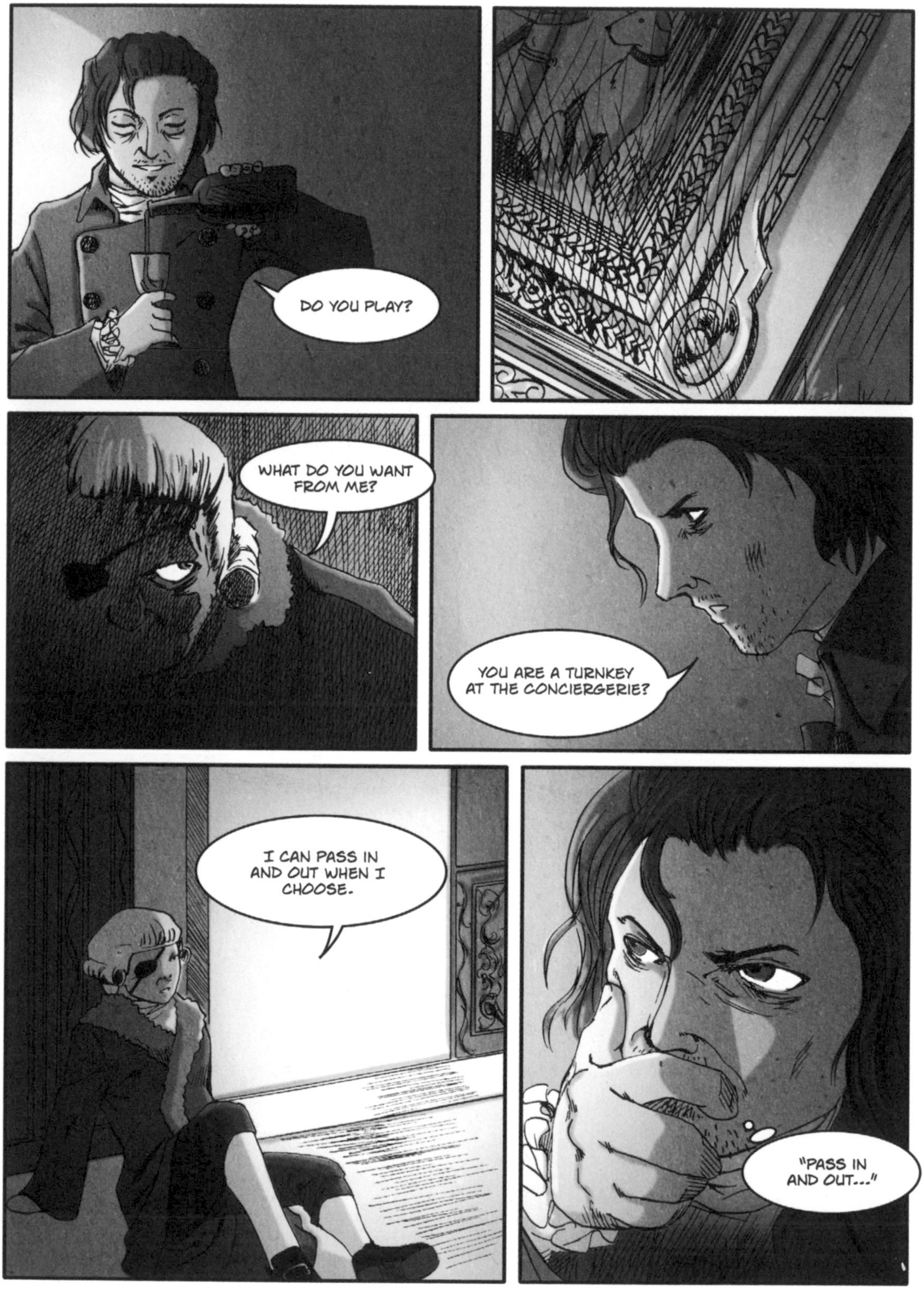
DO YOU PLAY?
WHAT DO YOU WANT FROM ME?
YOU ARE A TURNKEY AT THE CONCIERGERIE?
I CAN PASS IN AND OUT WHEN I CHOOSE.
"PASS IN AND OUT..."

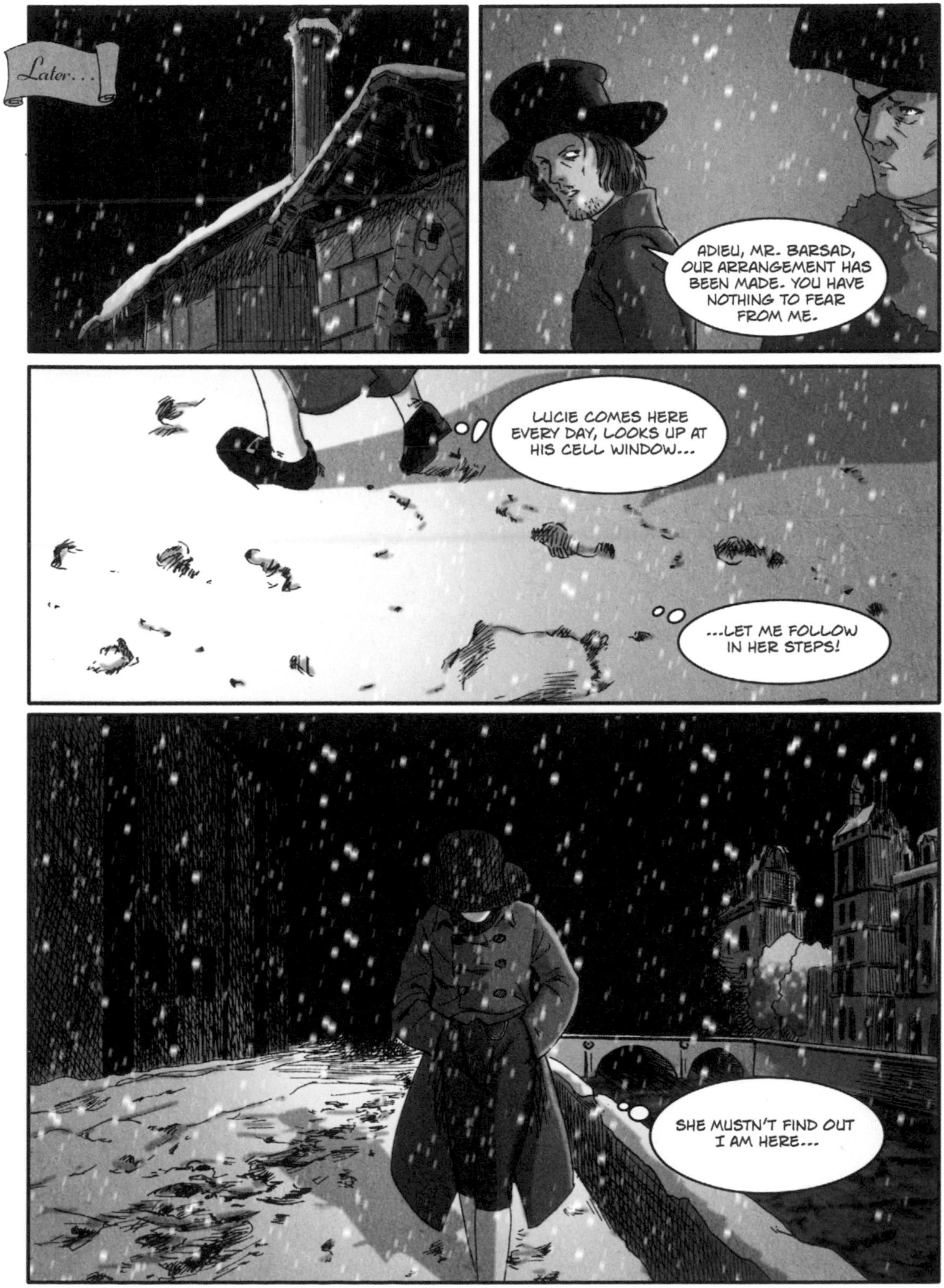
Later...
ADIEU, MR. BARSAD, OUR ARRANGEMENT HAS BEEN MADE. YOU HAVE NOTHING TO FEAR FROM ME.
LUCIE COMES HERE EVERY DAY, LOOKS UP AT HIS CELL WINDOW...
...LET ME FOLLOW IN HER STEPS!
SHE MUSTN'T FIND OUT I AM HERE...

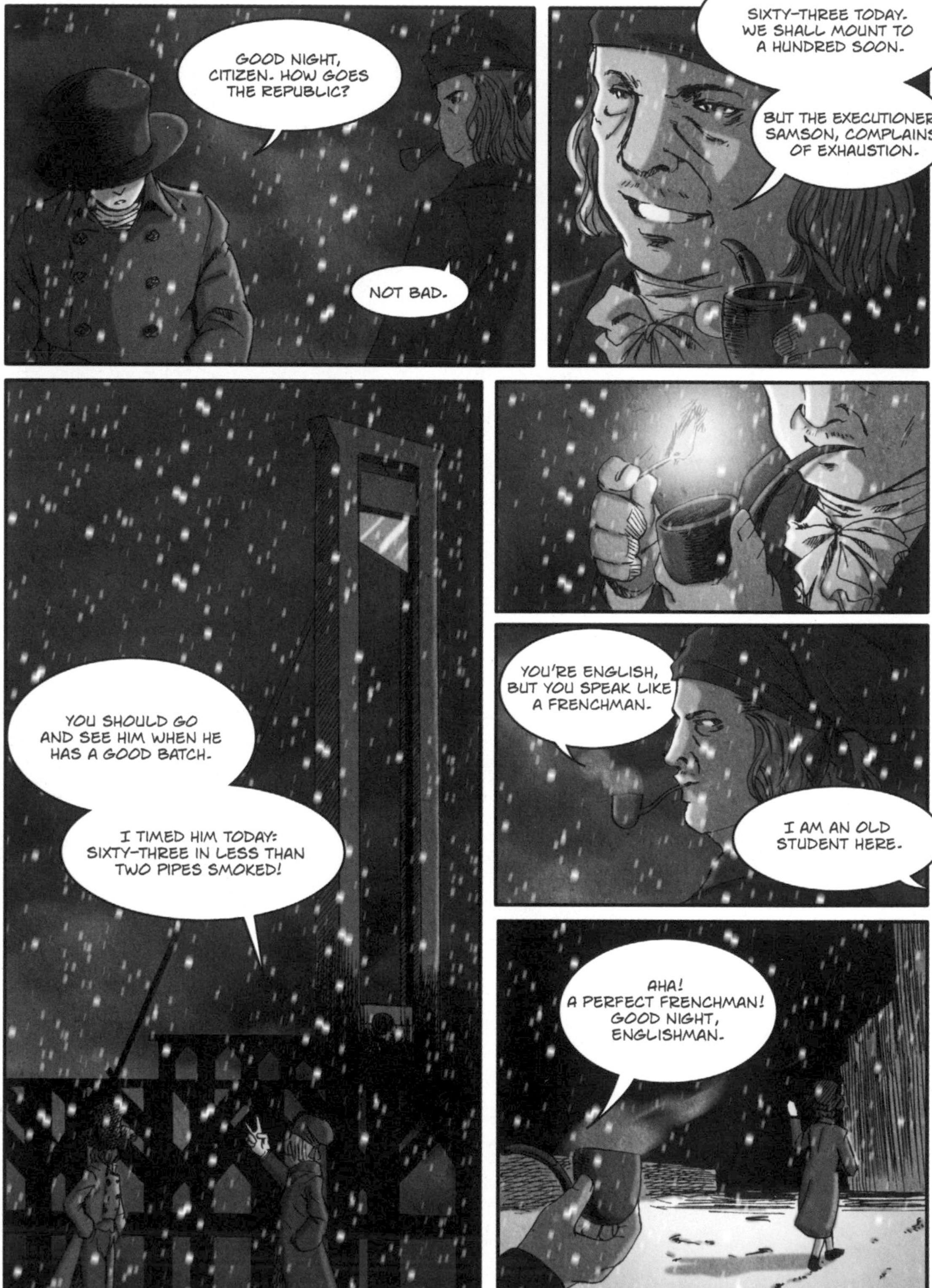
GOOD NIGHT, CITIZEN. HOW GOES THE REPUBLIC?
NOT BAD.
SIXTY-THREE TODAY. WE SHALL MOUNT TO A HUNDRED SOON.
BUT THE EXECUTIONER, SAMSON, COMPLAINS OF EXHAUSTION.
YOU SHOULD GO AND SEE HIM WHEN HE HAS A GOOD BATCH.
I TIMED HIM TODAY: SIXTY-THREE IN LESS THAN TWO PIPES SMOKED!
YOU'RE ENGLISH, BUT YOU SPEAK LIKE A FRENCHMAN.
I AM AN OLD STUDENT HERE.
AHA! A PERFECT FRENCHMAN! GOOD NIGHT, ENGLISHMAN.

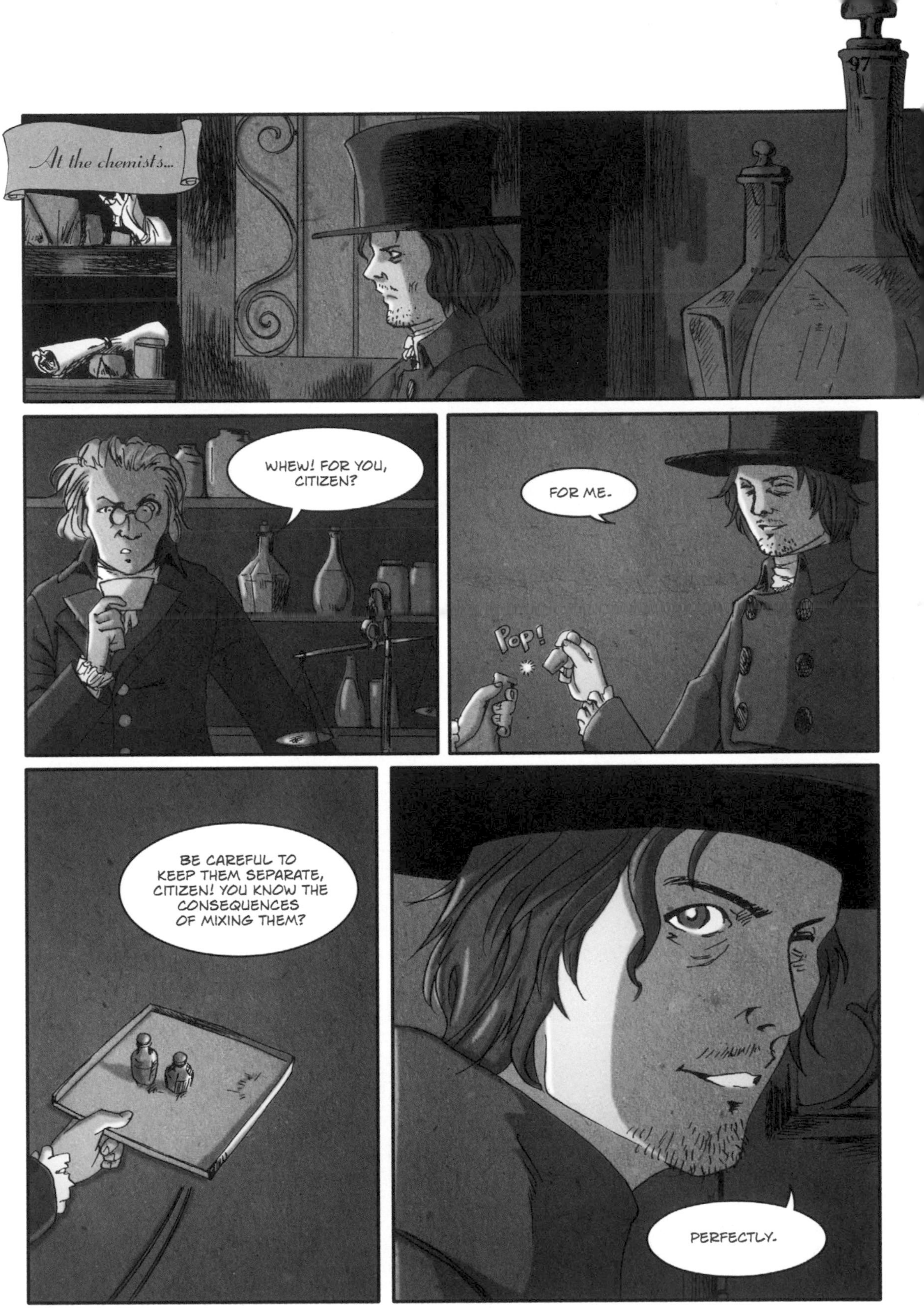
At the chemist's...
WHEW! FOR YOU, CITIZEN?
FOR ME.
POP!
BE CAREFUL TO KEEP THEM SEPARATE, CITIZEN! YOU KNOW THE CONSEQUENCES OF MIXING THEM?
PERFECTLY.

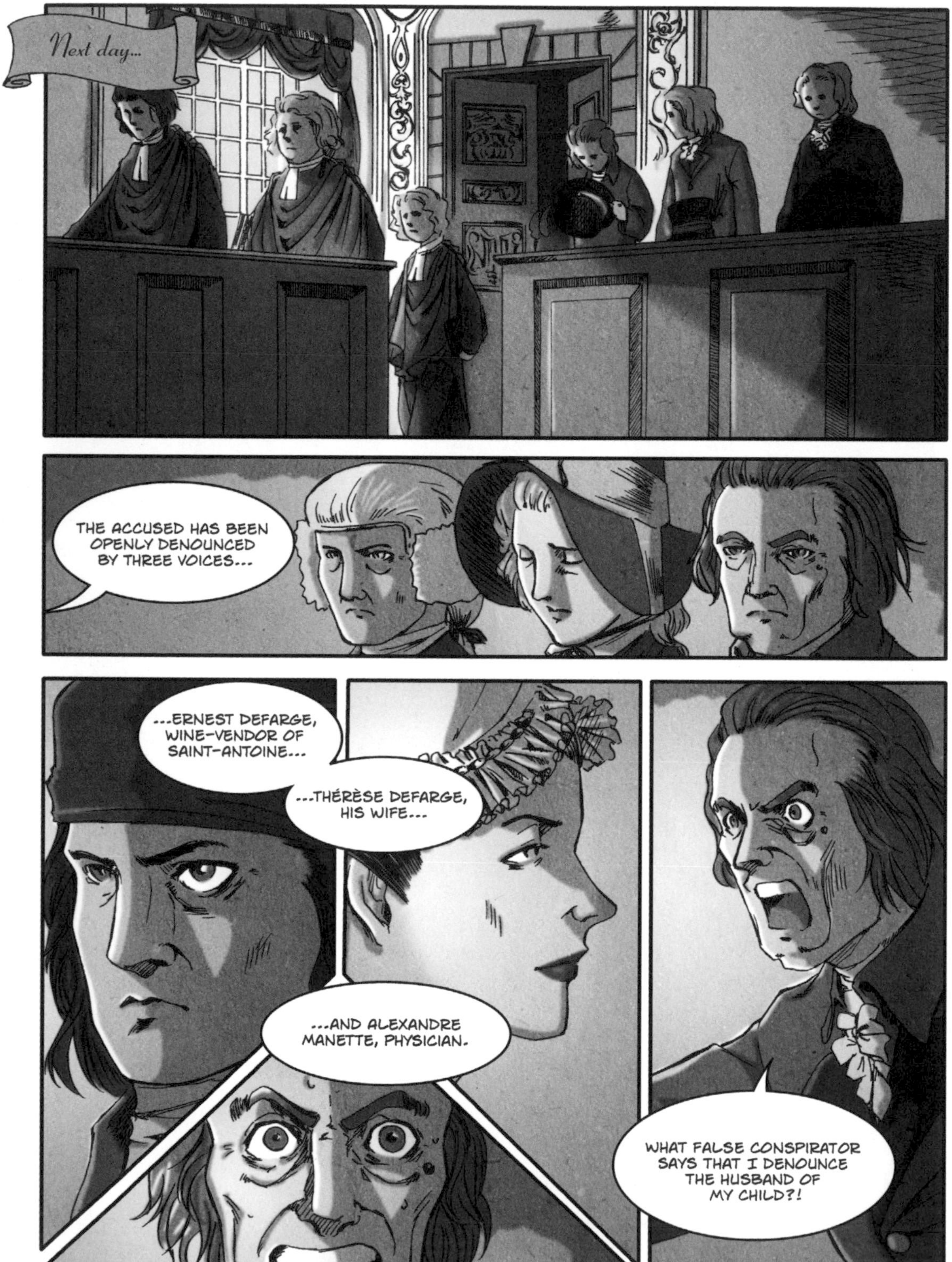
Next day...
THE ACCUSED HAS BEEN OPENLY DENOUNCED BY THREE VOICES...
...ERNEST DEFARGE, WINE-VENDOR OF SAINT-ANTOINE...
...THÉRÈSE DEFARGE, HIS WIFE...
...AND ALEXANDRE MANETTE, PHYSICIAN.
WHAT FALSE CONSPIRATOR SAYS THAT I DENOUNCE THE HUSBAND OF MY CHILD?!

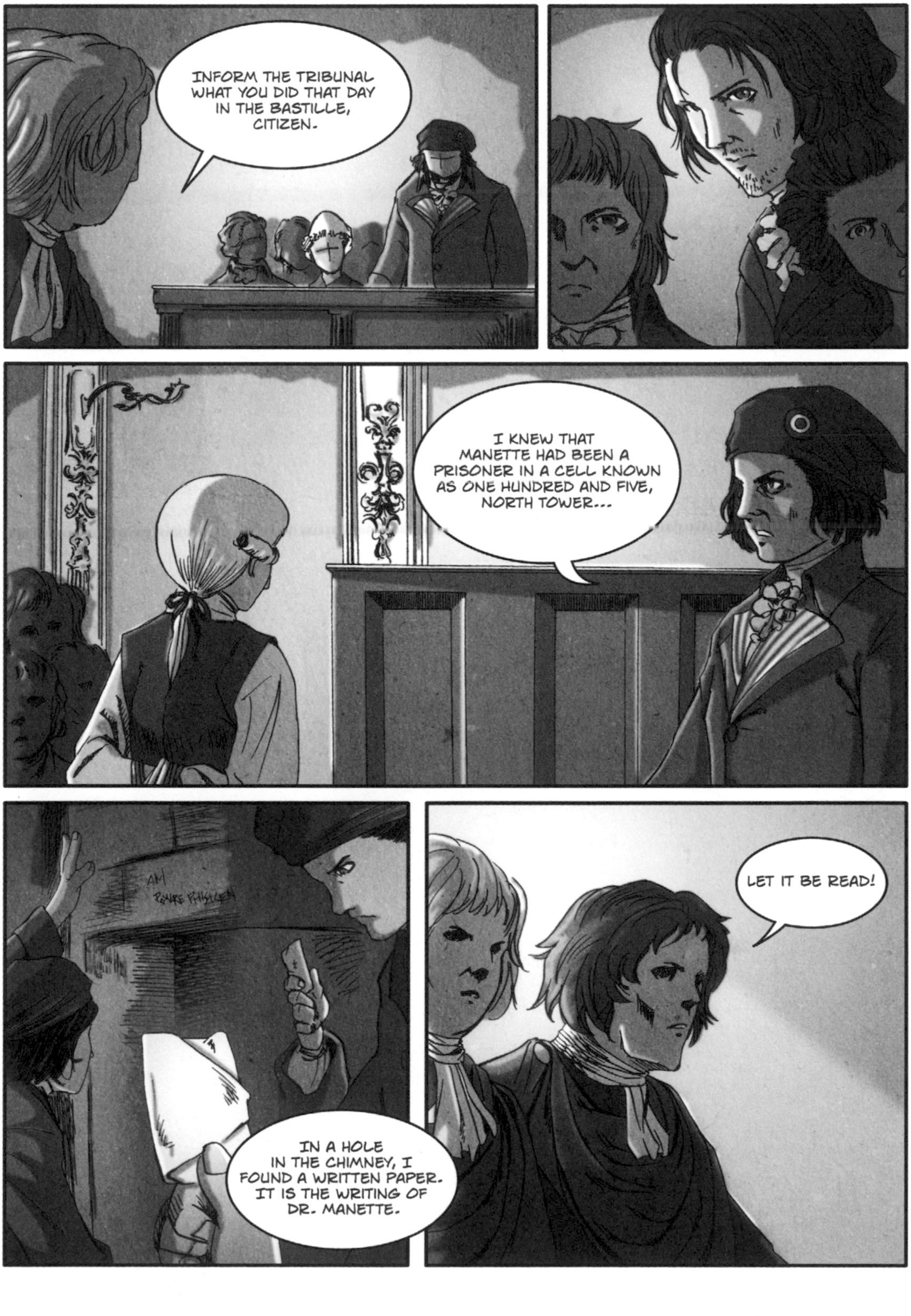
INFORM THE TRIBUNAL WHAT YOU DID THAT DAY IN THE BASTILLE, CITIZEN.
I KNEW THAT MANETTE HAD BEEN A PRISONER IN A CELL KNOWN AS ONE HUNDRED AND FIVE, NORTH TOWER...
IN A HOLE IN THE CHIMNEY, I FOUND A WRITTEN PAPER. IT IS THE WRITING OF DR. MANETTE.
LET IT BE READ!

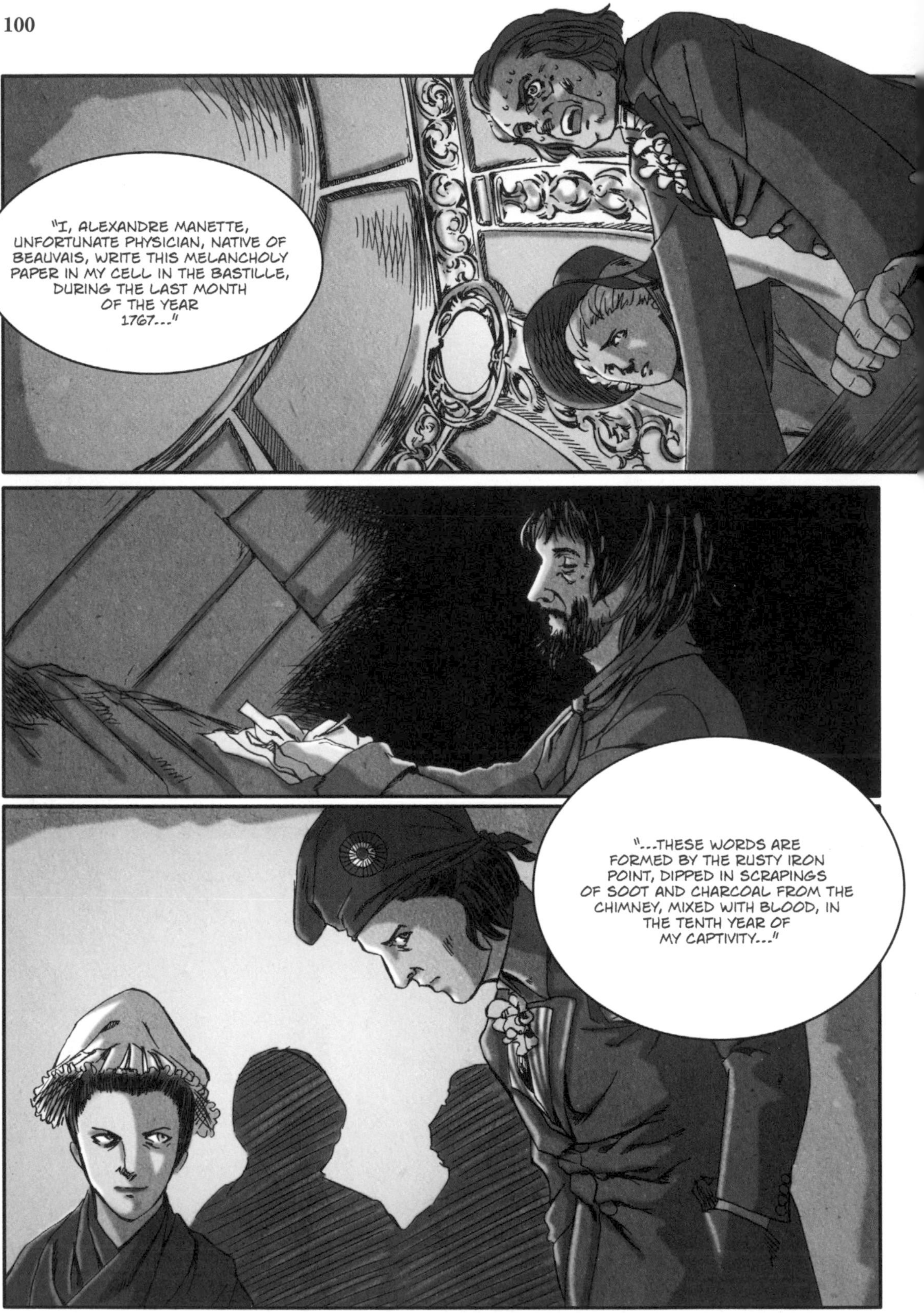
"I, ALEXANDRE MANETTE, UNFORTUNATE PHYSICIAN, NATIVE OF BEAUVAIS, WRITE THIS MELANCHOLY PAPER IN MY CELL IN THE BASTILLE, DURING THE LAST MONTH OF THE YEAR 1767..."
"...THESE WORDS ARE FORMED BY THE RUSTY IRON POINT, DIPPED IN SCRAPINGS OF SOOT AND CHARCOAL FROM THE CHIMNEY, MIXED WITH BLOOD, IN THE TENTH YEAR OF MY CAPTIVITY..."

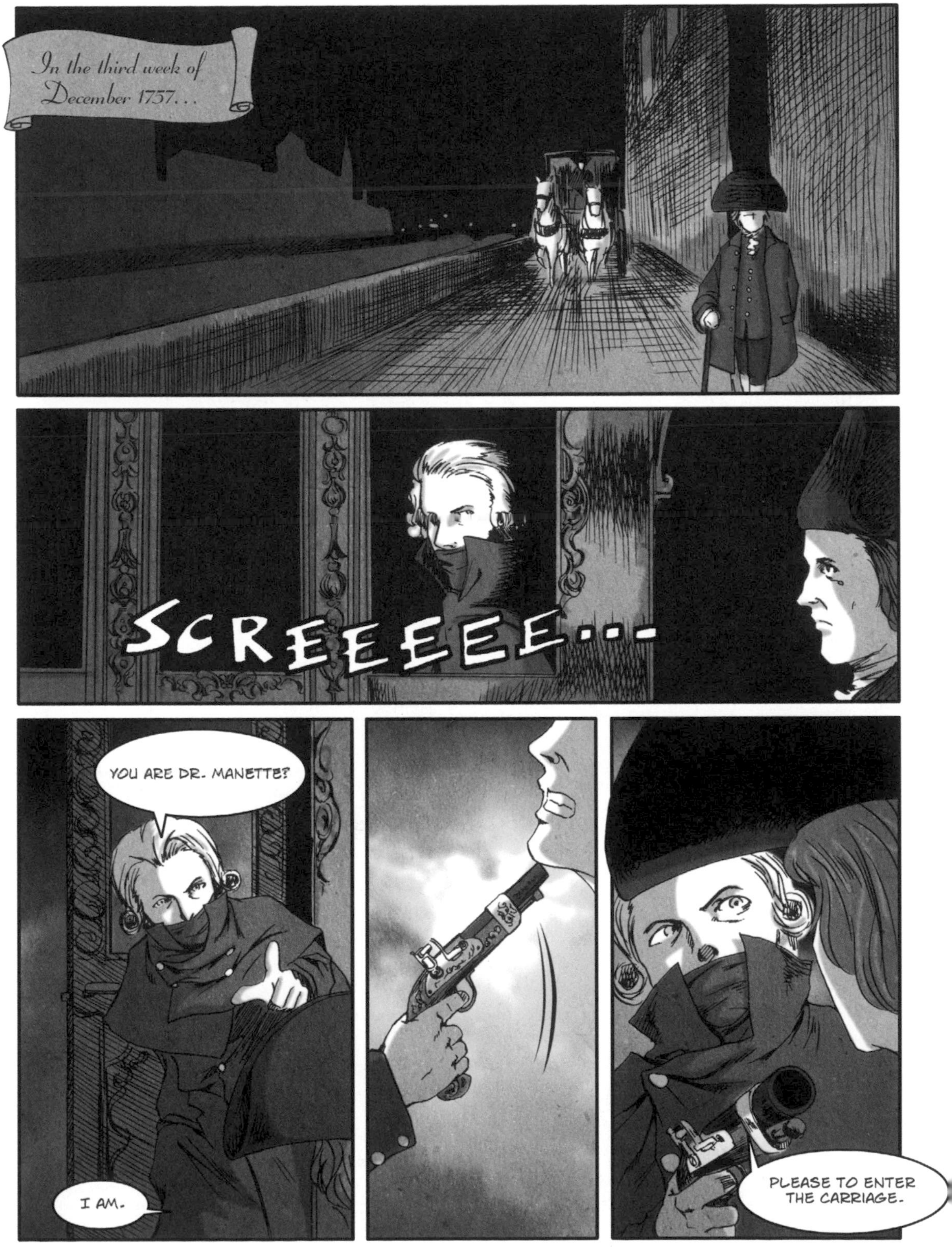
In the third week of December 1757. . .
SCREEEEE...
YOU ARE DR. MANETTE?
I AM.
PLEASE TO ENTER THE CARRIAGE.

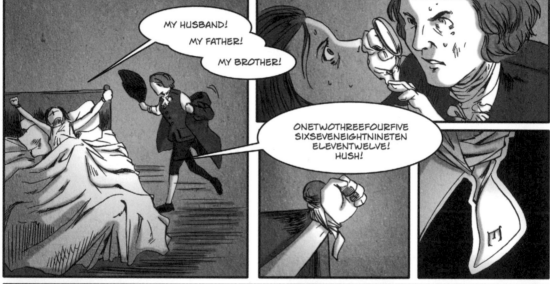

MY HUSBAND!

MY FATHER!

MY BROTHER!

ONETWOTHREEFOURFIVE SIXSEVENEIGHTNINETEN ELEVENTWELVE! HUSH!

SHE HAS SOME RECENT ASSOCIATION WITH THE NUMBER 12?

WITH TWELVE O'CLOCK.

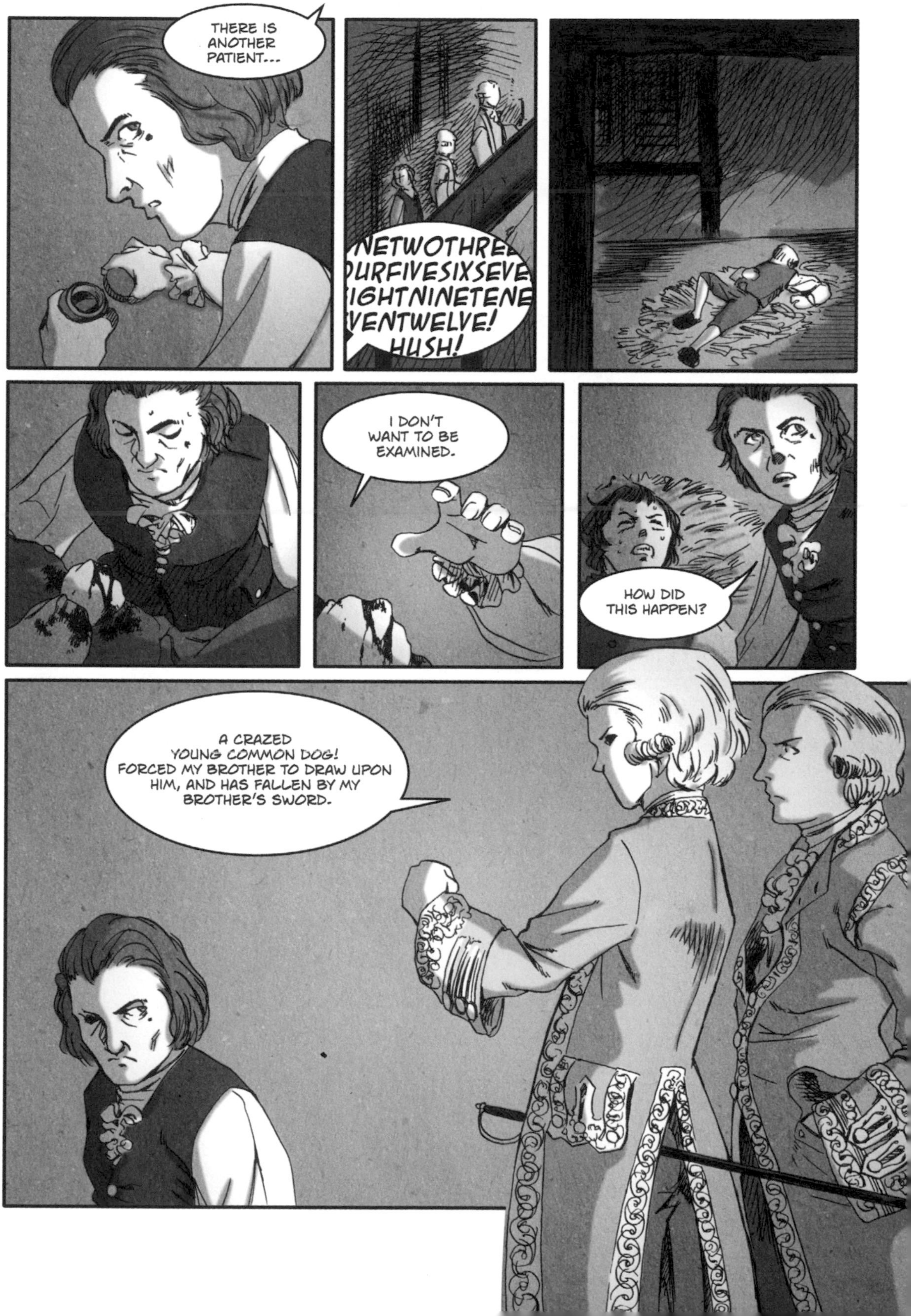
THERE IS ANOTHER PATIENT...
NETWOTHREE OURFIVESIXSEVE EIGHTNINETENE EVENTWELVE! HUSH!
I DON'T WANT TO BE EXAMINED.
HOW DID THIS HAPPEN?
A CRAZED YOUNG COMMON DOG! FORCED MY BROTHER TO DRAW UPON HIM, AND HAS FALLEN BY MY BROTHER'S SWORD.

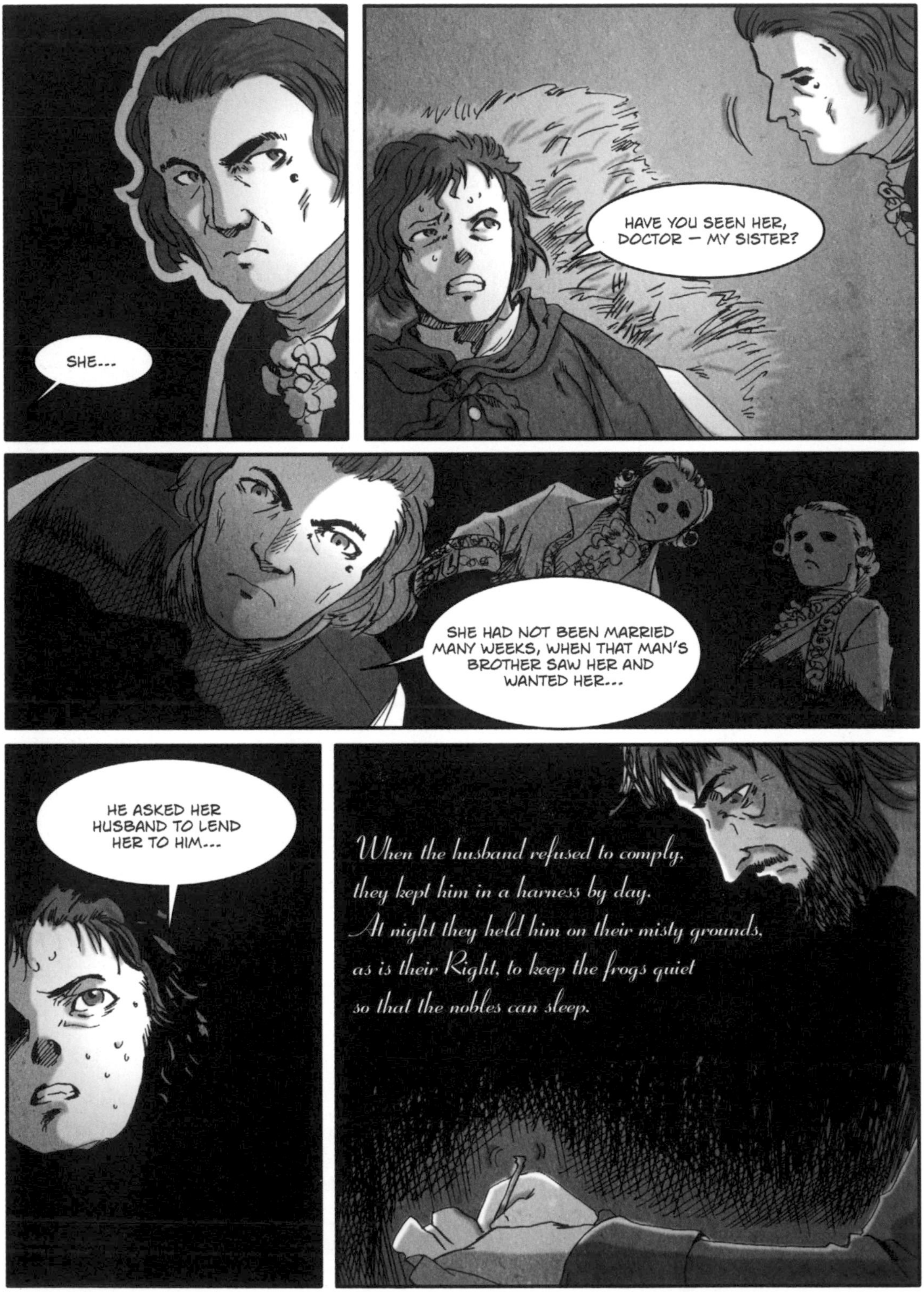
SHE...
HAVE YOU SEEN HER, DOCTOR — MY SISTER?
SHE HAD NOT BEEN MARRIED MANY WEEKS, WHEN THAT MAN'S BROTHER SAW HER AND WANTED HER...
HE ASKED HER HUSBAND TO LEND HER TO HIM...
When the husband refused to comply, they kept him in a harness by day. At night they held him on their misty grounds, as is their Right, to keep the frogs quiet so that the nobles can sleep.

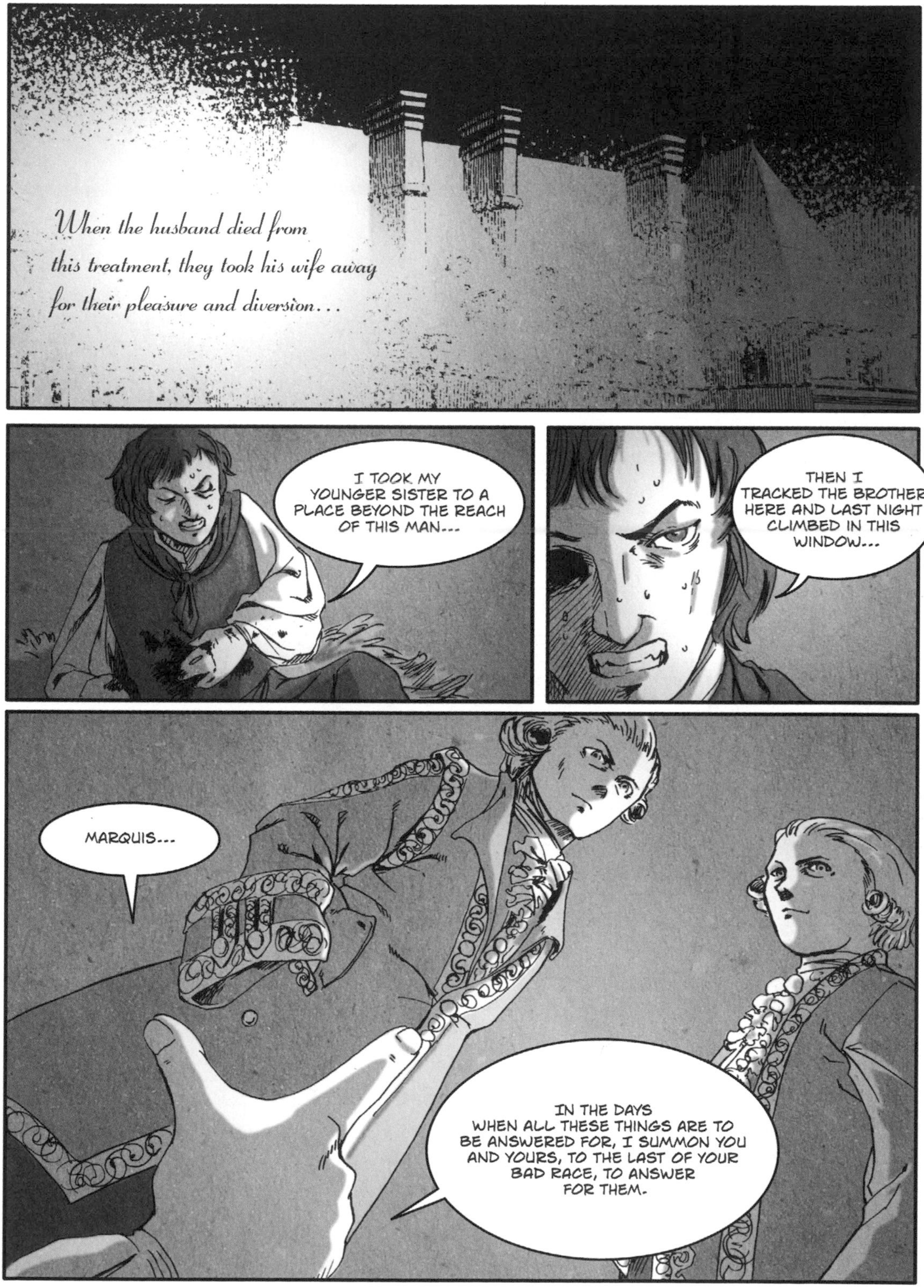
When the husband died from this treatment, they took his wife away for their pleasure and diversion...
I TOOK MY YOUNGER SISTER TO A PLACE BEYOND THE REACH OF THIS MAN...
THEN I TRACKED THE BROTHER HERE AND LAST NIGHT CLIMBED IN THIS WINDOW...
MARQUIS...
IN THE DAYS WHEN ALL THESE THINGS ARE TO BE ANSWERED FOR, I SUMMON YOU AND YOURS, TO THE LAST OF YOUR BAD RACE, TO ANSWER FOR THEM.

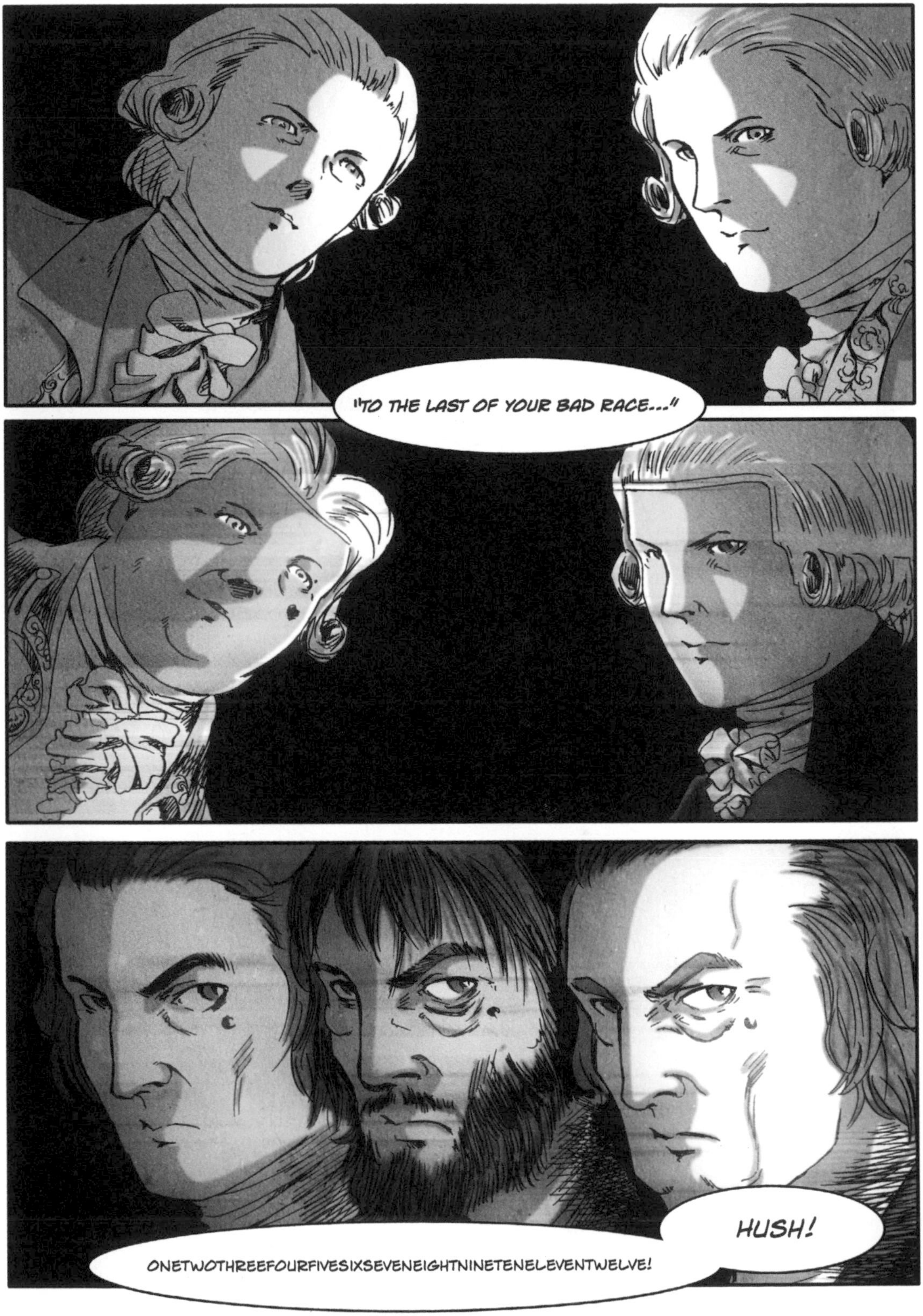
"TO THE LAST OF YOUR BAD RACE..."
HUSH!
ONETWOTHREEFOURFIVESIXSEVENEIGHTNINETENELEVENTWELVE!

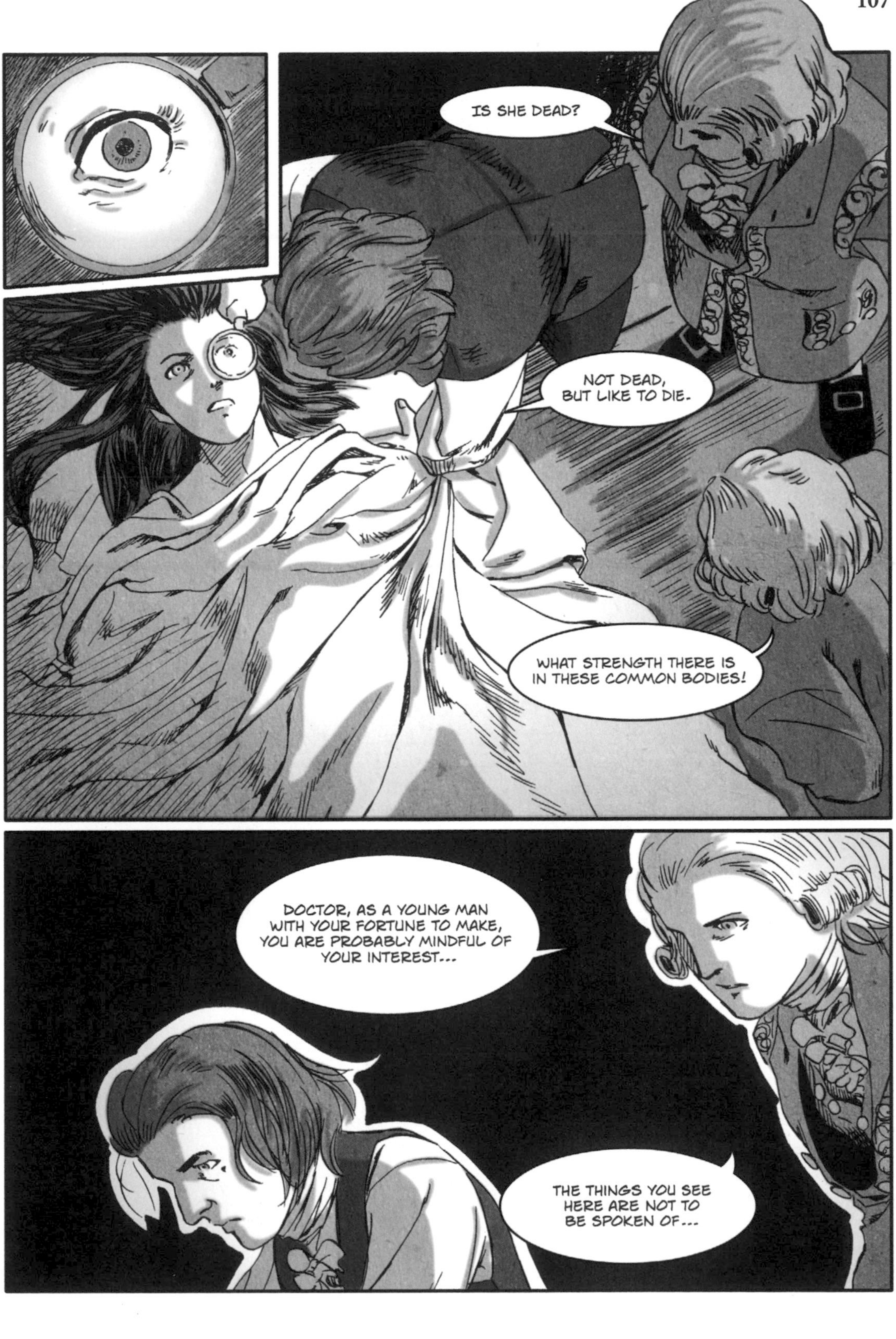
IS SHE DEAD?
NOT DEAD, BUT LIKE TO DIE.
WHAT STRENGTH THERE IS IN THESE COMMON BODIES!
DOCTOR, AS A YOUNG MAN WITH YOUR FORTUNE TO MAKE, YOU ARE PROBABLY MINDFUL OF YOUR INTEREST...
THE THINGS YOU SEE HERE ARE NOT TO BE SPOKEN OF...

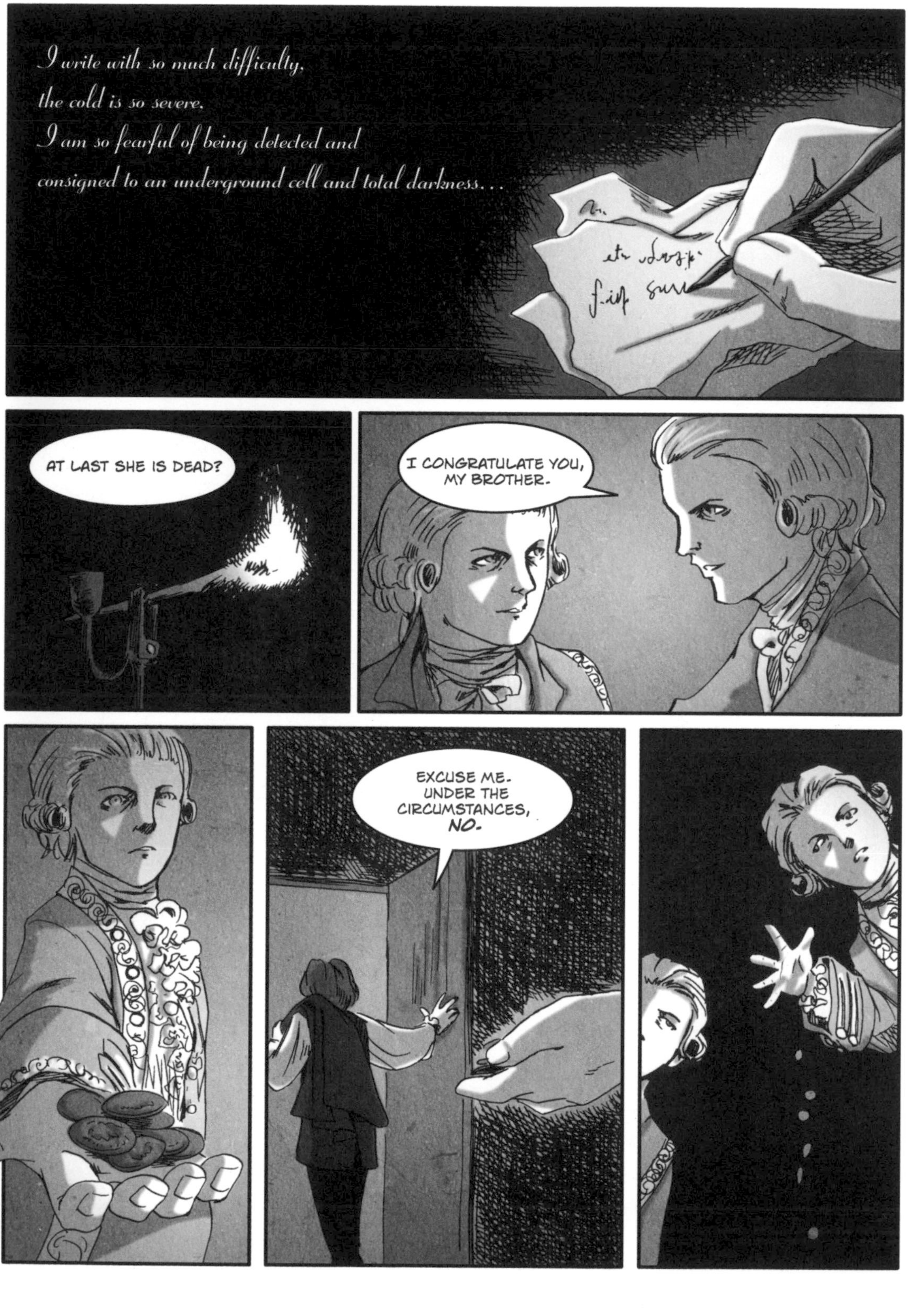
I write with so much difficulty,
the cold is so severe.
I am so fearful of being detected and
consigned to an underground cell and total darkness...
AT LAST SHE IS DEAD?
I CONGRATULATE YOU, MY BROTHER.
EXCUSE ME. UNDER THE CIRCUMSTANCES, NO.

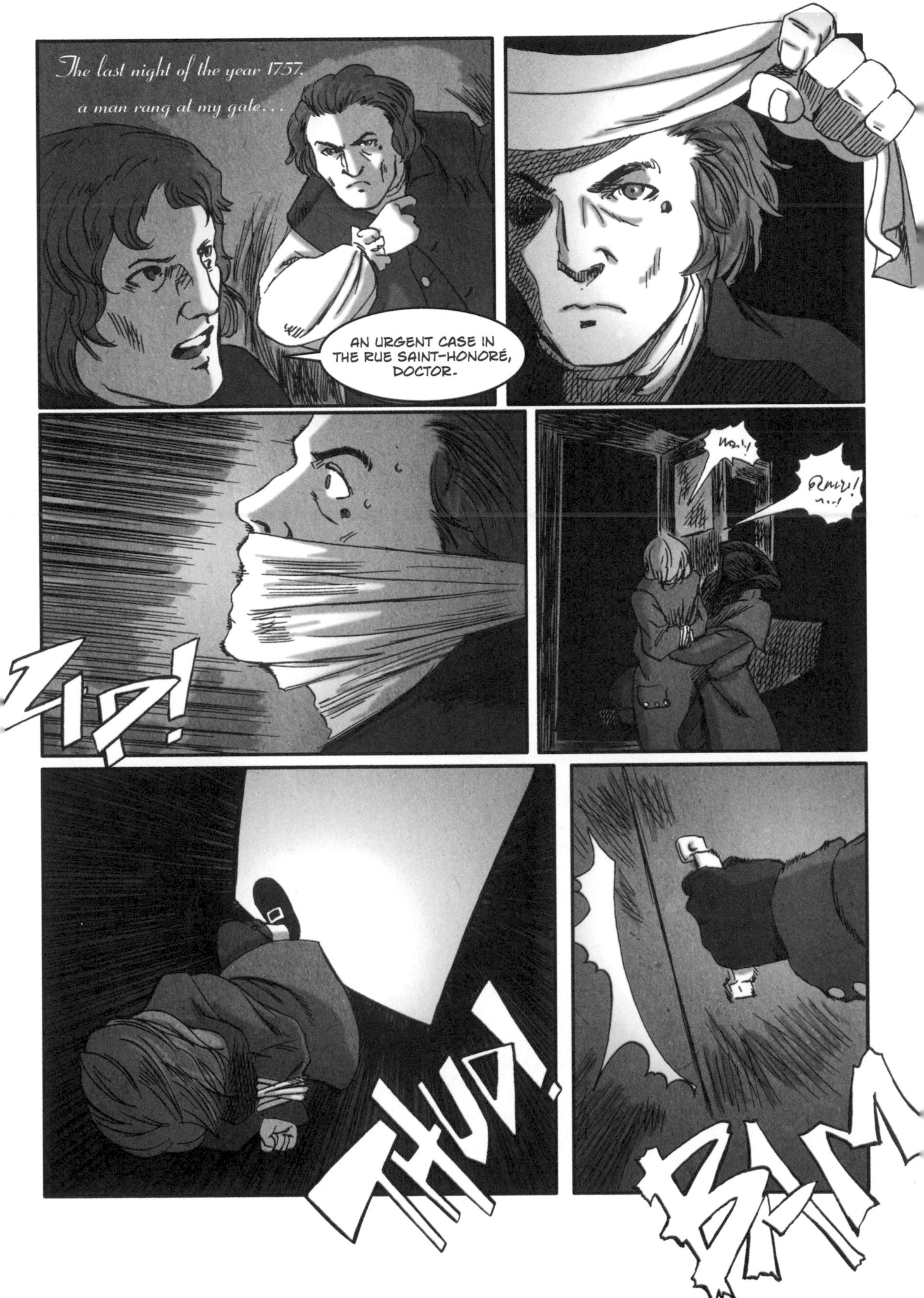
The last night of the year 1757, a man rang at my gate...
AN URGENT CASE IN THE RUE SAINT-HONORÉ, DOCTOR.
ZIP!
THUD!
BAM

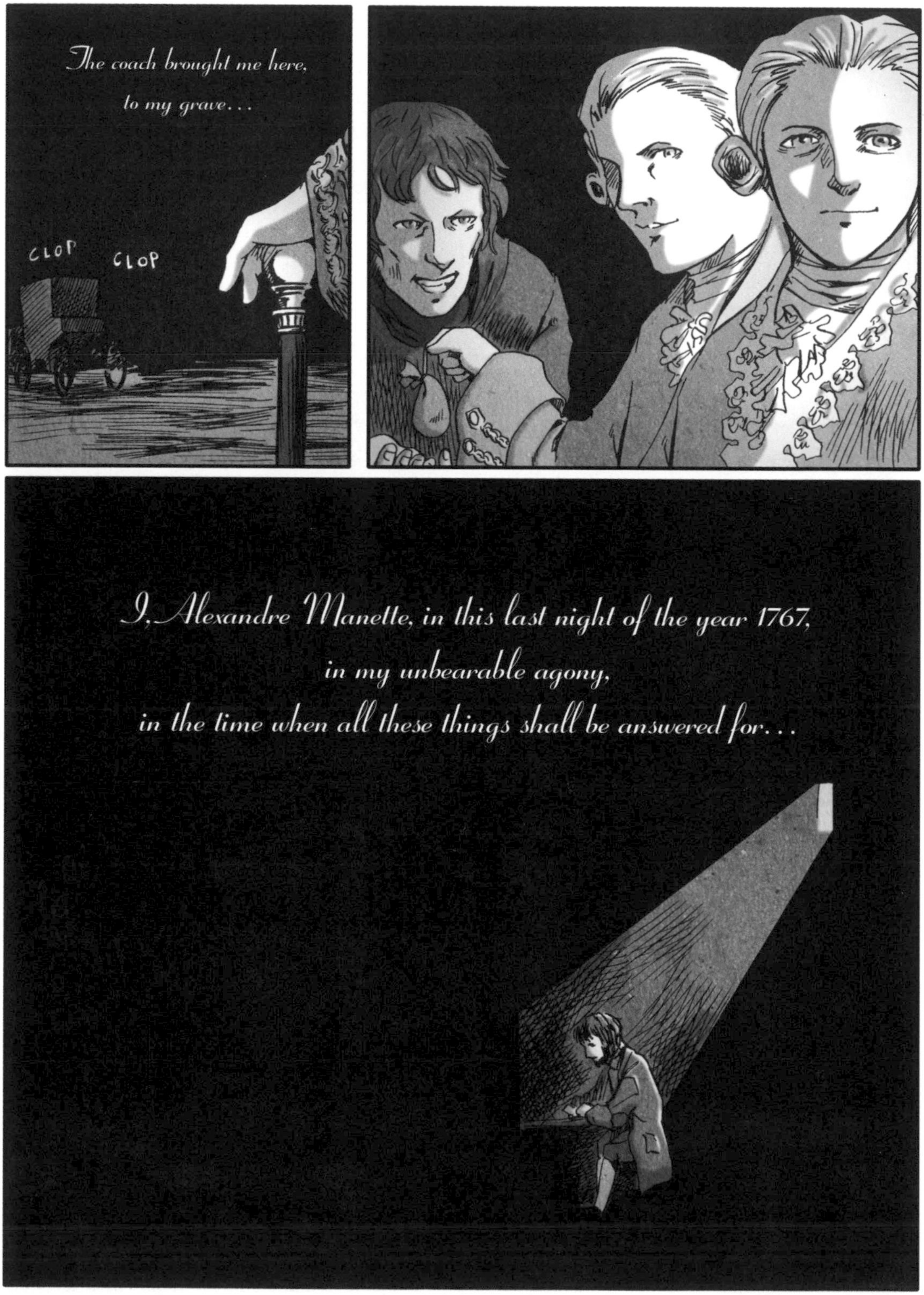
The coach brought me here,
to my grave...
CLOP
CLOP
I, Alexandre Manette, in this last night of the year 1767,
in my unbearable agony,
in the time when all these things shall be answered for...

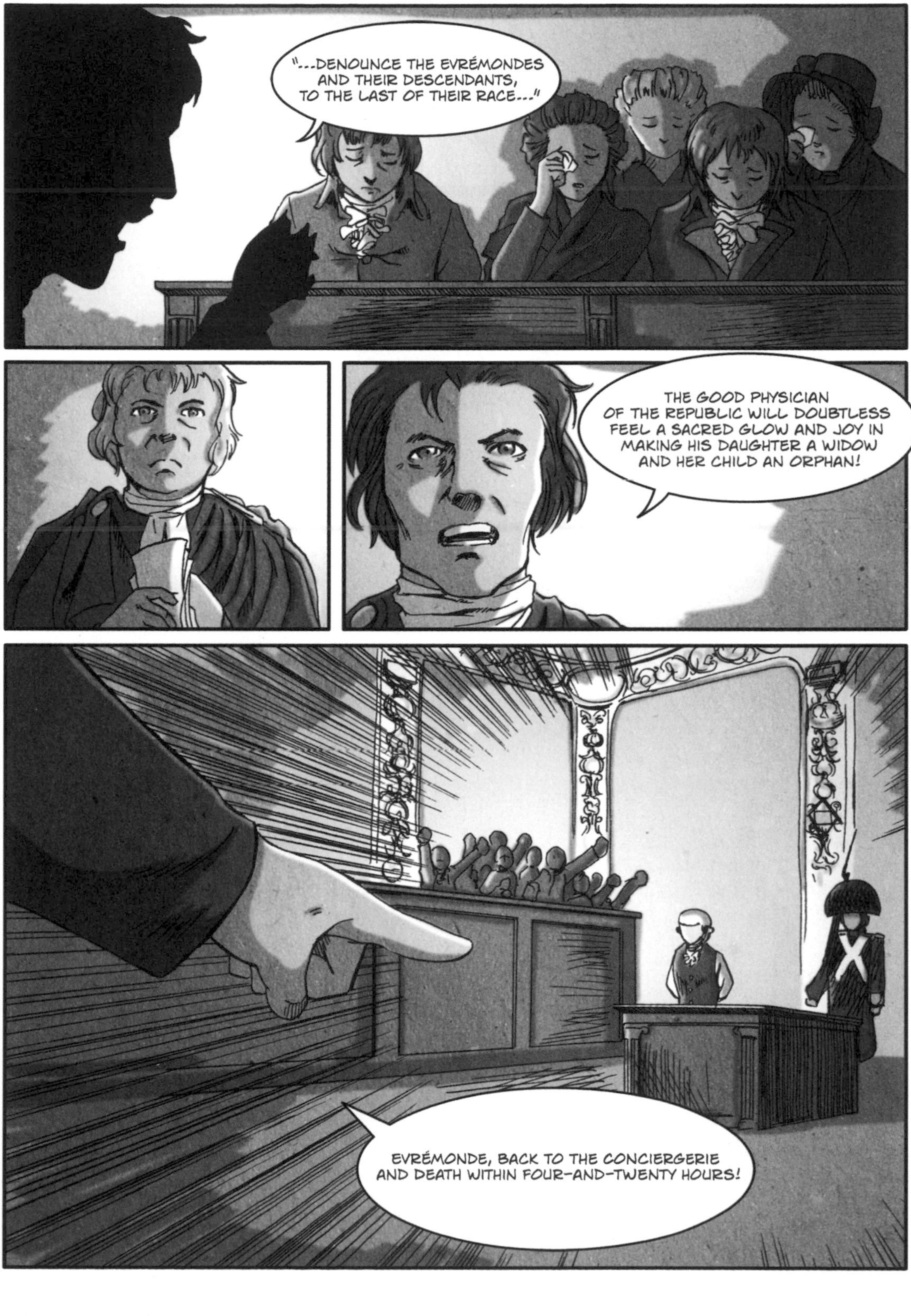
"...DENOUNCE THE EVRÉMONDES AND THEIR DESCENDANTS, TO THE LAST OF THEIR RACE..."
THE GOOD PHYSICIAN OF THE REPUBLIC WILL DOUBTLESS FEEL A SACRED GLOW AND JOY IN MAKING HIS DAUGHTER A WIDOW AND HER CHILD AN ORPHAN!
EVRÉMONDE, BACK TO THE CONCIERGERIE AND DEATH WITHIN FOUR-AND-TWENTY HOURS!

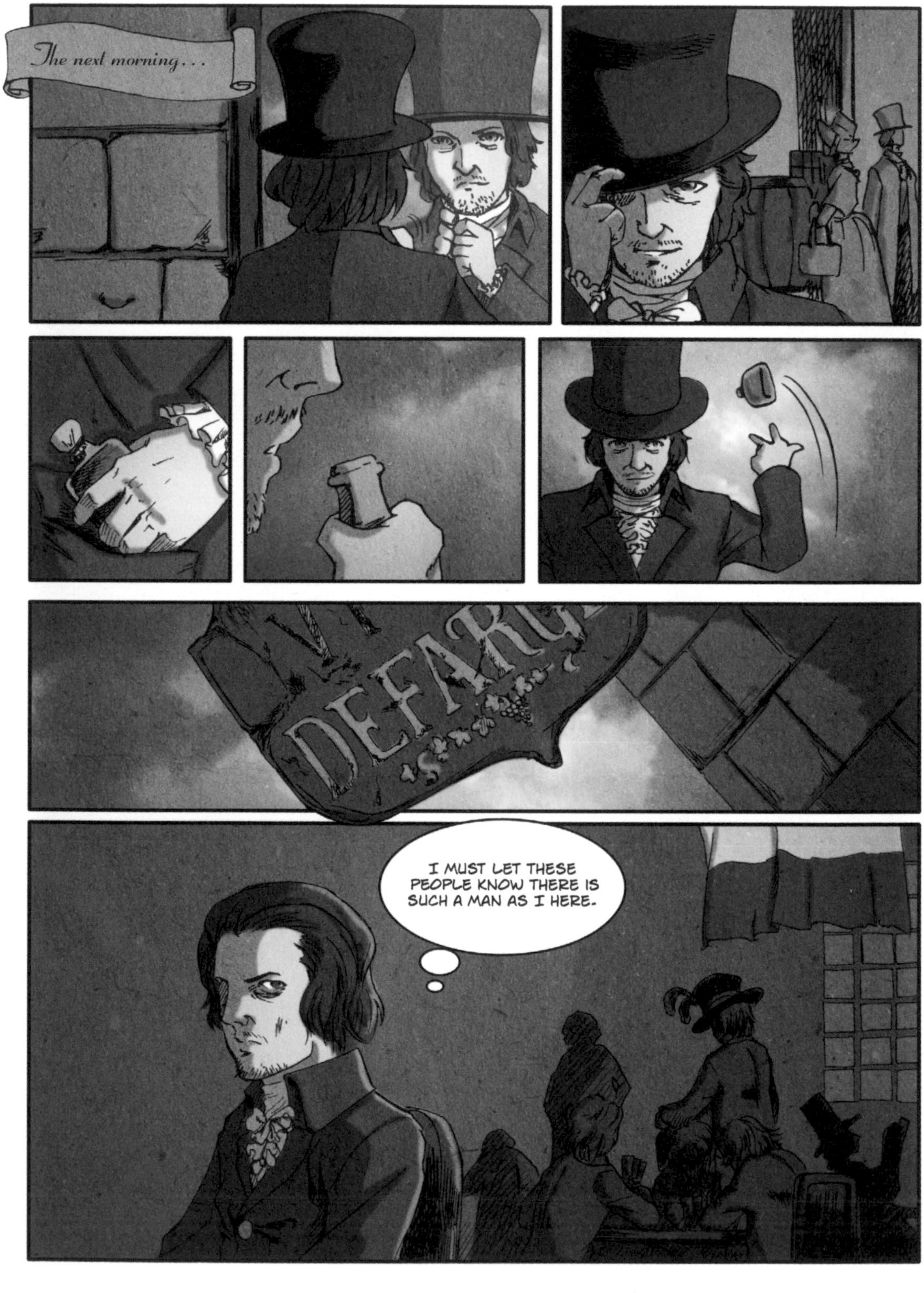
The next morning...
DEFARGE
I MUST LET THESE PEOPLE KNOW THERE IS SUCH A MAN AS I HERE.

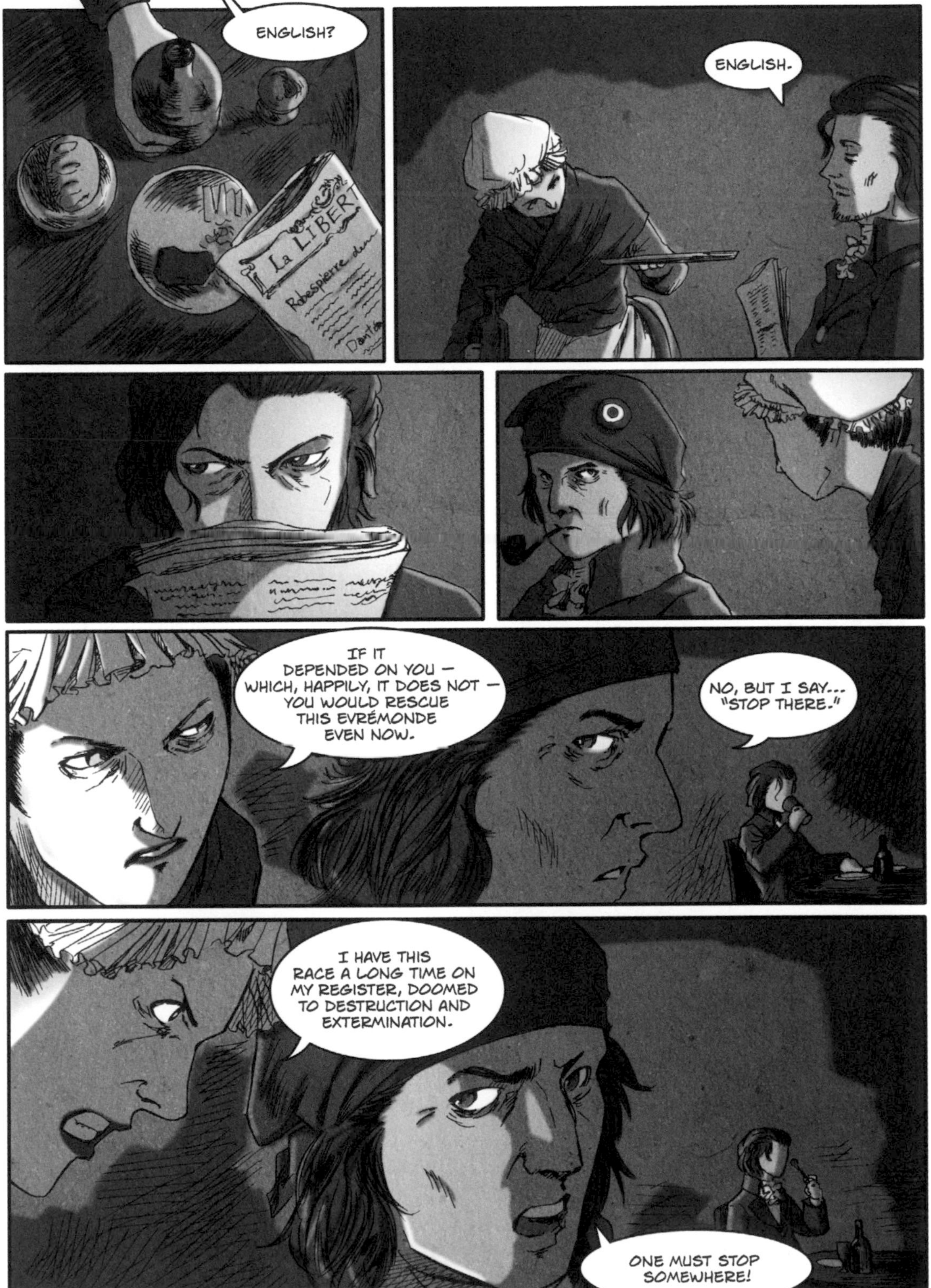
ENGLISH?
ENGLISH.
IF IT DEPENDED ON YOU — WHICH, HAPPILY, IT DOES NOT — YOU WOULD RESCUE THIS EVRÉMONDE EVEN NOW.
NO, BUT I SAY... "STOP THERE."
I HAVE THIS RACE A LONG TIME ON MY REGISTER, DOOMED TO DESTRUCTION AND EXTERMINATION.
ONE MUST STOP SOMEWHERE!

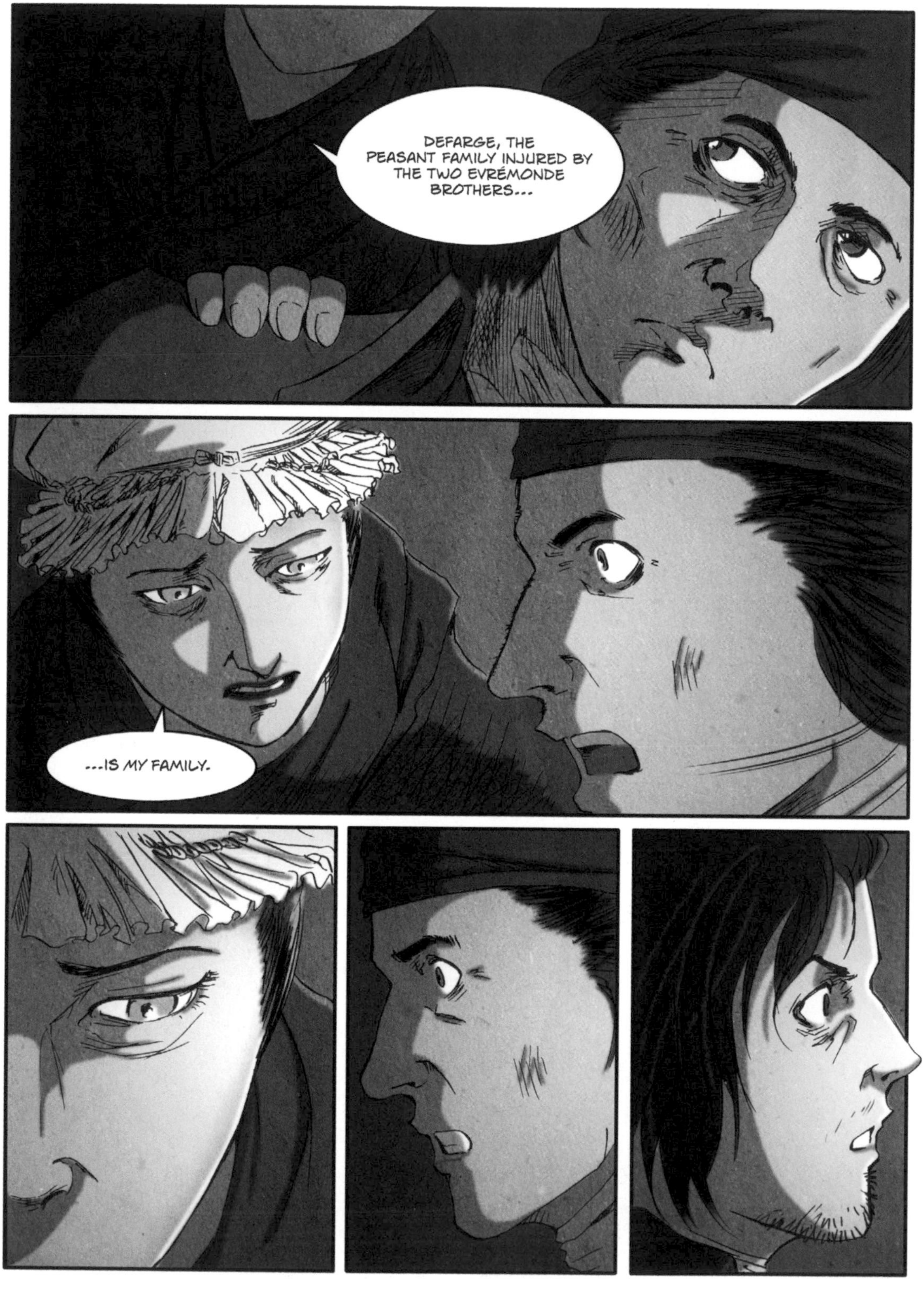
DEFARGE, THE PEASANT FAMILY INJURED BY THE TWO EVRÉMONDE BROTHERS...
...IS MY FAMILY.

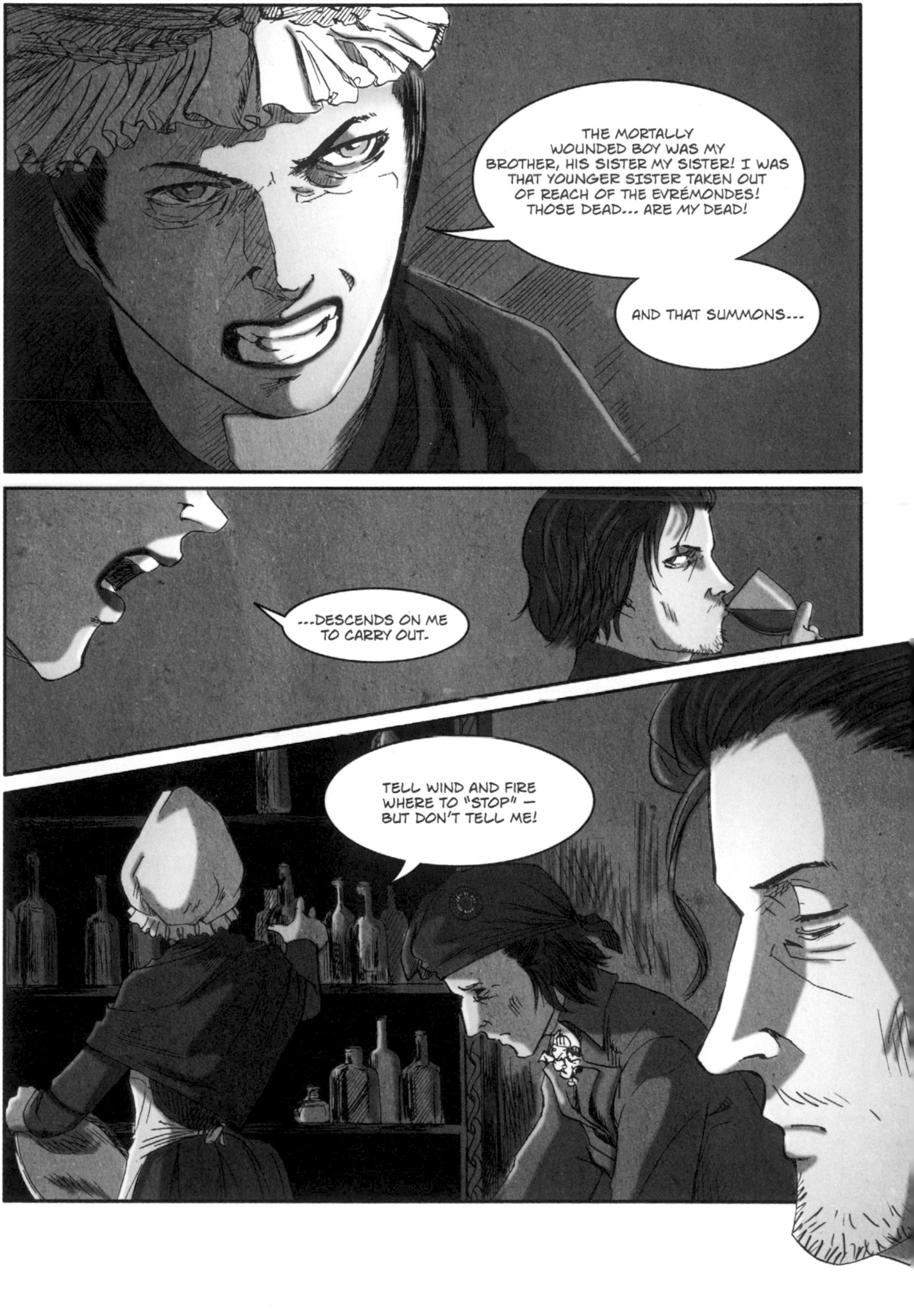
THE MORTALLY WOUNDED BOY WAS MY BROTHER, HIS SISTER MY SISTER! I WAS THAT YOUNGER SISTER TAKEN OUT OF REACH OF THE EVRÉMONDES! THOSE DEAD... ARE MY DEAD!
AND THAT SUMMONS...
...DESCENDS ON ME TO CARRY OUT.
TELL WIND AND FIRE WHERE TO "STOP" — BUT DON'T TELL ME!

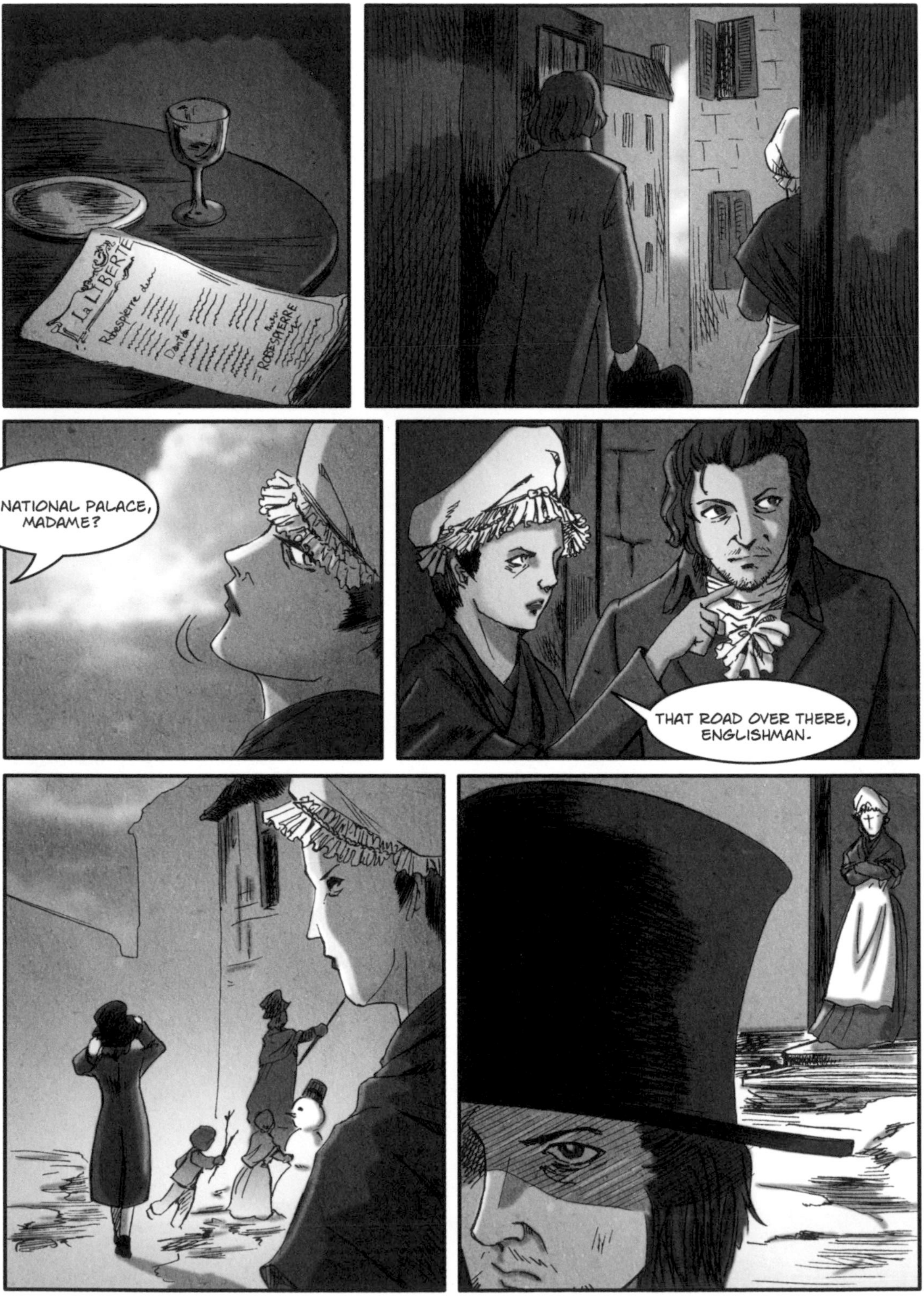
THE NATIONAL PALACE, MADAME?
THAT ROAD OVER THERE, ENGLISHMAN.

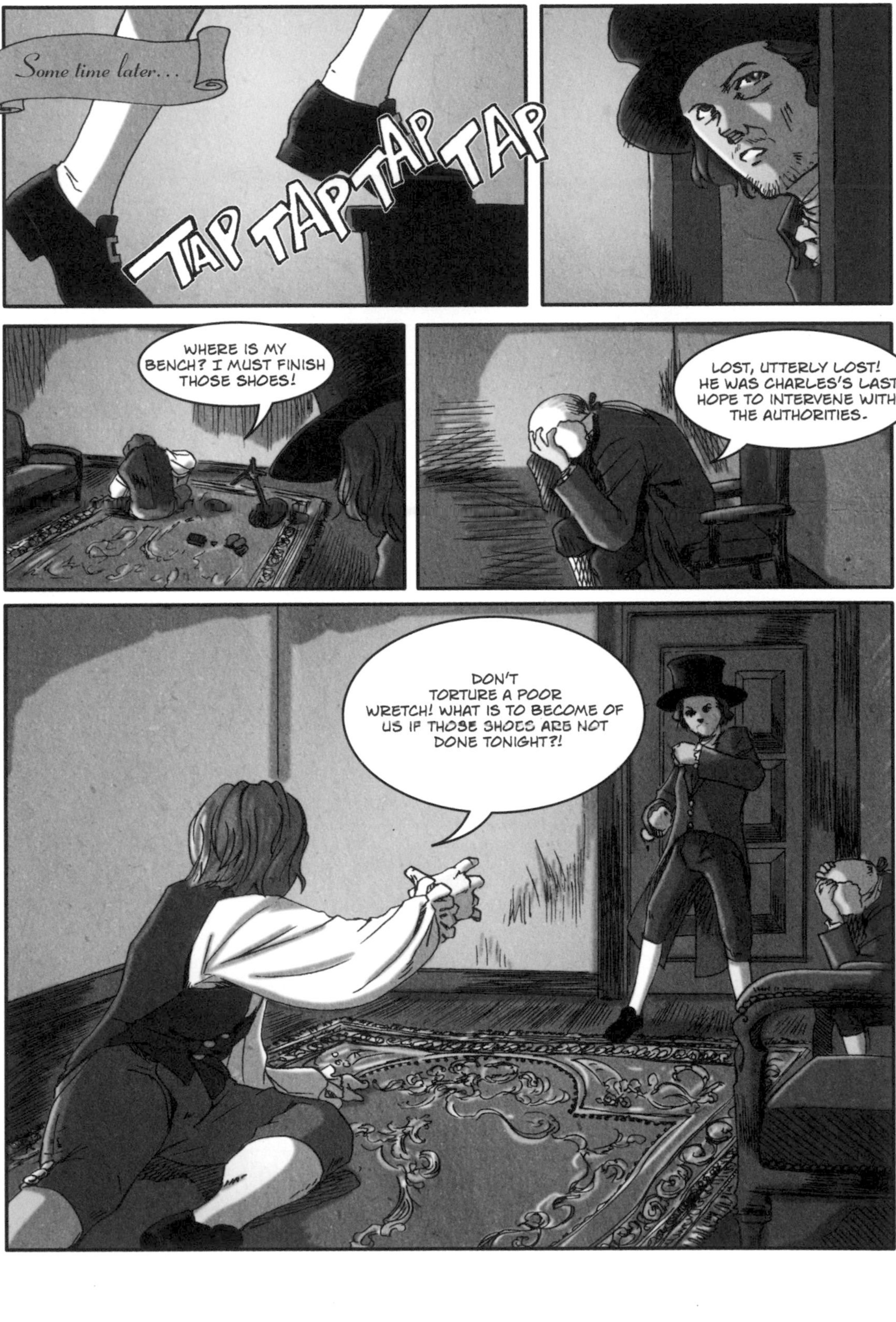
Some time later...
TAP TAP TAP TAP
WHERE IS MY BENCH? I MUST FINISH THOSE SHOES!
LOST, UTTERLY LOST! HE WAS CHARLES'S LAST HOPE TO INTERVENE WITH THE AUTHORITIES.
DON'T TORTURE A POOR WRETCH! WHAT IS TO BECOME OF US IF THOSE SHOES ARE NOT DONE TONIGHT?!

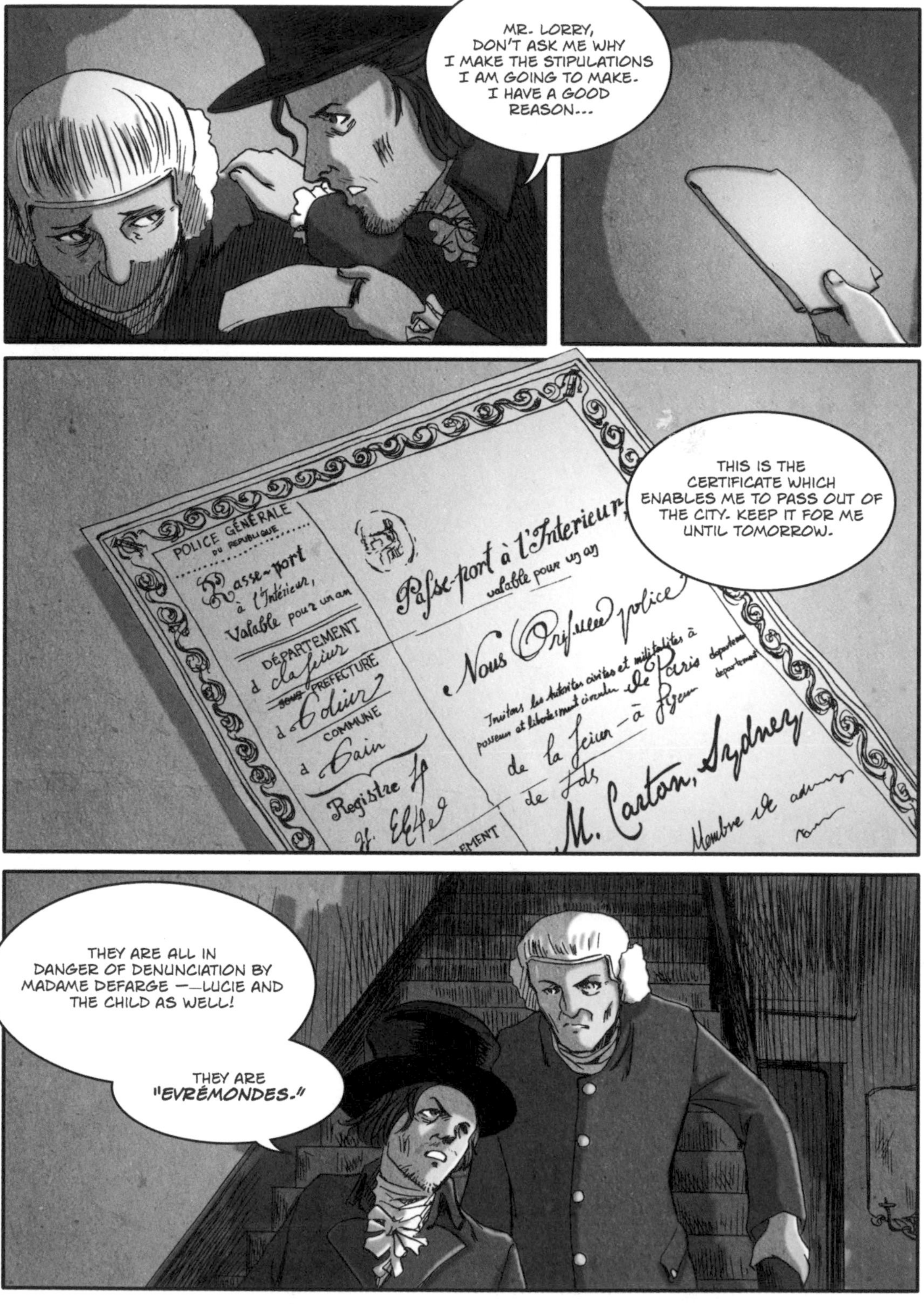
MR. LORRY, DON'T ASK ME WHY I MAKE THE STIPULATIONS I AM GOING TO MAKE. I HAVE A GOOD REASON...
THIS IS THE CERTIFICATE WHICH ENABLES ME TO PASS OUT OF THE CITY. KEEP IT FOR ME UNTIL TOMORROW.
THEY ARE ALL IN DANGER OF DENUNCIATION BY MADAME DEFARGE —LUCIE AND THE CHILD AS WELL!
THEY ARE "EVRÉMONDES."

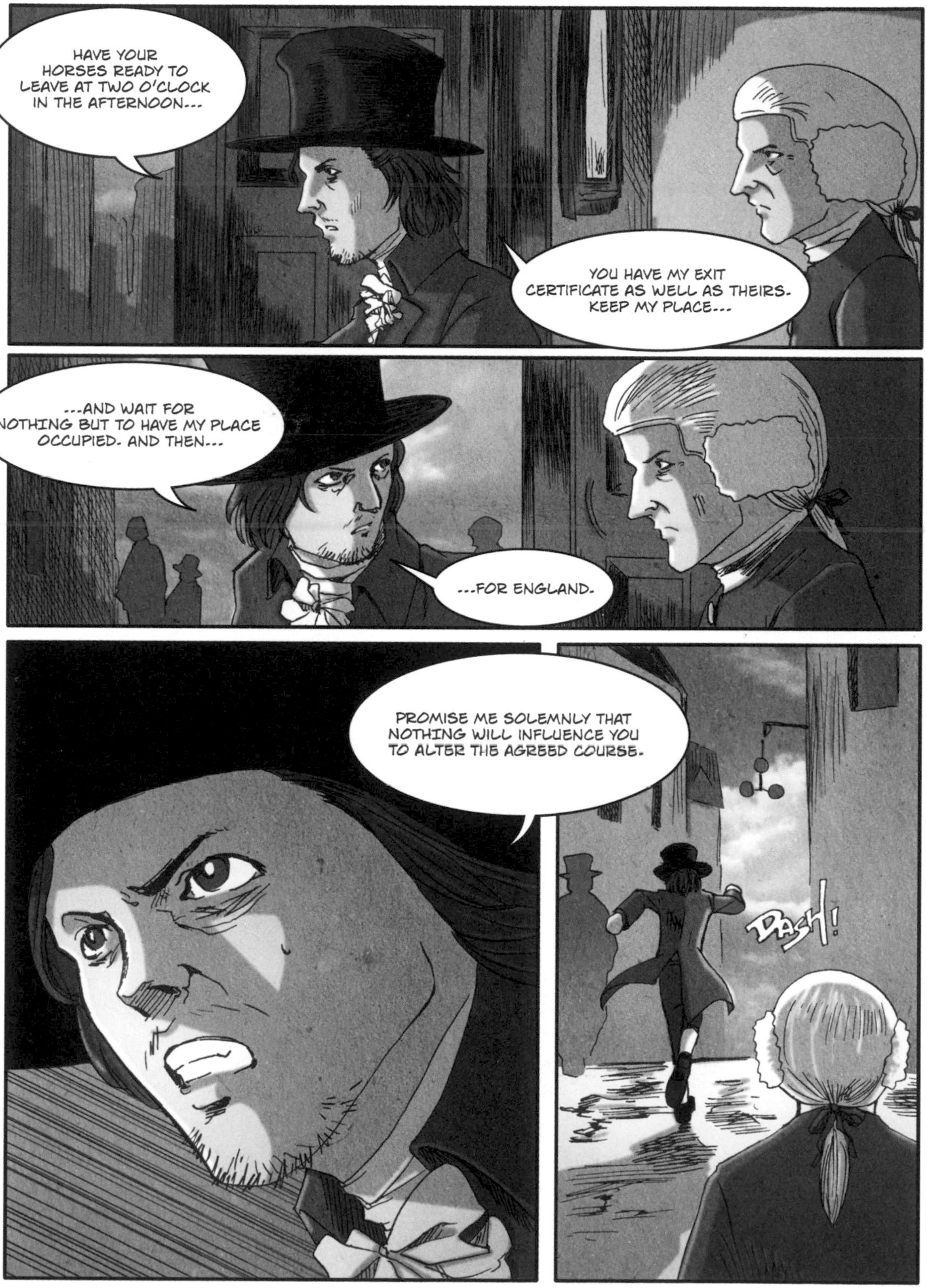
HAVE YOUR HORSES READY TO LEAVE AT TWO O'CLOCK IN THE AFTERNOON...
YOU HAVE MY EXIT CERTIFICATE AS WELL AS THEIRS. KEEP MY PLACE...
...AND WAIT FOR NOTHING BUT TO HAVE MY PLACE OCCUPIED. AND THEN...
...FOR ENGLAND.
PROMISE ME SOLEMNLY THAT NOTHING WILL INFLUENCE YOU TO ALTER THE AGREED COURSE.
DASH!

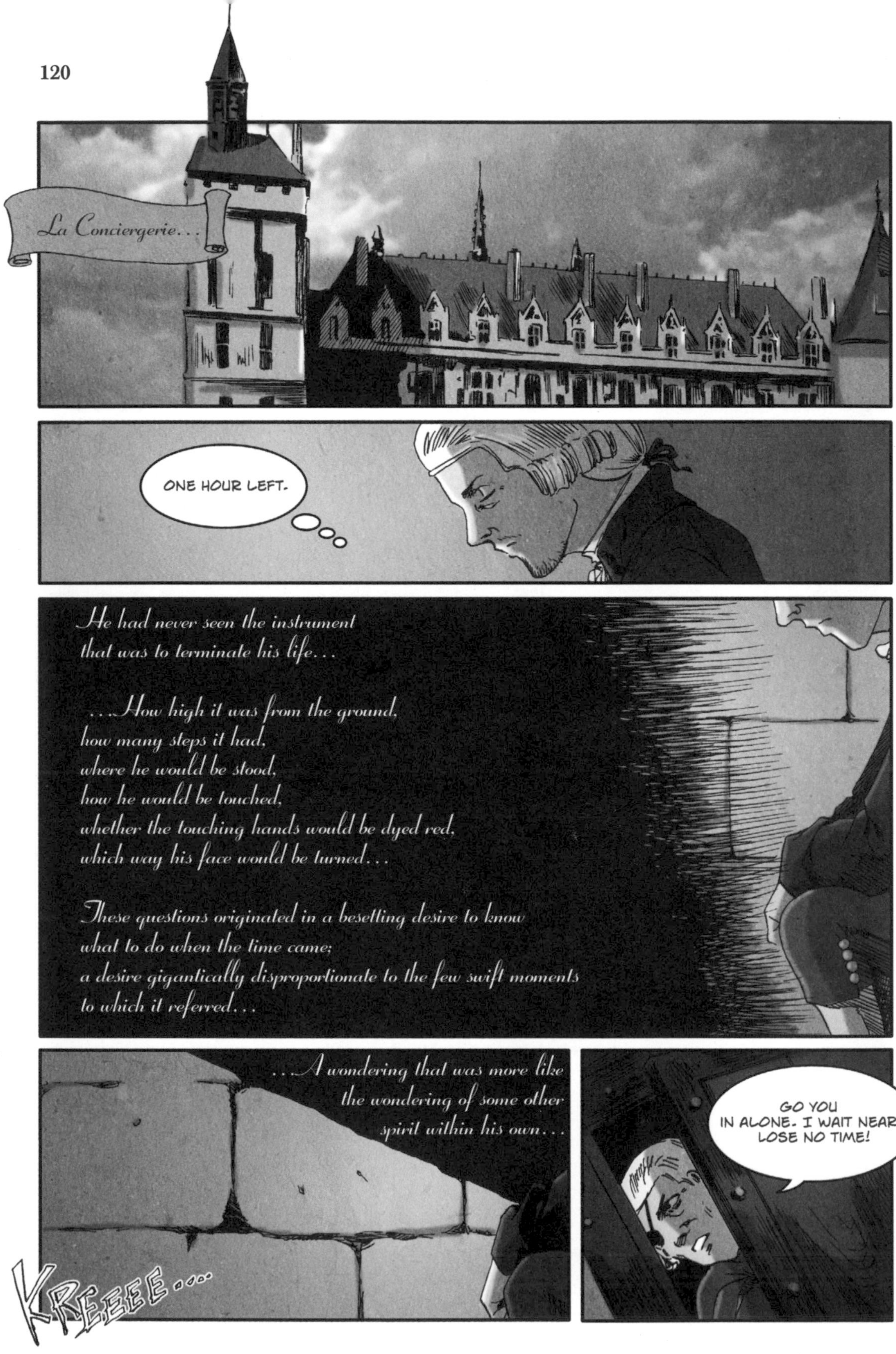
La Conciergerie...
ONE HOUR LEFT.
He had never seen the instrument
that was to terminate his life...
...How high it was from the ground,
how many steps it had,
where he would be stood,
how he would be touched,
whether the touching hands would be dyed red,
which way his face would be turned...
These questions originated in a besetting desire to know
what to do when the time came;
a desire gigantically disproportionate to the few swift moments
to which it referred...
...A wondering that was more like
the wondering of some other
spirit within his own...
KREEEE....
GO YOU
IN ALONE. I WAIT NEAR.
LOSE NO TIME!

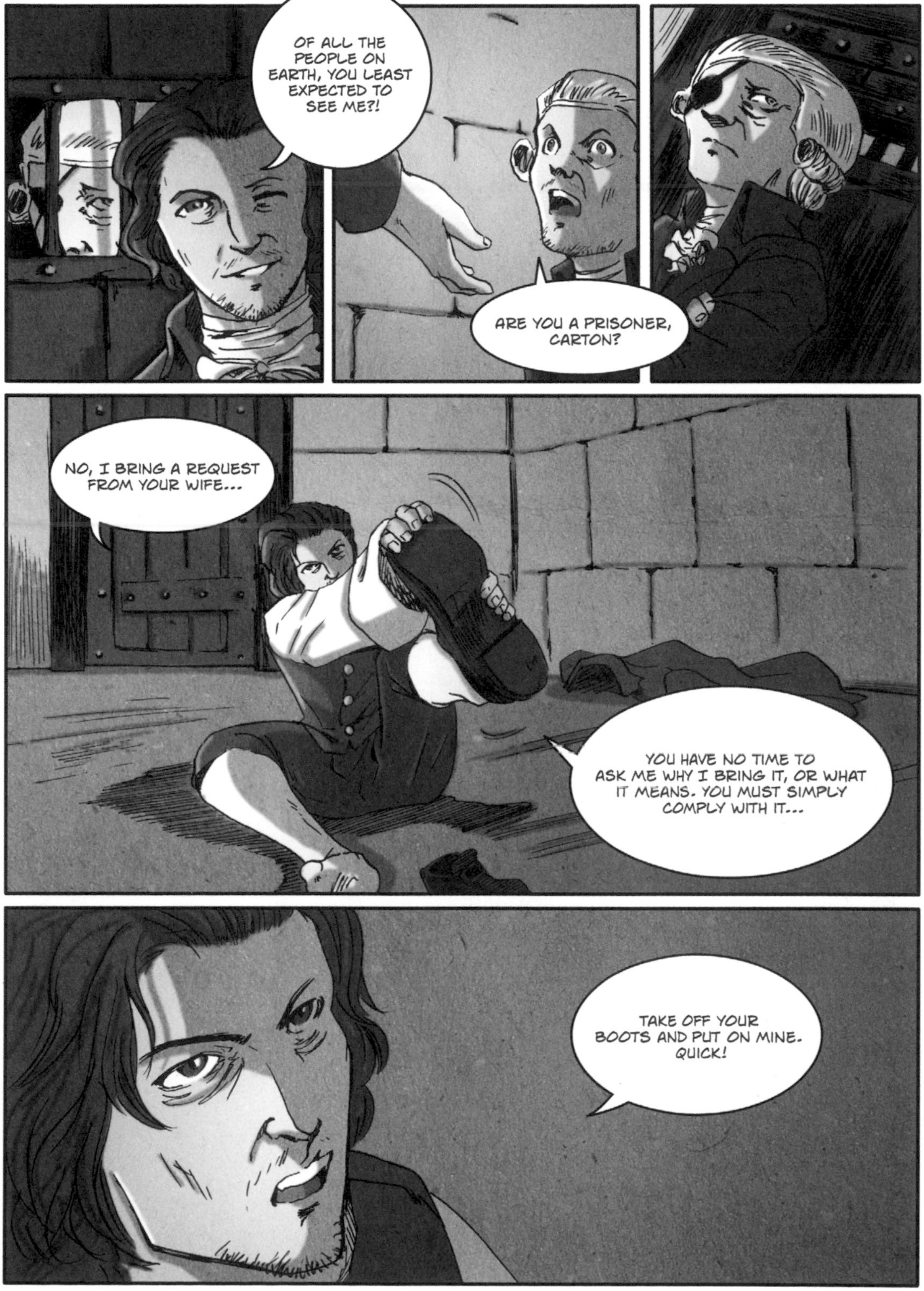
OF ALL THE PEOPLE ON EARTH, YOU LEAST EXPECTED TO SEE ME?!
ARE YOU A PRISONER, CARTON?
NO, I BRING A REQUEST FROM YOUR WIFE...
YOU HAVE NO TIME TO ASK ME WHY I BRING IT, OR WHAT IT MEANS. YOU MUST SIMPLY COMPLY WITH IT...
TAKE OFF YOUR BOOTS AND PUT ON MINE. QUICK!

CARTON, THERE'S NO ESCAPING FROM THIS PLACE. IT CAN'T BE DONE. IT'S MADNESS!

CHANGE THAT CRAVAT FOR MINE AND GIVE ME YOUR COAT.

CARTON, YOU'LL ONLY DIE WITH ME!

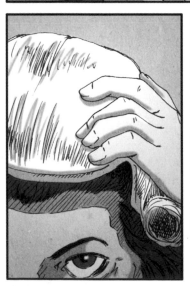

NOW SIT DOWN AND WRITE WHAT I SHALL DICTATE, DARNAY. QUICK!

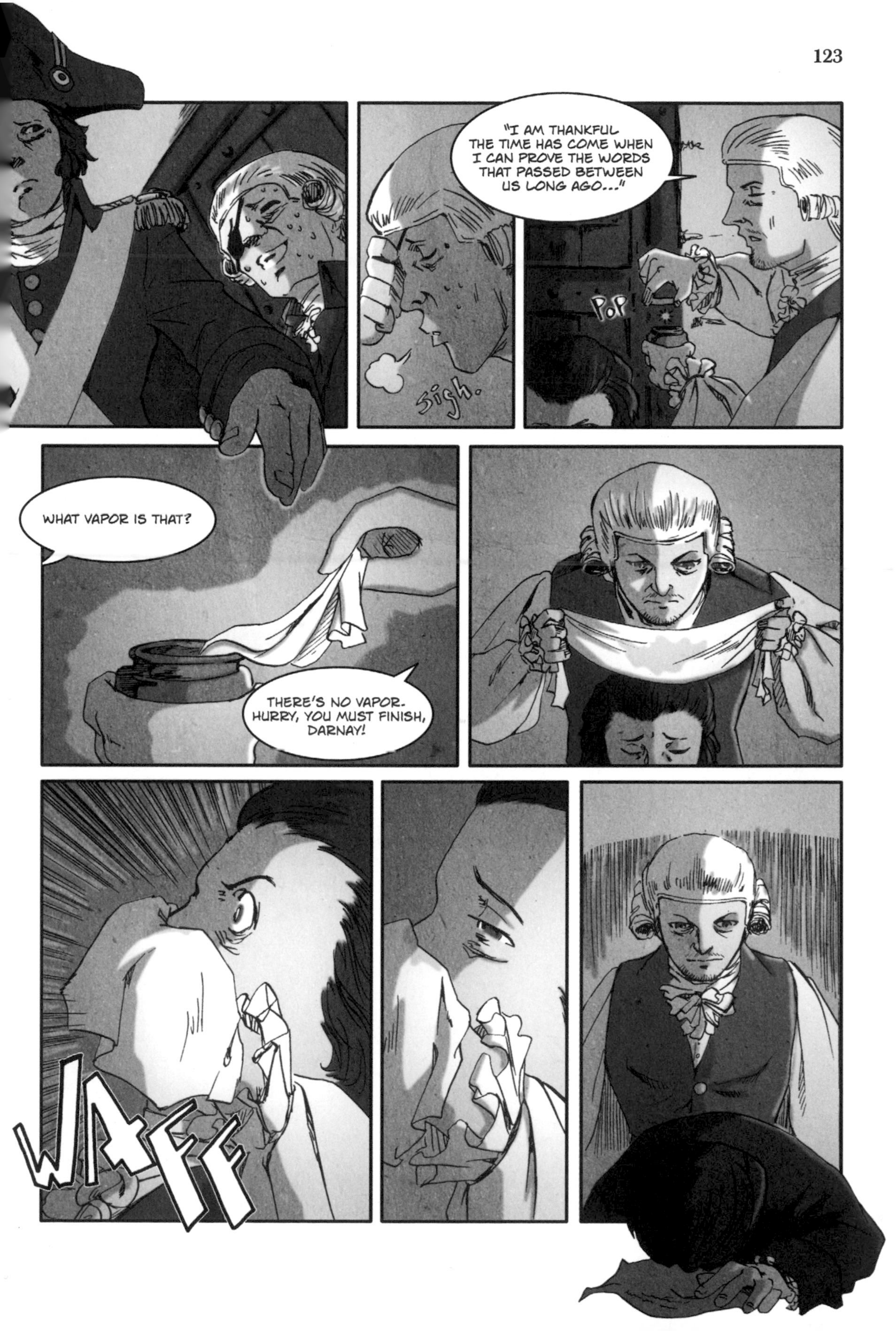
"I AM THANKFUL
THE TIME HAS COME WHEN
I CAN PROVE THE WORDS
THAT PASSED BETWEEN
US LONG AGO..."
SIGH.
POP
WHAT VAPOR IS THAT?
THERE'S NO VAPOR.
HURRY, YOU MUST FINISH,
DARNAY!
WAFF

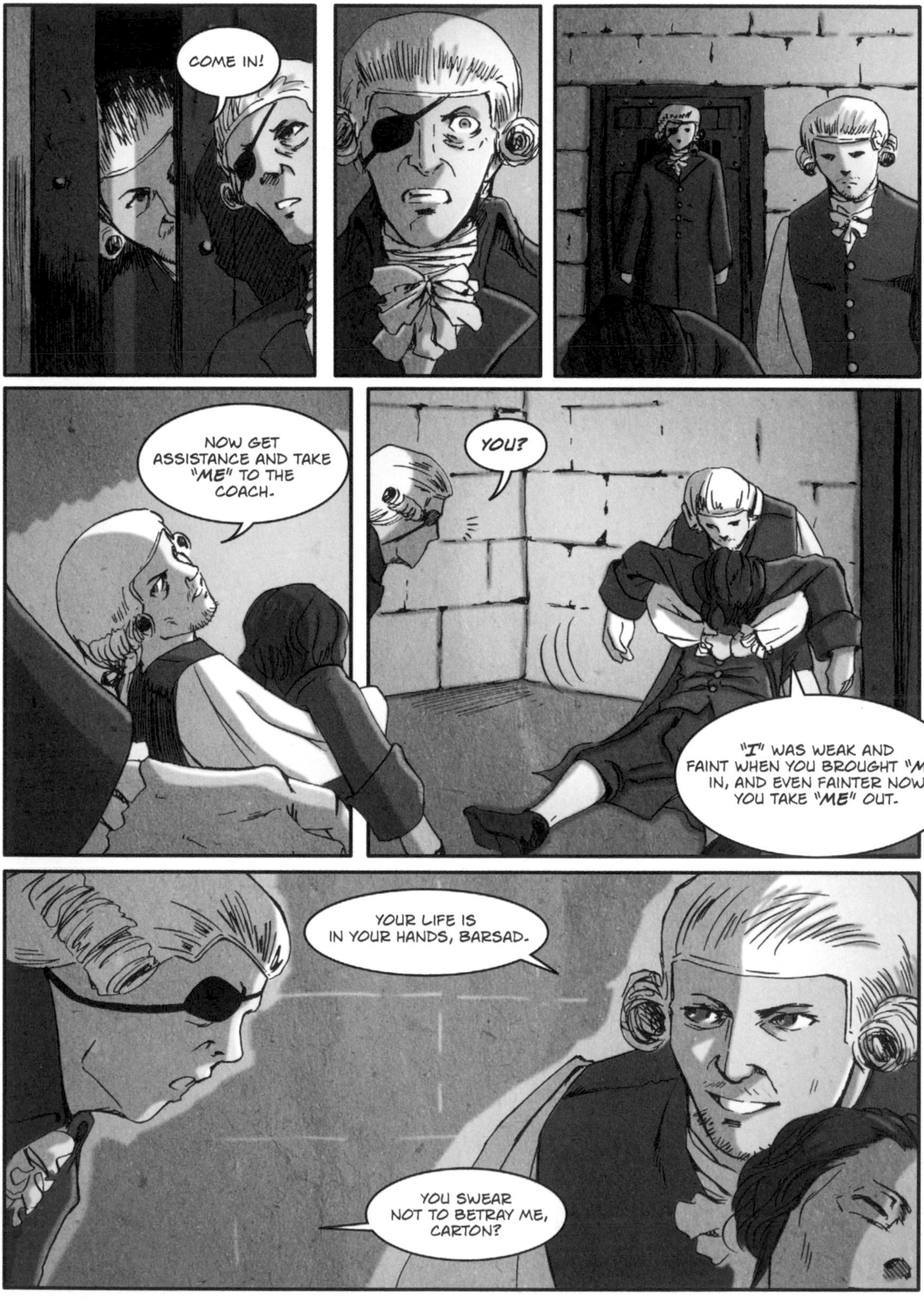
COME IN!
NOW GET ASSISTANCE AND TAKE "ME" TO THE COACH.
YOU?
"I" WAS WEAK AND FAINT WHEN YOU BROUGHT "ME" IN, AND EVEN FAINTER NOW YOU TAKE "ME" OUT.
YOUR LIFE IS IN YOUR HANDS, BARSAD.
YOU SWEAR NOT TO BETRAY ME, CARTON?

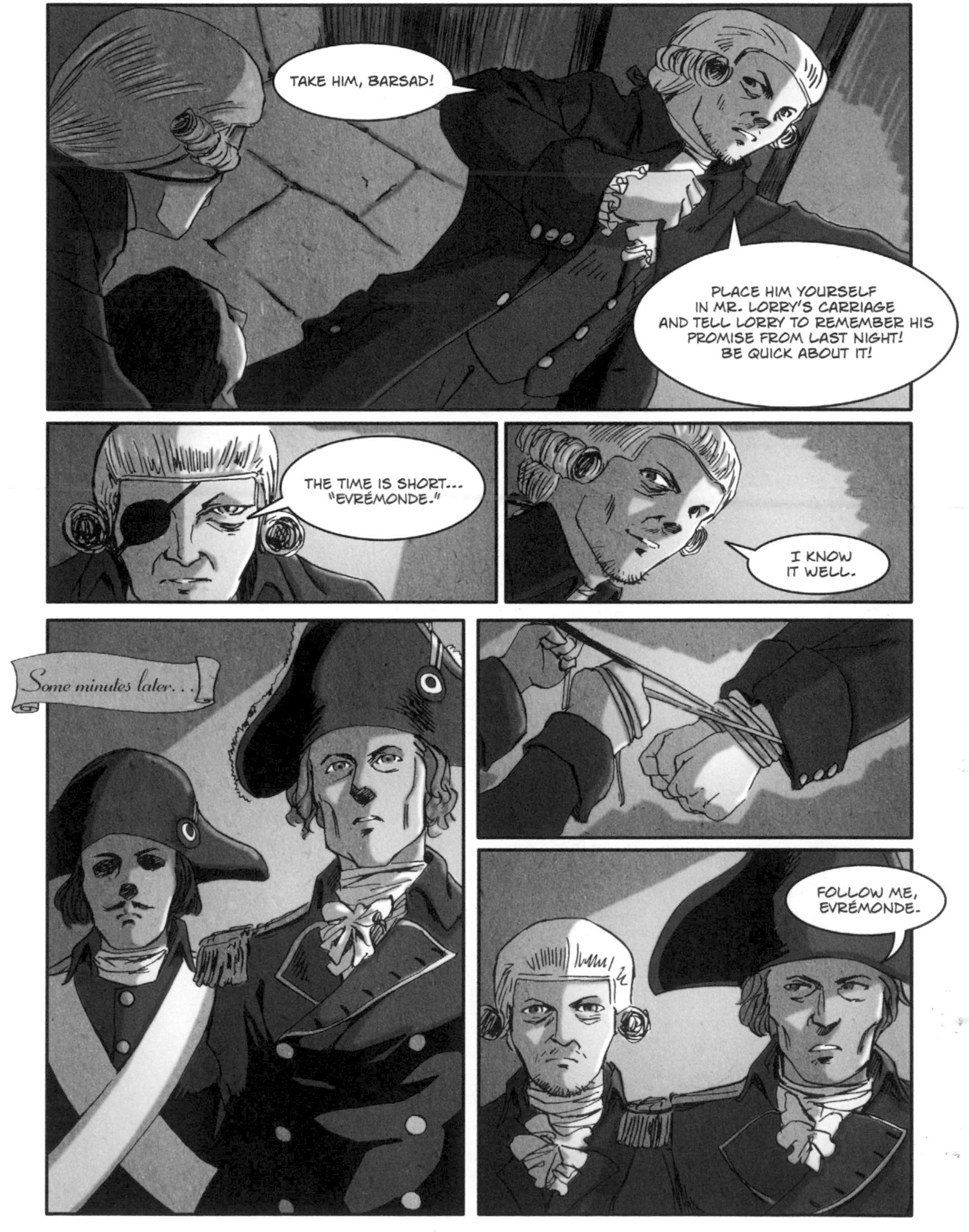
TAKE HIM, BARSAD!
PLACE HIM YOURSELF IN MR. LORRY'S CARRIAGE AND TELL LORRY TO REMEMBER HIS PROMISE FROM LAST NIGHT! BE QUICK ABOUT IT!
THE TIME IS SHORT... "EVRÉMONDE."
I KNOW IT WELL.
Some minutes later...
FOLLOW ME, EVRÉMONDE.

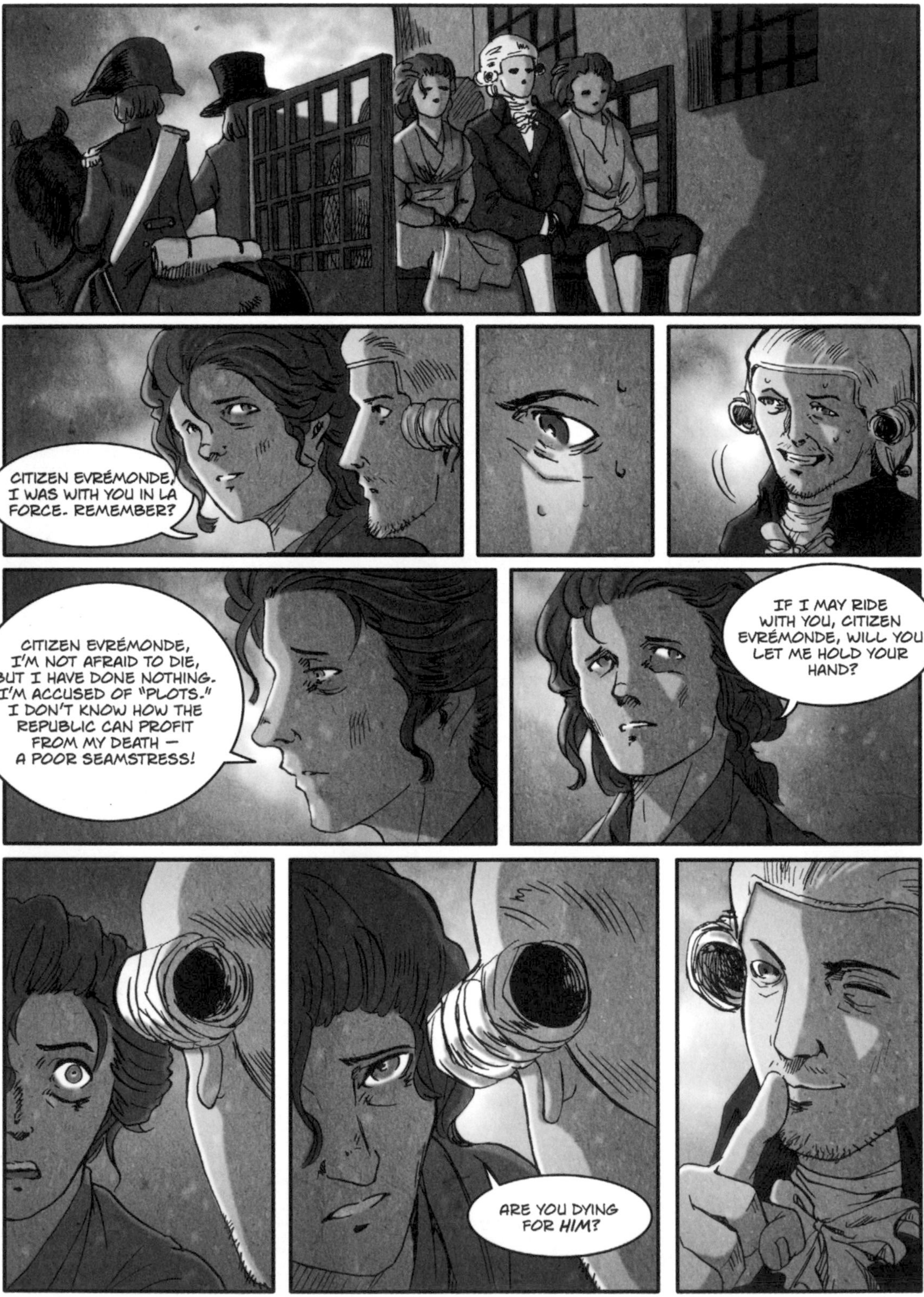
CITIZEN EVRÉMONDE, I WAS WITH YOU IN LA FORCE. REMEMBER?
CITIZEN EVRÉMONDE, I'M NOT AFRAID TO DIE, BUT I HAVE DONE NOTHING. I'M ACCUSED OF "PLOTS." I DON'T KNOW HOW THE REPUBLIC CAN PROFIT FROM MY DEATH — A POOR SEAMSTRESS!
IF I MAY RIDE WITH YOU, CITIZEN EVRÉMONDE, WILL YOU LET ME HOLD YOUR HAND?
ARE YOU DYING FOR *HIM*?

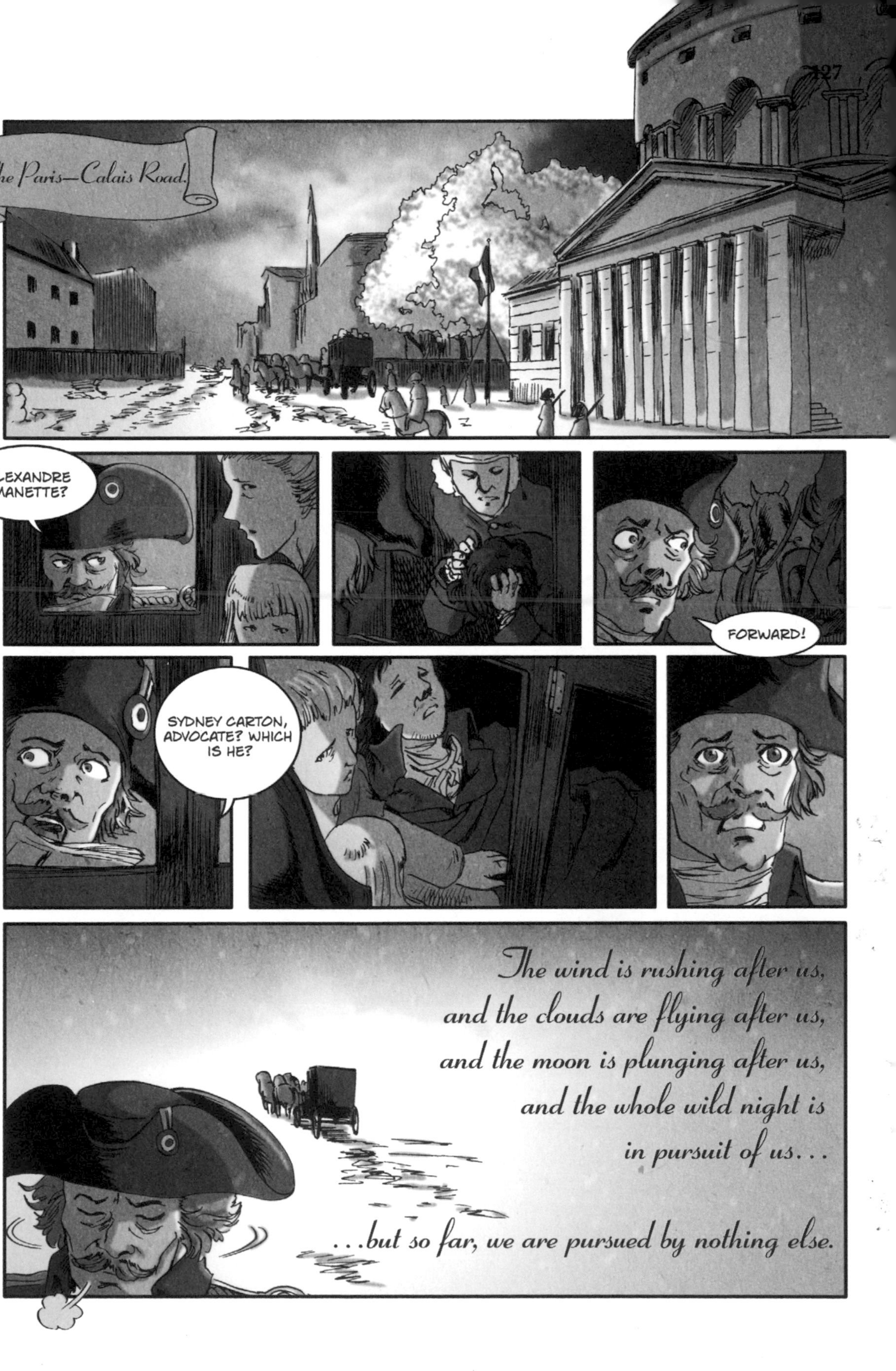
The Paris—Calais Road.
ALEXANDRE MANETTE?
FORWARD!
SYDNEY CARTON, ADVOCATE? WHICH IS HE?
The wind is rushing after us,
and the clouds are flying after us,
and the moon is plunging after us,
and the whole wild night is
in pursuit of us...
...but so far, we are pursued by nothing else.

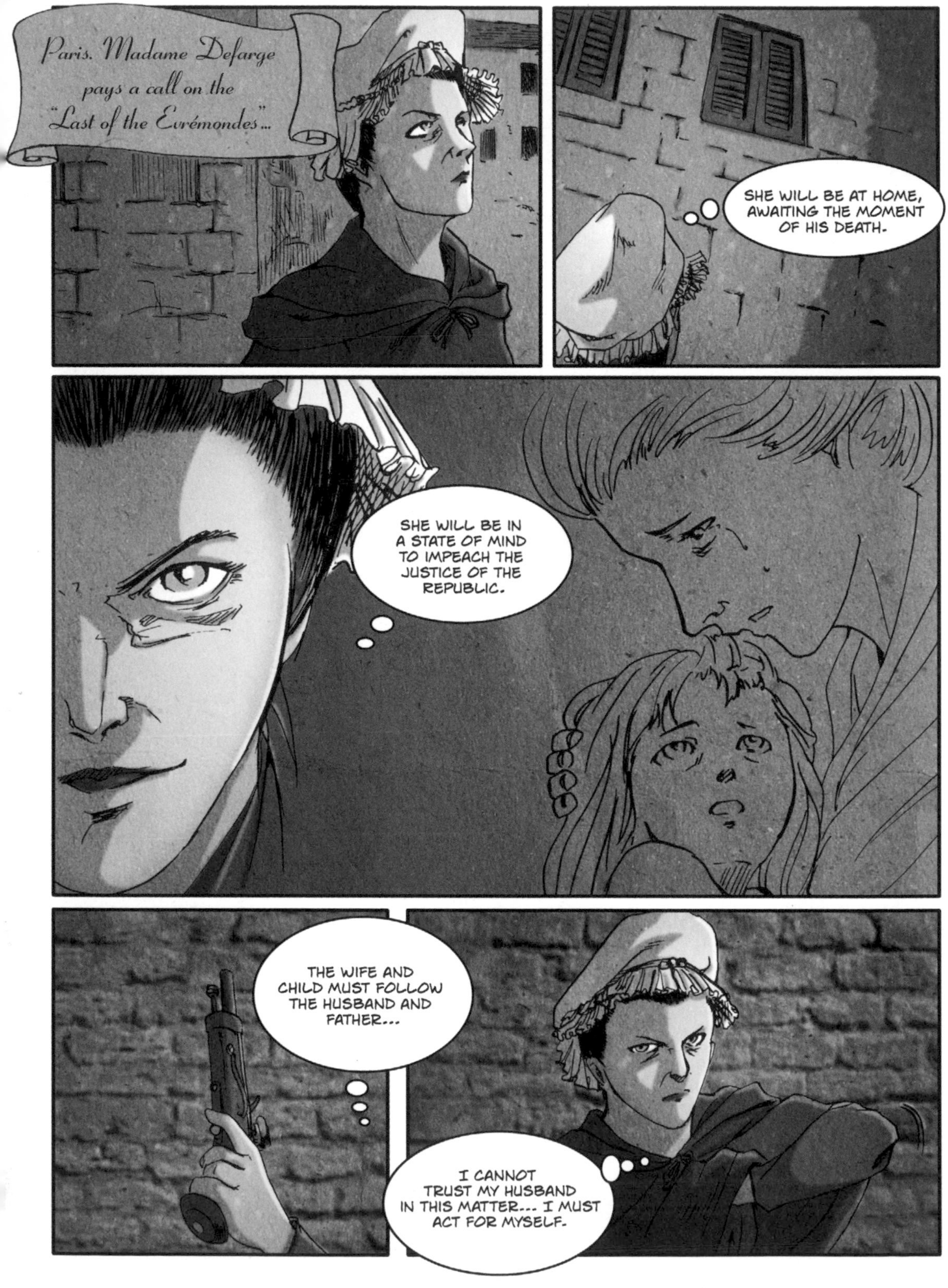
Paris. Madame Defarge pays a call on the "Last of the Evrémondes"...
SHE WILL BE AT HOME, AWAITING THE MOMENT OF HIS DEATH.
SHE WILL BE IN A STATE OF MIND TO IMPEACH THE JUSTICE OF THE REPUBLIC.
THE WIFE AND CHILD MUST FOLLOW THE HUSBAND AND FATHER...
I CANNOT TRUST MY HUSBAND IN THIS MATTER... I MUST ACT FOR MYSELF.

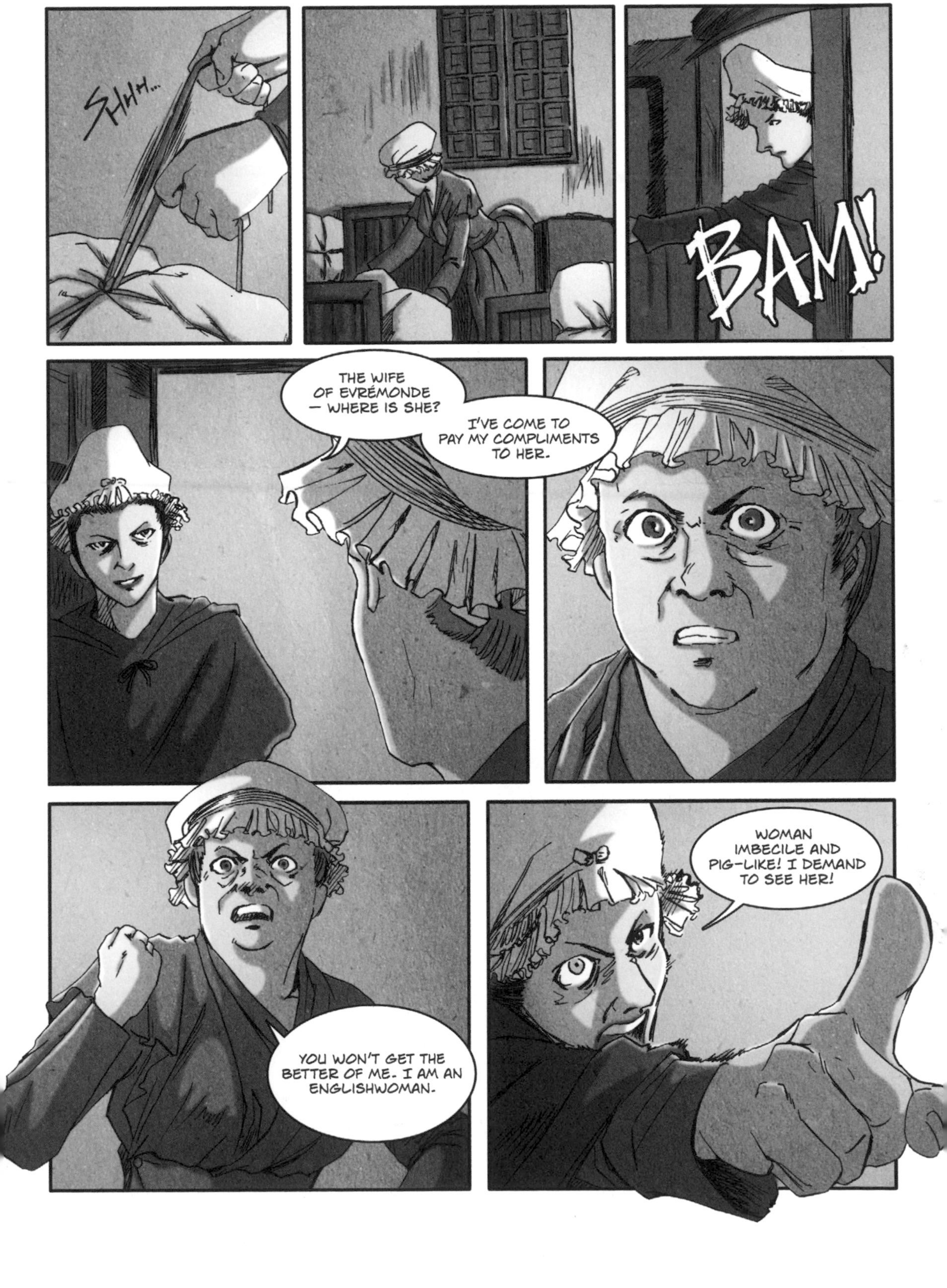
SHHH...
BAM!
THE WIFE OF EVRÉMONDE — WHERE IS SHE?
I'VE COME TO PAY MY COMPLIMENTS TO HER.
YOU WON'T GET THE BETTER OF ME. I AM AN ENGLISHWOMAN.
WOMAN IMBECILE AND PIG-LIKE! I DEMAND TO SEE HER!

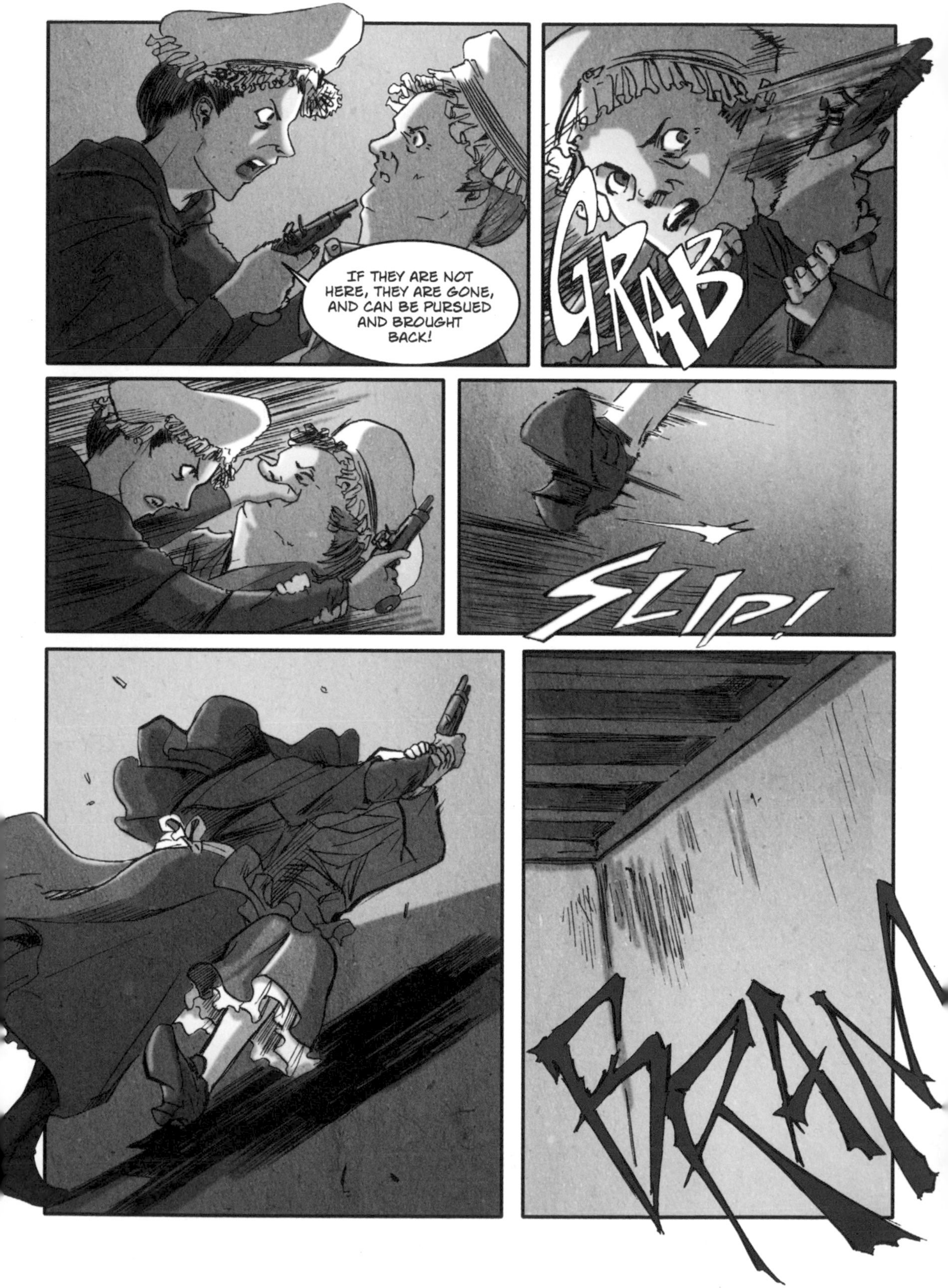
IF THEY ARE NOT HERE, THEY ARE GONE, AND CAN BE PURSUED AND BROUGHT BACK!
GRAB
SLIP!

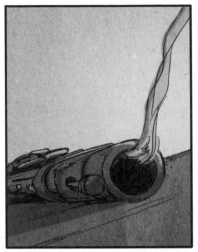

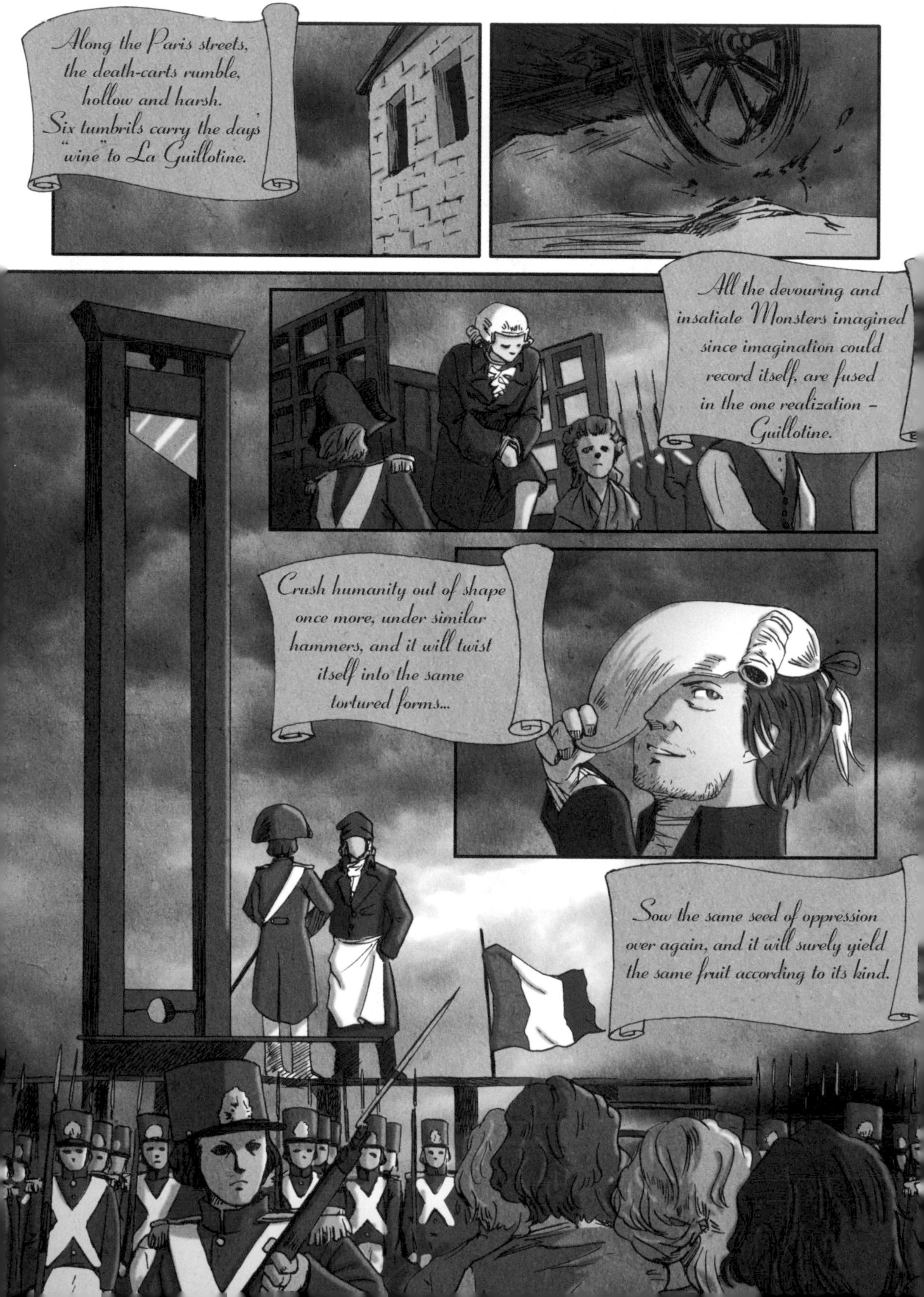
Along the Paris streets, the death-carts rumble, hollow and harsh. Six tumbrils carry the day's "wine" to La Guillotine.
All the devouring and insatiate Monsters imagined since imagination could record itself, are fused in the one realization – Guillotine.
Crush humanity out of shape once more, under similar hammers, and it will twist itself into the same tortured forms...
Sow the same seed of oppression over again, and it will surely yield the same fruit according to its kind.

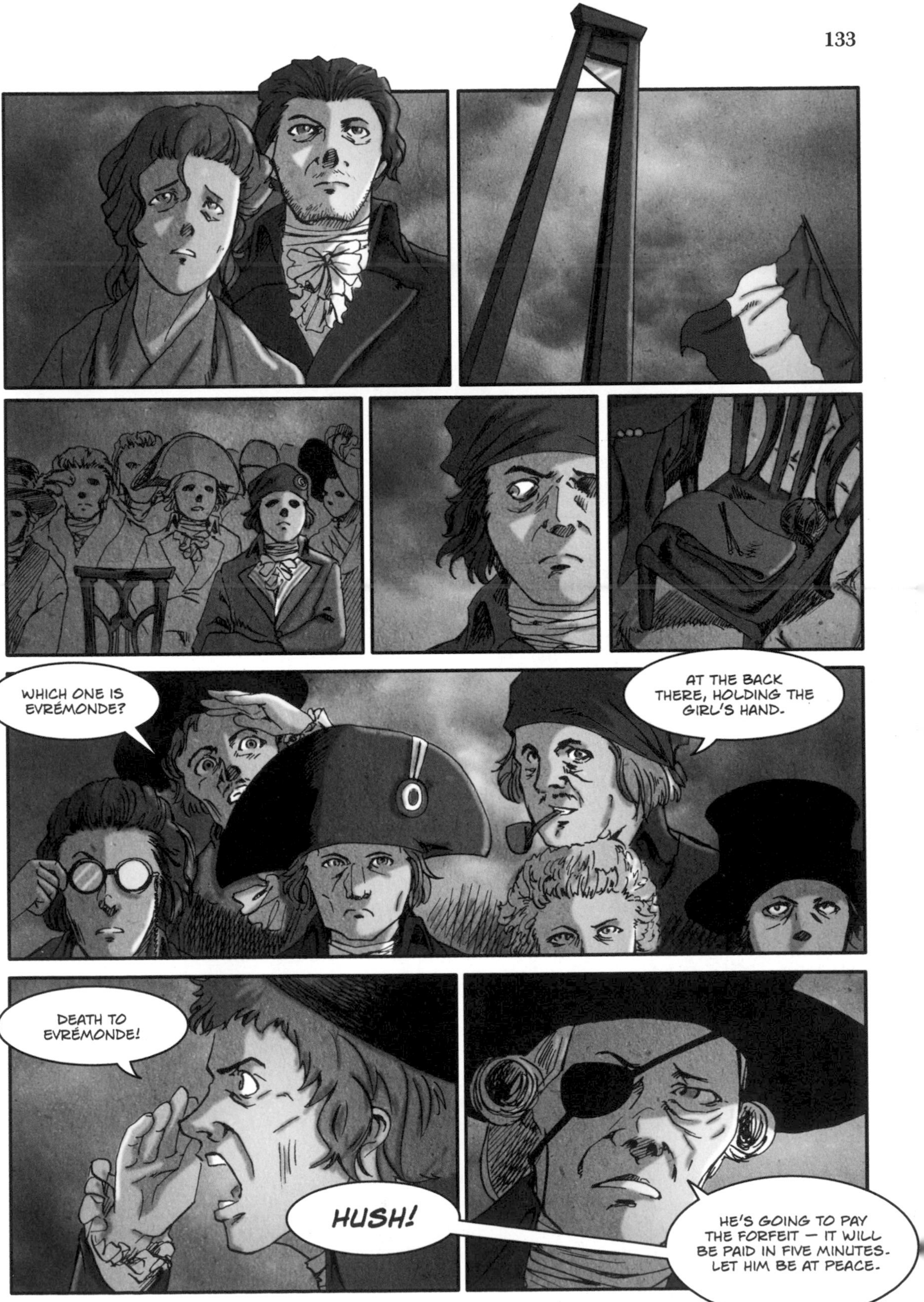
WHICH ONE IS EVRÉMONDE?
AT THE BACK THERE, HOLDING THE GIRL'S HAND.
DEATH TO EVRÉMONDE!
HUSH!
HE'S GOING TO PAY THE FORFEIT — IT WILL BE PAID IN FIVE MINUTES. LET HIM BE AT PEACE.

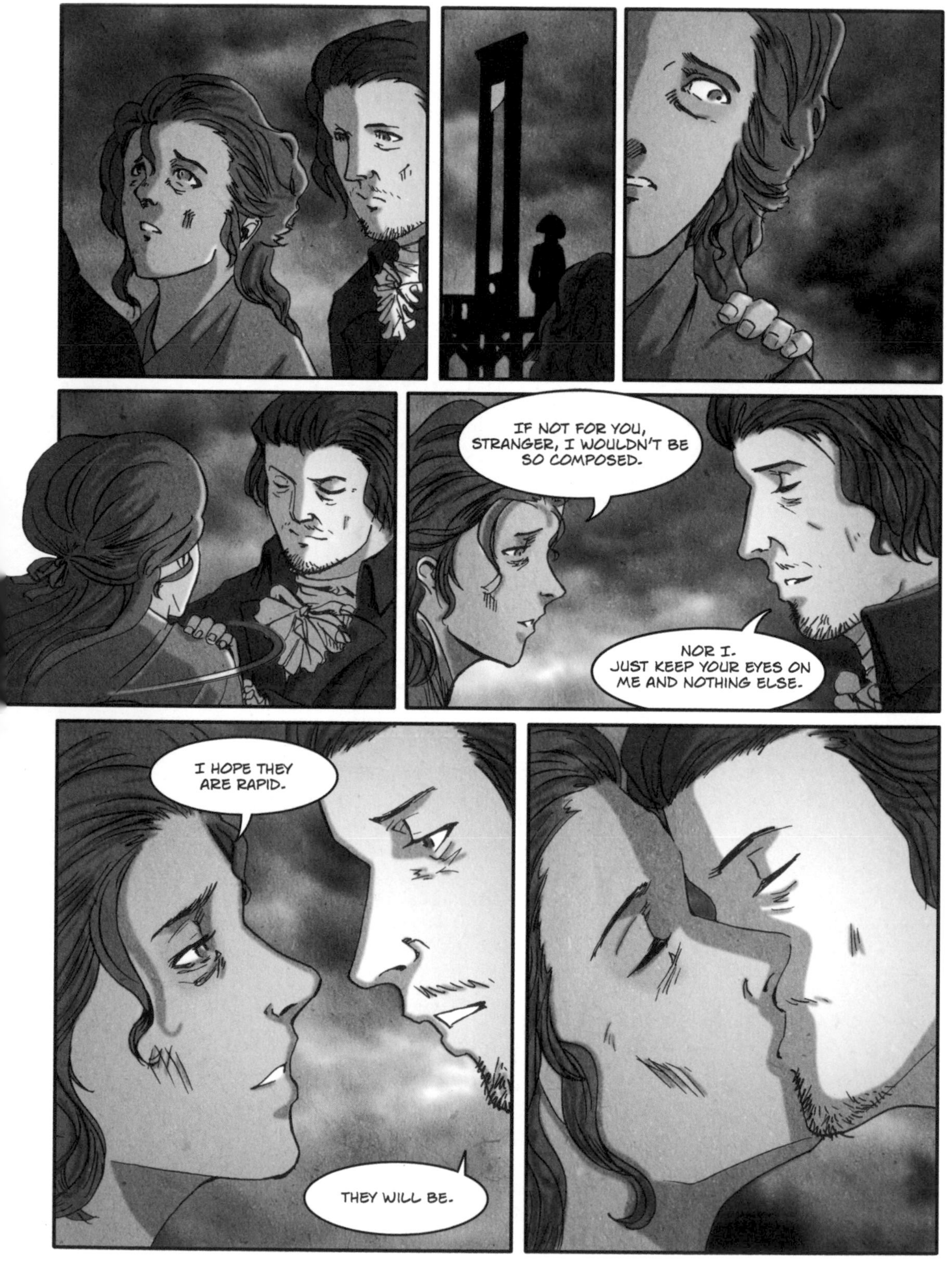
IF NOT FOR YOU, STRANGER, I WOULDN'T BE SO COMPOSED.
NOR I. JUST KEEP YOUR EYES ON ME AND NOTHING ELSE.
I HOPE THEY ARE RAPID.
THEY WILL BE.

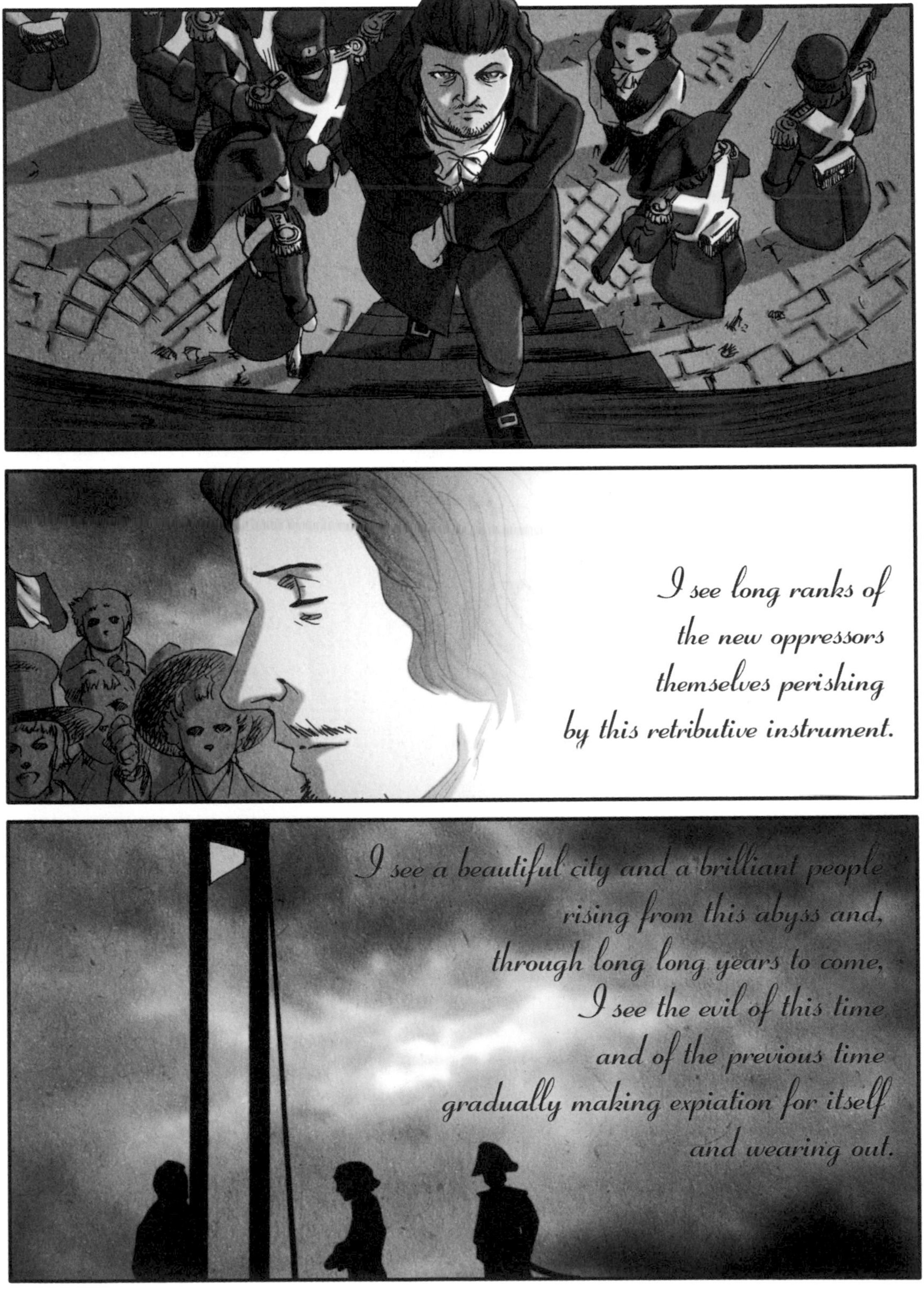
I see long ranks of
the new oppressors
themselves perishing
by this retributive instrument.
I see a beautiful city and a brilliant people
rising from this abyss and,
through long long years to come,
I see the evil of this time
and of the previous time
gradually making expiation for itself
and wearing out.

I see the lives for which
I lay down my life,
peaceful, useful,
prosperous, and happy...

I see HER,
an old woman,
weeping for me
on the anniversary
of this day.

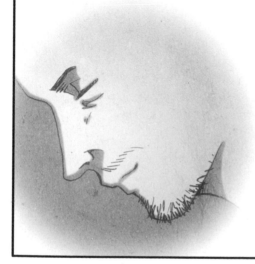

I see a child who bears my name,
now a man winning his way up
in that path of life which once was mine.

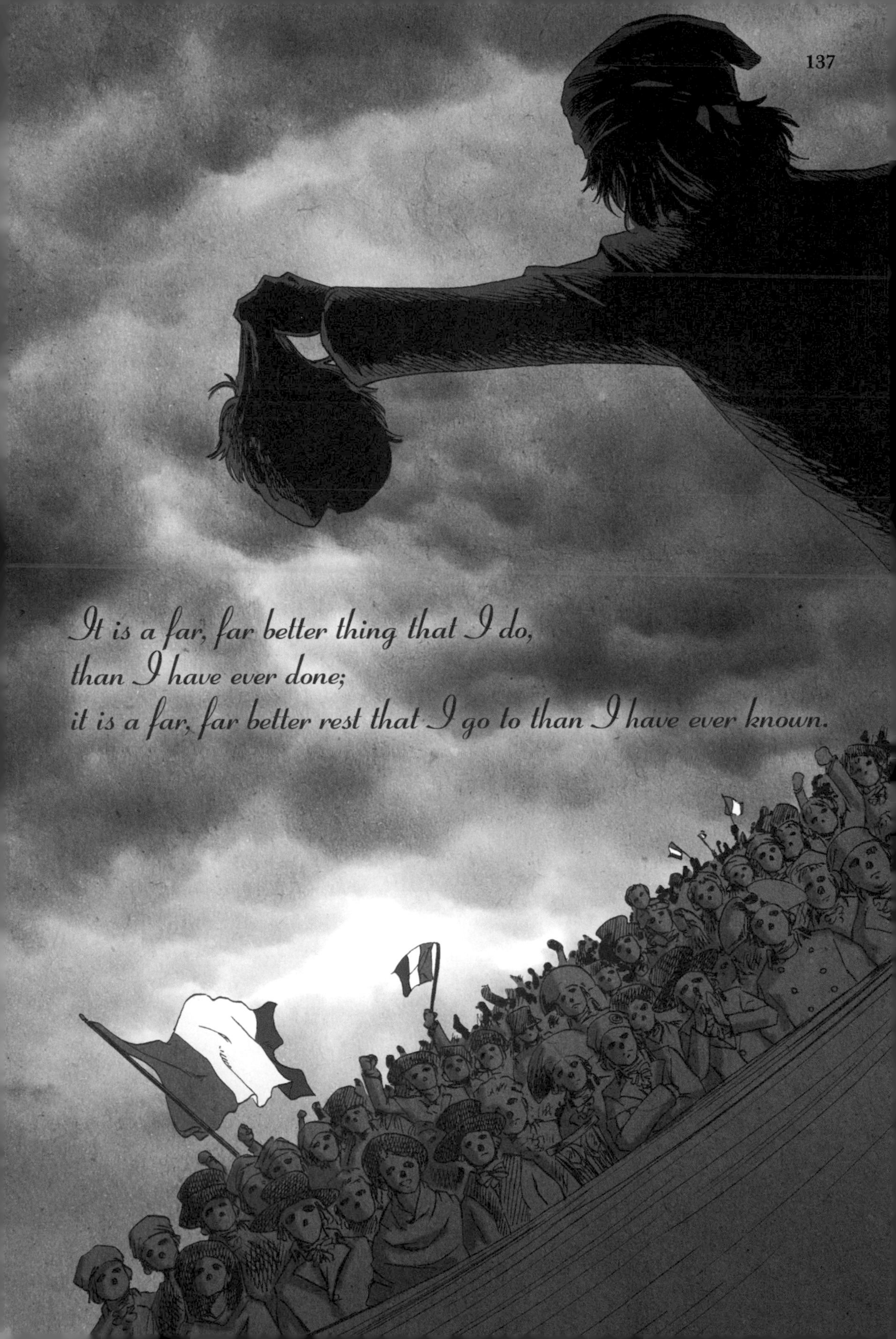
It is a far, far better thing that I do,
than I have ever done;
it is a far, far better rest that I go to than I have ever known.